military

THE ART OF WAR

By

Mao Tse-tung

Special Edition

The Art of War by Mao Tse-tung – Special Edition
By Mao Tse-tung
Translation by Foreign Language Press, Peking

Special Edition – April 2005

Published by
EL Paso Norte Press
El Paso, Texas

ISBN 10: 0-976072-67-X
ISBN 13: 978-0-976072-67-6

Printed in the United States of America

CONTENTS

The Art of War by Mao Tse-tung – Special Edition

Part 1: Problems of Strategy in China's Revolutionary War

Part 2: Problems of Strategy in Guerrilla War Against Japan

(Contents - Part 2 Continued)

Part 3: On Protracted War

Contents

Part 4: Problems of War and Strategy

THE ART OF WAR

PART 1

PROBLEMS OF STRATEGY

IN

CHINA'S REVOLUTIONARY WAR

by

Mao Tse-tung

December 1936

Mao Tse-tung

Preface

Mao Tse-tung wrote *Problems of Strategy in China's Revolutionary War* to sum up the experience of the Second Revolutionary Civil War and used it for his lectutes at the Red Army College in Northern Shensi. Only five chapters were completed. The chapters on the strategic offensive, political work and other problems were left undone because he was too busy in consequence of the Sian Incident.

This work, a result of a major inner-Party controversy on military questions during the Second Revolutionary Civil War, gives expression to one line in military affairs as against another. The enlarged meeting of the Political Bureau of the Central Committee held at Tsunyi in January 1935 settled the controversy about the military line, reaffirmed Comrade Mao Tse-tung's views and repudiated the erroneous line.

The Art of War

Mao Tse-tung

Chapter I

HOW TO STUDY WAR

1. THE LAWS OF WAR ARE DEVELOPMENTAL

The *laws of war* are a problem which anyone directing a war must study and solve.

The *laws of revolutionary war* are a problem which anyone directing a revolutionary war must study and solve.

The *laws of China's revolutionary war* are a problem which anyone directing China's revolutionary war must study and solve.

We are now engaged in a war; our war is a revolutionary war; and our revolutionary war is being waged in this semi-colonial and semi-feudal country of China. Therefore, we must study not only the laws of war in general, but the specific laws of revolutionary war, and the even more specific laws of revolutionary war in China.

It is well known that when you do anything, unless you understand its actual circumstances, its nature and its relations to other things, you will not know the laws governing it, or know how to do it, or be able to do it well.

War is the highest form of struggle for resolving contradictions, when they have developed to a certain stage, between classes, nations, states, or political groups, and it has existed ever since the emergence of private property and of classes. Unless you understand the actual circumstances of war, its nature and its relations to other things, you will not know the laws of war, or know how to direct war, or be able to win victory.

Revolutionary war, whether a revolutionary class war or a revolutionary national war, has its own specific circumstances and nature, in addition to the circumstances and nature of war in general. Therefore, besides the general laws of war, it has specific laws of its own. Unless you understand its specific circumstances and nature, unless you understand its specific laws, you will not be able to direct a revolutionary war and wage it successfully.

China's revolutionary war, whether civil war or national war, is waged in the specific environment of China and so has its own specific circumstances and nature distinguishing it both from war in general and from revolutionary war in general. Therefore, besides the laws of war in general and of revolutionary war in general, it has specific laws of its own. Unless you understand them, you will not be able to win in China's revolutionary war.

Therefore, we must study the laws of war in general, we must also study the laws of revolutionary war, and, finally, we must study the laws of China's revolutionary war.

Some people hold a wrong view, which we refuted long ago. They say that it is enough merely to study the laws of war in general, or, to put it more concretely, that it is enough merely to follow the military manuals published by the reactionary Chinese government or the reactionary military academies in China. They do not see that these manuals give merely the laws of war in general and moreover are wholly copied from abroad, and that if we copy and apply them exactly without the slightest change in form or content, we shall be "cutting the feet to fit the shoes" and be defeated. Their argument is: why should knowledge which has been acquired at the cost of blood be of no use? They fail to see that although we must cherish the earlier experience thus acquired, we must also cherish experience acquired at the cost of our own blood.

Others hold a second wrong view, which we also refuted long ago. They say that it is enough merely to study the experience of revolutionary war in Russia, or, to put it more concretely, that it is enough merely to follow the laws by which the civil war in the Soviet Union was directed and the military manuals published by Soviet military organizations. They do not see that these laws and manuals embody the specific characteristics of the civil war and the Red Army in the Soviet Union, and that if we copy and apply them without allowing any change, we shall also be "cutting the feet to fit the shoes" and be defeated. Their argument is: since our war, like the war in the Soviet Union, is a revolutionary war, and since the Soviet Union won victory, how then can there be any alternative but to follow the Soviet example? They fail to see that while we should set special store by the war experience of the Soviet Union, because it is the most recent experience of revolutionary war and was acquired under the guidance of Lenin and Stalin, we should likewise cherish the experience of China's revolutionary war, because there are many factors that are specific to the Chinese revolution and the Chinese Red Army.

Still others hold a third wrong view, which we likewise refuted long ago. They say that the most valuable experience is that of the Northern Expedition of 1926-27 and that we must learn from it, or, to put it more concretely, that we must imitate the Northern Expedition in driving straight ahead to seize the big cities. They fail to see that while the experience of the Northern Expedition should be studied, it should not be copied and applied mechanically, because the circumstances of our present war are different. We should take from the Northern Expedition only what still applies today, and work out something of our own in the light of present conditions.

Thus the different laws for directing different wars are determined by the different circumstances of those wars -- differences in their time, place and nature. As regards the time factor, both war and its laws develop; each historical stage has its special characteristics, and hence the laws of war in each historical stage have their special characteristics and cannot be mechanically applied in another stage. As for the nature of war, since revolutionary war and counterrevolutionary war both have their special characteristics, the laws governing them also have their own characteristics, and those applying to one cannot be mechanically transferred to the other. As for the factor of place, since each country or nation, especially a large country or nation, has its own characteristics, the laws of war for each country or nation also have their own characteristics, and here, too, those applying to one cannot be mechanically transferred to the other. In studying the laws for directing wars that occur at different historical stages, that differ in nature and that are waged in different places and by different nations, we must fix our attention on the characteristics and development of each, and must oppose a mechanical approach to the problem of war.

Nor is this all. It signifies progress and development in a commander who is initially capable of commanding only a small formation, if he becomes capable of commanding a big one. There is also a difference between operating in one locality and in many. It likewise signifies progress and development in a commander who is initially capable of operating only in a locality he knows well, if he becomes capable of operating in many other localities. Owing to technical, tactical and strategic developments on the enemy side and on our own, the circumstances also differ from stage to stage within a given war. It signifies still more progress and development in a commander who is capable of exercising command in a war at its lower stages, if he becomes capable of exercising command in its higher stages. A commander who remains capable of commanding only a formation of a certain size, only in a certain locality and at a certain stage in the development of a war shows that he has made no progress and has not developed. There are some people who, contented with a single skill or a peep-hole view, never make any progress, they may play some role in the revolution at a given place and time, but not a significant one. We need directors of war who can play a significant role. All the laws for directing war develop as history develops and as war develops; nothing is changeless.

2. THE AIM OF WAR IS TO ELIMINATE WAR

War, this monster of mutual slaughter among men, will be finally eliminated by the progress of human society, and in the not too distant future too. But there is only one way to eliminate it and that is to oppose war with war, to oppose counter-revolutionary war with revolutionary war, to oppose national counter-revolutionary war with national revolutionary war, and to oppose counter-revolutionary class war with revolutionary class war. History knows only two kinds of war, just and unjust. We support just wars and oppose unjust wars. All counter-revolutionary wars are unjust, all revolutionary wars are just. Mankind's era of wars will be brought to an end by our own efforts, and beyond doubt the war we wage is part of the final battle. But also beyond doubt the war we face will be part of the biggest and most ruthless of all wars. The biggest and most ruthless of unjust counter-revolutionary wars is hanging over us, and the vast majority of mankind will be ravaged unless we raise the banner of a just war. The banner of mankind's just war is the banner of mankind's salvation. The banner of China's just war is the banner of China's salvation. A war waged by the great majority of mankind and of the Chinese people is beyond doubt a just war, a most lofty and glorious undertaking for the salvation of mankind and China, and a bridge to a new era in world history. When human society advances to the point where classes and states are eliminated, there will be no more wars, counter-revolutionary or revolutionary, unjust or just; that will be the era of perpetual peace for mankind. Our study of the laws of revolutionary war springs from the desire to eliminate all wars; herein lies the distinction between us Communists and all the exploiting classes.

3. STRATEGY IS THE STUDY OF THE LAWS OF A WAR SITUATION AS A WHOLE

Wherever there is war, there is a war situation as a whole. The war situation as a whole may cover the entire world, may cover an entire country, or may cover an independent guerrilla zone or an independent major operational front. Any war situation which acquires a comprehensive consideration of its various aspects and stages forms a war situation as a whole.

The task of the science of strategy is to study those laws for directing a war that govern a war situation as a whole. The task of the science of campaigns and the science of tactics [1] is to study those laws for directing a war that govern a partial situation.

Why is it necessary for the commander of a campaign or a tactical operation to understand the laws of strategy to some degree? Because an understanding of the whole facilitates the handling of the part, and because the part is subordinate to the whole. The view that strategic victory is determined by tactical successes alone is wrong because it overlooks the fact that victory or defeat in a war is first and foremost a question of whether the situation as a whole and its various stages are properly taken into account. If there are serious defects or mistakes in taking the situation as a whole and its various stages into account, the war is sure to be lost. "One careless move loses the whole game" refers to a move affecting the situation as a whole, a move decisive for the whole situation, and not to a move of a partial nature, a move which is not decisive for the whole situation. As in chess, so in war.

But the situation as a whole cannot be detached from its parts and become independent of them, for it is made up of all its parts. Sometimes certain parts may suffer destruction or defeat without seriously affecting the situation as a whole, because they are not decisive for it. Some defeats or failures in tactical operations or campaigns do not lead to deterioration in the war situation as a whole, because they are not of decisive significance. But the loss of most of the campaigns making up the war situation as a whole, or of one or two decisive campaigns, immediately changes the whole situation. Here, "most of the campaigns" or "one or two campaigns" are decisive. In the history of war, there are instances where defeat in a single battle nullified all the advantages of a series of victories, and there are also instances where victory in a single battle after many defeats opened up a new situation. In those instances the "series of victories" and the "many defeats" were partial in nature and not decisive for the situation as a whole, while "defeat in a single battle" or "victory in a single battle" played the decisive role. All this explains the importance of taking into account the situation as a whole. What is most important for the person in over-all command is to concentrate on attending to the war situation as a whole. The main point is that, according to the circumstances, he should concern himself with the problems of the grouping of his military units and formations, the relations between campaigns, the relations between various operational stages, and the relations between our activities as a whole and the enemy's activities as a whole -- all these problems demand his greatest care and effort, and if he ignores them and immerses himself in secondary problems, he can hardly avoid setbacks.

The relationship between the whole and the part holds not only for the relationship between strategy and campaign but also for that between campaign and tactics. Examples are to be found in the relation between the operations of a division and those of its regiments and battalions, and in the relation between the operations of a company and those of its platoons and squads. The commanding officer at any level should centre his attention on the most important and decisive problem or action in the whole situation he is handling, and not on other problems or actions.

What is important or decisive should be determined not by general or abstract considerations, but according to the concrete circumstances. In a military operation the direction and point of assault should be selected according to the actual situation of the enemy, the terrain, and the strength of our own forces at the moment. One must see to it that the soldiers do not overeat when supplies are abundant, and take care that they do not go hungry when supplies are short. In the White areas the mere leakage of a piece of information may cause defeat in a subsequent engagement, but in the Red areas such leakage is often not a very serious matter. It is necessary for the high commanders to participate personally in certain battles but not in others. For a military school, the most important question is the selection of a director and instructors and the adoption of a training programme. For a mass meeting, the main thing is mobilizing the masses to attend and putting forward suitable slogans. And so on and so forth. In a word, the principle is to centre our attention on the important links that have a bearing on the situation as a whole.

The only way to study the laws governing a war situation as a whole is to do some hard thinking. For what pertains to the situation as a whole is not visible to the eye, and we can understand it only by hard thinking; there is no other way. But because the situation as a whole is made up of parts, people with experience of the parts, experience of campaigns and tactics, can understand matters of a higher order provided they are willing to think hard. The problems of strategy include the following:

Giving proper consideration to the relation between the enemy and ourselves.

Giving proper consideration to the relation between various campaigns or between various operational stages.

Giving proper consideration to those parts which have a bearing on (are decisive for) the situation as a whole.

Giving proper consideration to the special features contained in the general situation.

Giving proper consideration to the relation between the front and the rear.

Giving proper consideration to the distinction as well as the connection between losses and replacements, between fighting and resting, between concentration and dispersion, between attack and defence, between advance and retreat, between concealment and exposure, between the main attack and supplementary attacks, between assault and containing action, between centralized command and decentralized command, between protracted war and war of quick decision, between positional war and mobile war, between our own forces and friendly forces, between one military arm and another, between higher and lower levels, between cadres and the rank and file, between old and new soldiers, between senior and junior cadres, between old and new cadres, between Red areas and White areas, between old Red areas and new ones, between the central district and the borders of a given base area, between the warm season and the cold season, between victory and defeat, between large and small troop formations, between the regular army and the guerrilla forces, between destroying the enemy and winning over the masses, between expanding the Red Army and consolidating it, between military work and political work, between past and present tasks, between present and future tasks, between tasks arising from one set of circumstances and tasks arising from another, between fixed fronts and fluid fronts, between civil war and national war, between one historical stage and another, etc., etc.

None of these problems of strategy is visible to the eye, and yet, if we think hard, we can comprehend, grasp and master them all, that is, we can raise the important problems concerning a war or concerning military operations to the higher plane of principle and solve them. Our task in studying the problems of strategy is to attain this goal.

4. THE IMPORTANT THING IS TO BE GOOD AT LEARNING

Why have we organized the Red Army? For the purpose of defeating the enemy. Why do we study the laws of war? For the purpose of applying them in war.

To learn is no easy matter and to apply what one has learned is even harder. Many people appear impressive when discoursing on military science in classrooms or in books, but when it comes to actual fighting, some win battles and others lose them. Both the history of war and our own experience in war have proved this point.

Where then does the crux lie?

In real life, we cannot ask for "ever-victorious generals", who are few and far between in history. What we can ask for is generals who are brave and sagacious and who normally win their battles in the course of a war, generals who combine wisdom with courage. To become both wise and courageous one must acquire a method, a method to be employed in learning as well as in applying what has been learned.

What method? The method is to familiarize ourselves with all aspects of the enemy situation and our own, to discover the laws governing the actions of both sides and to make use of these laws in our own operations.

The military manuals issued in many countries point both to the necessity of a "flexible application of principles according to circumstances" and to the measures to be taken in case of defeat. They point to the former in order to warn a commander against subjectively committing mistakes through too rigid an application of principles, and to the latter in order to enable him to cope with the situation after he has committed subjective mistakes or after unexpected and irresistible changes have occurred in the objective circumstances.

Why are subjective mistakes made? Because the way the forces in a war or a battle are disposed or directed does not fit the conditions of the given time and place, because subjective direction does not correspond to, or is at variance with, the objective conditions, in other words, because the contradiction between the subjective and the objective has not been resolved. People can hardly avoid such situations whatever they are doing, but some people prove themselves more competent than others. As in any job we demand a comparatively high degree of competence, so in war we demand more victories or, conversely, fewer defeats. Here the crux is to bring the subjective and the objective into proper correspondence with each other.

Take an example in tactics. If the point chosen for attack is on one of the enemy's flanks and it is located precisely where his weak spot happens to be, and in consequence the assault succeeds, then the subjective corresponds with the objective, that is, the commander's reconnaissance, judgement and decision have corresponded with the enemy's actual situation and dispositions. If the point chosen for attack is on another flank or in the centre and the attack hits a snag and makes no headway, then such correspondence is lacking. If the attack is properly timed, if the reserves are used neither too late nor too early, and if all the other dispositions and operations in the battle are such as to favour us and not the enemy, then the subjective direction throughout the battle completely corresponds with the objective situation. Such complete correspondence is extremely rare in a war or a battle, in which the belligerents are groups of live human beings bearing arms and keeping their secrets from each other; this is quite unlike handling inanimate objects or routine matters. But if the direction given by the commander corresponds in the main with the actual situation, that is, if the decisive elements in the direction correspond with the actual situation, then there is a basis for victory.

A commander's correct dispositions stem from his correct decisions, his correct decisions stem from his correct judgements, and his correct judgements stem from a thorough and necessary reconnaissance and from pondering on and piecing together the data of various kinds gathered through reconnaissance. He applies all possible and necessary methods of reconnaissance, and ponders on the information gathered about the enemy's situation, discarding the dross and selecting the essential, eliminating the false and retaining the true, proceeding from the one to the other and from the outside to the inside; then, he takes the conditions on his own side into account, and makes a study of both sides and their interrelations, thereby forming his judgements, making up his mind and working out his plans. Such is the complete process of knowing a situation which a military man goes through before he formulates a strategic plan, a campaign plan or a battle plan. But instead of doing this, a careless military man bases his military plans on his own wishful thinking, and hence his plans are fanciful and do not correspond with reality. A rash military man relying solely upon enthusiasm is bound to be tricked by the enemy, or lured on by some superficial or partial aspect of the enemy's situation, or swayed by irresponsible suggestions from subordinates that are not based on real knowledge or deep insight, and so he runs his head against a brick wall, because he does not know or does not want to know that every military plan must be based on the necessary reconnaissance and on careful consideration of the enemy's situation, his own situation, and their interrelations.

The process of knowing a situation goes on not only before the formulation of a military plan but also after. In carrying out the plan from the moment it is put into effect to the end of the operation, there is another process of knowing the situation, namely, the process of practice. In the course of this process, it is necessary to examine anew whether the plan worked out in the preceding process corresponds with reality. If it does not correspond with reality, or if it does not fully do so, then in the light of our new knowledge, it becomes necessary to form new judgements, make new decisions and change the original plan so as to meet the new situation. The plan is partially changed in almost every operation, and sometimes it is even changed completely. A rash man who does not understand the need for such alterations or is unwilling to make them, but who acts blindly, will inevitably run his head against a brick wall.

The above applies to a strategic action, a campaign or a battle. Provided he is modest and willing to learn, an experienced military man will be able to familiarize himself with the character of his own forces (commanders, men, arms, supplies, etc., and their sum total), with the character of the enemy forces (likewise, commanders, men, arms, supplies, etc., and their sum total) and with all other conditions related to the war, such as politics, economics, geography and weather; such a military man will have a better grasp in directing a war or an operation and will be more likely to win victories. He will achieve this because, over a long period of time, he has come to know the situation on the enemy side and his own, discovered the laws of action, and resolved the contradictions between the subjective and the objective. This process of knowing is extremely important; without such a long period of experience, it would be difficult to understand and grasp the laws of an entire war. Neither a beginner nor a person who fights only on paper can become a really able high-ranking commander; only one who has learned through actual fighting in war can do so.

All military laws and military theories which are in the nature of principles are the experience of past wars summed up by people in former days or in our own times. We should seriously study these lessons, paid for in blood, which are a heritage of past wars. That is one point. But there is another. We should put these conclusions to the test of our own experience, assimilating what is useful, rejecting what is useless, and adding what is specifically our own. The latter is very important, for otherwise we cannot direct a war.

Reading is learning, but applying is also learning and the more important kind of learning at that. Our chief method is to learn warfare through warfare. A person who has had no opportunity to go to school can also learn warfare -- he can learn through fighting In war. A revolutionary war is a mass undertaking, it is often n a matter of first learning and then doing, but of doing and the learning, for doing is itself learning. There is a gap between the ordinary civilian and the soldier, but it is no Great Wall, and it can be quickly closed, and the way to close it is to take part in revolution in war. By saying that it is not easy to learn and to apply, we mean that It Is hard to learn thoroughly and to apply skillfully. By saying that civilians can very quickly become soldiers, we mean that it is not difficult to cross the threshold. To put the two statements together we may cite the Chinese adage, "Nothing in the world is difficult for one who sets his mind to it." To cross the threshold is not difficult and mastery, too, is possible provided one sets one's mind to the task and is good at learning.

The laws of war, like the laws governing all other things, are reflections in our minds of objective realities; everything outside of the mind is objective reality. Consequently what has to be learned and known includes the state of affairs on the enemy side and that on our side, both of which should be regarded as the object of study, while the mind (the capacity to think) alone is the subject performing the study. Some people are good at knowing themselves and poor at knowing their enemy, and some are the other way round, neither can solve the problem of learning and applying the laws of war. There is a saying in the book of Sun Wu Tzu, the great military scientist of ancient China, "Know the enemy and know yourself, and you can fight a hundred battles with no danger of defeat", [2] which refers both to the stage of learning and to the stage of application, both to knowing the laws of the development of objective reality and to deciding on our own action in accordance with these laws in order to overcome the enemy facing us. We should not take this saying lightly.

War is the highest form of struggle between nations, states, classes, or political groups, and all the laws of war are applied by warring nations, states, classes, or political groups for the purpose of achieving victory for themselves. Unquestionably, victory or defeat in war is determined mainly by the military, political, economic and natural conditions on both sides. But not by these alone. It is also determined by each side's subjective ability in directing the war. In his endeavour to win a war, a military man cannot overstep the limitations imposed by the material conditions; within these limitations, however, he can and must strive for victory. The stage of action for a military man is built upon objective material conditions, but on that stage he i can direct the performance of many a drama, full of sound and colour, power and grandeur. Therefore, given the objective material foundations, i.e., the military, political, economic and natural conditions, our Red Army commanders must display their prowess and marshal all their forces to crush the national and class enemies and to transform this evil world. Here is where our subjective ability in directing war can and must be exercised. We do not permit any of our Red Army commanders to become a blundering hothead; we decidedly want every Red Army commander to become a hero who is both brave and sagacious, who possesses both all-conquering courage and the ability to remain master of the situation throughout the changes and vicissitudes of the entire war. Swimming in the ocean of war, he not only must not flounder but must make sure of reaching the opposite shore with measured strokes. The laws for directing war constitute the art of swimming in the ocean of war.

So much for our methods.

Chapter II

THE CHINESE COMMUNIST PARTY AND CHINA'S REVOLUTIONARY WAR

China's revolutionary war, which began in 1924, has passed through two stages, the first from 1924 to 1927, and the second from 1927 to 1936; the stage of national revolutionary war against Japan will now commence. In all three of its stages this revolutionary war has been, is and will be fought under the leadership of the Chinese proletariat and its party, the Chinese Communist Party. The chief enemies in China's revolutionary war are imperialism and the feudal forces. Although the Chinese bourgeoisie may take part in the revolutionary war at certain historical junctures, yet its selfishness and lack of political and economic independence render it both unwilling and unable to lead China's revolutionary war on to the road of complete victory. The masses of China's peasantry and urban petty bourgeoisie wish to take an active part in the revolutionary war and to carry it to complete victory. They are the main forces in the revolutionary war, but, being small-scale producers, they are limited in their political outlook (and some of the unemployed masses have anarchist views), so that they are unable to give correct leadership in the war. Therefore, in an era when the proletariat has already appeared on the political stage, the responsibility for leading China's revolutionary war inevitably falls on the shoulders of the Chinese Communist Party. In this era, any revolutionary war will definitely end in defeat if it lacks, or runs counter to, the leadership of the proletariat and the Communist Party. Of all the social strata and political groupings in semi-colonial China, the proletariat and the Communist Party are the ones most free from narrow-mindedness and selfishness, are politically the most far-sighted, the best organized and the readiest to learn with an open mind from the experience of the vanguard class, the proletariat, and its political party throughout the world and to make use of this experience in their own cause Hence only the proletariat and the Communist Party can lead the peasantry, the urban petty bourgeoisie and bourgeoisie, can overcome the narrow-mindedness of the peasants and the petty bourgeoisie, the destructiveness of the unemployed masses, and also (provided the Communist Party does not err in its policy) the vacillation and lack of thoroughness of the bourgeoisie can lead the revolution and the war on to the road of victory.

The revolutionary war of 1924-27 was waged, basically speaking, in conditions in which the international proletariat and the Chinese proletariat and its party exerted political influence on the Chinese national bourgeoisie and its parties and entered into political cooperation with them. However, this revolutionary war failed at the critical juncture, first of all because the big bourgeoisie turned traitor, and at the same time because the opportunists within the revolutionary ranks voluntarily surrendered the leadership of the revolution.

The Agrarian Revolutionary War, lasting from 1927 to the present, has been waged under new conditions. The enemy in this war is not imperialism alone but also the alliance of the big bourgeoisie and the big landlords. And the national bourgeoisie has become a tail to the big bourgeoisie. This revolutionary war is led by the Communist Party alone, which has established absolute leadership over it. This absolute leadership is the most important condition enabling the revolutionary war to be carried through firmly to the end. Without it, it is inconceivable that the revolutionary war could have been carried on with such perseverance.

The Chinese Communist Party has led China's revolutionary war courageously and resolutely, and for fifteen long years [3] has demonstrated to the whole nation that it is the people's friend, fighting at all times in the forefront of the revolutionary war in defence of the people's interests and for their freedom and liberation.

By its arduous struggles and by the martyrdom of hundreds of thousands of its heroic members and tens of thousands of its heroic cadres, the Communist Party of China has played a great educative role among hundreds of millions of people throughout the country. The Party's great historic achievements in its revolutionary struggles have provided the prerequisite for the survival and salvation of China at this critical juncture when she is being invaded by a national enemy; and this prerequisite is the existence of a political leadership enjoying the confidence of the vast majority of the people and chosen by them after long years of testing. Today, the people accept what the Communist Party says more readily than what any other political party says. Were it not for the arduous struggles of the Chinese Communist Party in the last fifteen years, it would be impossible to save China in the face of the new menace of subjugation.

Besides the errors of the Right opportunism of Chen Tu-hsiu [4] and the "Left" opportunism of Li Li-san, [5] the Chinese Communist Party has committed two other errors in the course of the revolutionary war. The first error was the "Left" opportunism of 1931-34 [6] which resulted in serious losses in the Agrarian Revolutionary War so that, instead of our defeating the enemy's fifth campaign of "encirclement and suppression", we lost our base areas and the Red Army was weakened. This error was corrected at the enlarged meeting of the Political Bureau of the Central Committee at Tsunyi in January 1935. The second was the Right opportunism of Chang Kuo-tao in 1935-36 [7] which grew to such an extent that it undermined the discipline of the Party and of the Red Army and caused serious losses to part of the Red Army's main forces. But this error was also finally rectified, thanks to the correct leadership of the Central Committee and the political consciousness of Party members, commanders and fighters in the Red Army. Of course all these errors were harmful to our Party, to our revolution and the war, but in the end we overcame them, and in doing so our Party and our Red Army have steeled themselves and become still stronger.

The Chinese Communist Party has led and continues to lead the stirring, magnificent and victorious revolutionary war. This war is not only the banner of China's liberation, but has international revolutionary significance as well. The eyes of the revolutionary people the world over are upon us. In the new stage, the stage of the anti-Japanese national revolutionary war, we shall lead the Chinese revolution to It's completion and exert a profound influence on the revolution in the East and in the whole world. Our revolutionary war has proved that we need a correct Marxist military line as well as a correct Marxist political line. Fifteen years of revolution and war have hammered out such political and military lines. We believe that from now on, in the new stage of the war, these lines will be further developed, filled out and enriched in new circumstances, so that we can attain our aim of defeating the national enemy. History tells us that correct political and military lines do not emerge and develop spontaneously and tranquilly, but only in the course of struggle. These lines must combat left opportunism on the one hand and Right opportunism on the other. Without combating and thoroughly overcoming these harmful tendencies which damage the revolution and the revolutionary war, it would be impossible to establish a correct line and win victory in this war. It is for this reason that I often refer to erroneous views in this pamphlet.

Chapter III

CHARACTERISTICS OF
CHINA'S REVOLUTIONARY WAR

1. THE IMPORTANCE OF THE SUBJECT

People who do not admit, do not know, or do not want to know t at China's revolutionary war has its own characteristics have equated the war waged by the Red Army against the Kuomintang forces with war in general or with the civil war in the Soviet Union. The experience of the civil war in the Soviet Union directed by Lenin and Stalin has a world-wide significance. All Communist Parties, including the Chinese Communist Party, regard this experience and its theoretical summing-up by Lenin and Stalin as their guide. But this does not mean that we should apply it mechanically to our own conditions. In many of its aspects China's revolutionary war has characteristics distinguishing it from the civil war in the Soviet Union. Of course it is wrong to take no account of these characteristics or deny their existence. This point has been fully borne out in our ten years of war.

Our enemy has made similar mistakes. He did not recognize that fighting against the Red Army required a different strategy and different tactics from those used in fighting other forces. Relying on his superiority in various respects, he took us lightly and stuck to his old methods of warfare. This was the case both before and during his fourth "encirclement and suppression" campaign in 1933, with the result that he suffered a series of defeats. In the Kuomintang army a new approach to the problem was suggested first by the reactionary Kuomintang general Liu Wei-yuan and then by Tai Yueh. Their idea was eventually accepted by Chiang Kai-shek. That was how Chiang Kai-shek's Officers' Training Corps at Lushan [8] came into being and how the new reactionary military principles [9] applied in the fifth campaign of "encirclement and suppression" were evolved.

But when the enemy changed his military principles to suit operations against the Red Army, there appeared in our ranks a group of people who reverted to the "old ways". They urged a return to ways suited to the general run of things, refused to go into the specific circumstances of each case, rejected the experience gained in the Red Army's history of sanguinary battles, belittled the strength of imperialism and the Kuomintang as well as that of the Kuomintang army, and turned a blind eye to the new reactionary principles adopted by the enemy. As a result, all the revolutionary bases except the Shensi-Kansu border area were lost, the Red Army was reduced from 300,000 to a few tens of thousands, the membership of the Chinese Communist Party fell from 300,000 to a few tens of thousands, and the Party organizations in the Kuomintang areas were almost all destroyed. In short, we paid a severe penalty, which was historic in its significance. This group of people called themselves Marxist-Leninists, but actually they had not learned an iota of Marxism-Leninism. Lenin said that the most essential thing in Marxism, the living soul of Marxism, is the concrete analysis of concrete conditions. [10] That was precisely the point these comrades of ours forgot.

Hence one can see that, without an understanding of the characteristics of China's revolutionary war, it is impossible to direct it and lead It to victory.

2. WHAT ARE THE CHARACTERISTICS OF CHINA'S REVOLUTIONARY WAR?

What then are the characteristics of China's revolutionary war?

I think there are four principal ones.

The first is that China is a vast, semi-colonial country which is unevenly developed politically and economically and which has gone through the revolution of 1924-27.

This characteristic indicates that it is possible for China's revolutionary war to develop and attain victory. We already pointed this out (at the First Party Congress of the Hunan-Kiangsi Border Area) when in late 1927 and early 1928 soon after guerrilla warfare was started in China, some comrades in the Chingkang Mountains in the Hunan-Kiangsi border area raised the question, "How long can we keep the Red Flag flying?" For this was a most fundamental question. Without answering this question of whether China's revolutionary base areas and the Chinese Red Army could survive and develop, we could not have advanced a single step. The Sixth National Congress of the Chinese Communist Party in 1928 again gave the answer to the question. Since then the Chinese revolutionary movement has had a correct theoretical basis.

Let us now analyse this characteristic.

China's political and economic development is uneven -- a weak capitalist economy coexists with a preponderant semi-feudal economy; a few modern industrial and commercial cities coexist with a vast stagnant countryside; several million industrial workers coexist with several hundred millions of peasants and handicraftsmen labouring under the old system; big warlords controlling the central government coexist with small warlords controlling the provinces; two kinds of reactionary armies, the so-called Central Army under Chiang Kai-shek and - miscellaneous troops" under the warlords in the provinces, exist side by side; a few railways, steamship lines and motor roads exist side by side with a vast number of wheelbarrow paths and foot-paths many of which are difficult to negotiate even on foot.

China is a semi-colonial country -- disunity among the imperialist powers makes for disunity among the ruling groups in China. There is a difference between a semi-colonial country controlled by several countries and a colony controlled by a single country.

China is a vast country -- "When it is dark in the east, it is light in the west; when things are dark in the south, there is still light in the north." Hence one need not worry about lack of room for manoeuvre.

China has gone through a great revolution -- this has provided the seeds from which the Red Army has grown, provided the leader of the Red Army, namely, the Chinese Communist Party, and provided the masses with experience of participation in a revolution.

We say, therefore, that the first characteristic of China's revolutionary war is that it is waged in a vast semi-colonial country which is unevenly developed politically and economically and which has gone through a revolution. This characteristic basically determines our military strategy and tactics as well as our political strategy and tactics.

The second characteristic is that our enemy is big and powerful.

How do matters stand with the Kuomintang, the enemy of the Red Army? It is a party that has seized political power and has more or less stabilized its power. It has gained the support of the world's principal counter-revolutionary states. It has remodeled its army which has thus become different from any other army in Chinese history and on the whole similar to the armies of modern states; this army is much better supplied with weapons and matériel than the Red Army, and is larger than any army in Chinese history, or for that matter than the standing army of any other country. There is a world of difference between the Kuomintang army and the Red Army. The Kuomintang controls the key positions or lifelines in the politics, economy, communications and culture of China; its political power is nation-wide.

The Chinese Red Army is thus confronted with a big and powerful enemy. This is the second characteristic of China's revolutionary war. It necessarily makes the military operations of the Red Army different in many ways from those of wars in general and from those of the civil war in the Soviet Union or of the Northern Expedition.

The third characteristic is that the Red Army is small and weak. The Chinese Red Army, starting as guerrilla units, came into being after the defeat of the first great revolution. This occurred in a period of relative political and economic stability in the reactionary capitalist countries of the world as well as in a period of reaction in China.

Our political power exists in scattered and isolated mountainous or remote regions and receives no outside help whatsoever. Economic and cultural conditions in the revolutionary base areas are backward compared with those in the Kuomintang areas. The revolutionary base areas embrace only rural districts and small towns. These areas were extremely small in the beginning and have not grown much larger since. Moreover, they are fluid and not stationary, and the Red Army has no really consolidated bases.

The Red Army is numerically small, its arms are poor, and it has great difficulty in obtaining supplies such as food, bedding and clothing.

This characteristic presents a sharp contrast to the preceding one. Prom this sharp contrast have arisen the strategy and tactics of the Red Army.

The fourth characteristic is Communist Party leadership and the agrarian revolution.

This characteristic is the inevitable consequence of the first one. It has given rise to two features. On the one hand, despite the fact that China's revolutionary war is taking place in a period of reaction in China and throughout the capitalist world, victory is possible because it is under the leadership of the Communist Party and has the support of the peasantry. Thanks to this support, our base areas, small as they are, are politically very powerful and stand firmly opposed to the enormous Kuomintang regime, while militarily they place great difficulties in the way of the Kuomintang attacks. Small as it is, the Red Army has great fighting capacity, because its members, led by the Communist Party, are born of the agrarian revolution and are fighting for their own interests, and because its commanders and fighters are politically united.

The Kuomintang, on the other hand, presents a sharp contrast. It opposes the agrarian revolution and therefore has no support from the peasantry. Though it has a large army, the Kuomintang cannot make its soldiers and the many lower-ranking officers, who were originally small producers, risk their lives willingly for it. Its officers and men are politically divided, which reduces its fighting capacity.

3. OUR STRATEGY AND TACTICS ENSUING FROM THESE CHARACTERISTICS

Thus the four principal characteristics of China's revolutionary war are: a vast semi-colonial country which is unevenly developed politically and economically and which has gone through a great revolution; a big and powerful enemy; a small and weak Red Army; and the agrarian revolution. These characteristics determine the line for guiding China's revolutionary war as well as many of its strategic and tactical principles. It follows from the first and fourth characteristics that it is possible for the Chinese Red Army to grow and defeat its enemy. It follows from the second and third characteristics that it is impossible for the Chinese Red Army to grow very rapidly or defeat its enemy quickly; in other words, the war will be protracted and may even be lost if it is mishandled.

These are the two aspects of China's revolutionary war. They exist simultaneously, that is, there are favourable factors and there are difficulties. This is the fundamental law of China's revolutionary war, from which many other laws ensue. The history of our ten years of war has proved the validity of this law. He who has eyes but fails to see this fundamental law cannot direct China's revolutionary war, cannot lead the Red Army to victories.

It is clear that we must correctly settle all the following matters of principle:

Determine our strategic orientation correctly, oppose adventurism when on the offensive, oppose conservatism when on the defensive, and oppose flightism when shifting from one place to another.

Oppose guerrilla-ism in the Red Army, while recognizing the guerrilla character of its operations.

Oppose protracted campaigns and a strategy of quick decision, and uphold the strategy of protracted war and campaigns of quick decision.

Oppose fixed battle lines and positional warfare, and favour fluid battle lines and mobile warfare.

Oppose fighting merely to rout the enemy, and uphold fighting to annihilate the enemy.

Oppose the strategy of striking with two "fists" in two directions at the same time, and uphold the strategy of striking with one "fist" in one direction at one time. [12]

Oppose the principle of maintaining one large rear area, and uphold the principle of small rear areas.

Oppose an absolutely centralized command, and favour a relatively centralized command.

Oppose the purely military viewpoint and the ways of roving rebels, [13] and recognize that the Red Army is a propagandist and organizer of the Chinese revolution.

Oppose bandit ways, [14] and uphold strict political discipline.

Oppose warlord ways, and favour both democracy within proper limits and an authoritative discipline in the army.

Oppose an incorrect, sectarian policy on cadres, and uphold the correct policy on cadres.

Oppose the policy of isolation, and affirm the policy of winning over all possible allies.

Oppose keeping the Red Army at its old stage, and strive to develop it to a new stage.

Our present discussion of the problems of strategy is intended to elucidate these matters carefully in the light of the historical experience gained in China's ten years of bloody revolutionary war.

Chapter IV

"ENCIRCLEMENT AND SUPPRESSION" AND COUNTER-CAMPAIGNS AGAINST IT -- THE MAIN PATTERN OF CHINA'S CIVIL WAR

In the ten years since our guerrilla war began, every independent Red guerrilla unit, every Red Army unit or every revolutionary base area has been regularly subjected by the enemy to "encirclement and suppression". The enemy looks upon the Red Army as a monster and seeks to capture it the moment it shows itself. He is for ever pursuing the Red Army and for ever trying to encircle it. For ten years this pattern of warfare has not changed, and unless the civil war gives place to a national war, the pattern will remain the same till the day the enemy becomes the weaker contestant and the Red Army the stronger.

The Red Army's operations take the form of counter-campaigns against "encirclement and suppression". For us victory means chiefly victory in combating "encirclement and suppression", that is, strategic victory and victories in campaigns. The fight against each "encirclement and suppression" campaign constitutes a counter-campaign, which usually comprises several or even scores of battles, big and small. Until an "encirclement and suppression" campaign has been basically smashed, one cannot speak of strategic victory or of victory in the counter-campaign as a whole, even though many battles may have been won. The history of the Red Army's decade of war is a history of counter-campaigns against "encirclement and suppression".

In the enemy's "encirclement and suppression" campaigns and the Red Army's counter-campaigns against them, the two forms of fighting, offensive and defensive, are both employed, and here there is no difference from any other war, ancient or modern, in China or elsewhere. The special characteristic of China's civil war, however, is the repeated alternation of the two forms over a long period of time. In each "encirclement and suppression" campaign, the enemy employs the offensive against the Red Army's defensive, and the Red Army employs the defensive against his offensive; this is the first stage of a counter-campaign against "encirclement and suppression". Then the enemy employs the defensive against the Red Army's offensive, and the Red Army employs the offensive against his defensive; this is the second stage of the counter-campaign. Every "encirclement and suppression" campaign has these two stages, and they alternate over a long period.

By repeated alternation over a long period we mean the repetition of this pattern of warfare and these forms of fighting. This is a fact obvious to everybody. An "encirclement and suppression" campaign and a counter-campaign against it -- such is the repeated pattern of the war. In each campaign the alternation in the forms of fighting consists of the first stage in which the enemy employs the offensive against our defensive and we meet his offensive with our defensive, and of the second stage in which the enemy employs the defensive against our offensive and we meet his defensive with our offensive.

As for the content of a campaign or of a battle, it does not consist of mere repetition but is different each time. This, too, is a fact and obvious to everybody. In this connection it has become a rule that with each campaign and each counter-campaign, the scale becomes larger, the situation more complicated and the fighting more intense.

But this does not mean that there are no ups and downs. After the enemy's fifth "encirclement and suppression" campaign, the Red Army was greatly weakened, and all the base areas in the south were lost. Having shifted to the northwest, the Red Army now no longer holds a vital position threatening the internal enemy as it did in the south and as a result the scale of the "encirclement and suppression" campaigns has become smaller, the situation simpler and the fighting less intense.

What constitutes a defeat for the Red Army? Strategically speaking, there is a defeat only when a counter-campaign against "encirclement and suppression" fails completely, but even then the defeat is only partial and temporary. For only the total destruction of the Red Army would constitute complete defeat in the civil war; but this has never happened. The loss of extensive base areas and the shift of the Red Army constituted a temporary and partial defeat, not a final and complete one, even though this partial defeat entailed losing go per cent of the Party membership, of the armed forces and of the base areas. We call this shift the continuation of our defensive and the enemy's pursuit the continuation of his offensive. That is to say, in the course of the struggle between the enemy's "encirclement and suppression" and our counter-campaign we allowed our defensive to be broken by the enemy's offensive instead of turning from the defensive to the offensive; and so our defensive turned into a retreat and the enemy's offensive into a pursuit. But when the Red Army reached a new area, as for example when we shifted from Kiangsi Province and various other regions to Shensi Province, the repetition of "encirclement and suppression" campaigns began afresh. That is why we say that the Red Army's strategic retreat (the Long March) was a continuation of its strategic defensive and the enemy's strategic pursuit was a continuation of his strategic offensive.

In the Chinese civil war, as in all other wars, ancient or modern, in China or abroad, there are only two basic forms of fighting, attack and defence. The special characteristic of China's civil war consists in the long-term repetition of "encirclement and suppression" campaigns and of our counter-campaigns together with the long-term alternation in the two forms of fighting, attack and defence, with the inclusion of the phenomenon of the great strategic shift of more than ten thousand kilometres (the Long March). [15]

A defeat for the enemy is much the same. It is a strategic defeat for the enemy when his "encirclement and suppression" campaign is broken and our defensive becomes an offensive, when the enemy turns to the defensive and has to reorganize before launching another "encirclement and suppression" campaign. The enemy has not had to make a strategic shift of more than ten thousand kilometres such as we have, because he rules the whole country and is much stronger than we are. But there have been partial shifts of his forces. Sometimes, enemy forces in White strongholds encircled by the Red Army in some base areas have broken through our encirclement and withdrawn to the White areas to organize new offensives. If the civil war is prolonged and the Red Army's victories become more extensive, there will be more of this sort of thing. But the enemy cannot achieve the same results as the Red Army, because he does not have the help of the people and because his officers and men are not united. If he were to imitate the Red Army's long-distance shift, he would certainly be wiped out.

In the period of the Li Li-san line in 1930, Comrade Li Li-san failed to understand the protracted nature of China's civil war and for that reason did not perceive the law that in the course of this war there is repetition over a long period of "encirclement and suppression" campaigns and of their defeat (by that time there had already been three in the Hunan-Kiangsi border area and two in Fukien). Hence, in an attempt to achieve rapid victory for the revolution, he ordered the Red Army, which was then still in its infancy, to attack Wuhan, and also ordered a nation-wide armed uprising. Thus he committed the error of "Left" opportunism.

Likewise the "Left" opportunists of 1931-1934 did not believe in the law of the repetition of "encirclement and suppression" campaigns. Some responsible comrades in our base area along the Hupeh-Honan-Anhwei border held an "auxiliary force" theory, maintaining that the Kuomintang army had become merely an auxiliary force after the defeat of its third "encirclement and suppression" campaign and that the imperialists themselves would have to take the field as the main force in further attacks on the Red Army. The strategy based on this estimate was that the Red Army should attack Wuhan. In principle, this fitted in with the views of those comrades in Kiangsi who called for a Red Army attack on Nanchang, were against the work of linking up the base areas and the tactics of luring the enemy in deep, regarded the seizure of the capital and other key cities of a province as the starting point for victory in that province, and held that "the fight against the fifth 'encirclement and suppression' campaign represents the decisive battle between the road of revolution and the road of colonialism". This "Left" opportunism was the source of the wrong line adopted in the struggles against the fourth "encirclement and suppression" campaign in the Hupeh-Honan-Anhwei border area and in those against the fifth in the Central Area in Kiangsi; and it rendered the Red Army helpless before these fierce enemy campaigns and brought enormous losses to the Chinese revolution.

The view that the Red Army should under no circumstances adopt defensive methods was directly related to this "Left" opportunism which denied the repetition of "encirclement and suppression" campaigns, and it, too, was entirely erroneous.

The proposition that a revolution or a revolutionary war is an offensive is of course correct. A revolution or a revolutionary war in its emergence and growth from a small force to a big force, from the absence of political power to the seizure of political power, from the absence of a Red Army to the creation of a Red Army, and from the absence of revolutionary base areas to their establishment must be on the offensive and cannot be conservative; and tendencies towards conservatism must be opposed.

The only entirely correct proposition is that a revolution or a revolutionary war is an offensive but also involves defence and retreat To defend in order to attack, to retreat in order to advance, to move against the flanks in order to move against the front, and to take a roundabout route in order to get on to the direct route -- this is inevitable in the process of development of many phenomena, especially military movements.

Of the two propositions stated above, the first may be correct in the political sphere, but it is incorrect when transposed to the military sphere. Moreover, it is correct politically only in one situation (when the revolution is advancing), but incorrect when transposed to another situation (when the revolution is in retreat, in general retreat as in Russia in 1906, [16] and in China in 1927 or in partial retreat as in Russia at the time of the Treaty of Brest-Litovsk in 1918). [17] Only the second proposition is entirely correct and true. The "Left" opportunism of 1931-34, which mechanically opposed the employment of defensive military measures, was nothing but infantile thinking.

When will the pattern of repeated "encirclement and suppression" campaigns come to an end? In my opinion, if the civil war is prolonged, this repetition will cease when a fundamental change takes place in the balance of forces. It will cease when the Red Army has become stronger than the enemy. Then we shall be encircling and suppressing the enemy and he will be resorting to counter-campaigns, but political and military conditions will not allow him to attain the same position as that of the Red Army in its counter-campaigns. It can be definitely asserted that by then the pattern of repeated "encirclement and suppression" campaigns will have largely, if not completely, come to an end.

Chapter V

THE STRATEGIC DEFENSIVE

Under this heading I would like to discuss the following problems: (I) active and passive defence; (2) preparations for combating "encirclement and suppression" campaigns; (3) strategic retreat; (4) strategic counter-offensive; (5) starting the counter-offensive; (6) concentration of troops; (7) mobile warfare; (8) war of quick decision; and (9) war of annihilation.

1. ACTIVE AND PASSIVE DEFENCE

Why do we begin by discussing defence? After the failure of China's first national united front of 1994-27, the revolution became a most intense and ruthless class war. While the enemy ruled the whole country, we had only small armed forces; consequently, from the very beginning we have had to wage a bitter struggle against his "encirclement and suppression" campaigns. Our offensives have been closely linked with our efforts to break them, and our fate depends entirely on whether or not we are able to do so. The process of breaking an "encirclement and suppression" campaign is usually circuitous and not as direct as one would wish. The primary problem, and a serious one too, is how to conserve our strength and await an opportunity to defeat the enemy. Therefore, the strategic defensive is the most complicated and most important problem facing the Red Army in its operations.

In our ten years of war two deviations often arose with regard to the strategic defensive; one was to belittle the enemy, the other was to be terrified of him.

As a result of belittling the enemy, many guerrilla units suffered defeat, and on several occasions the Red Army was unable to break the enemy's "encirclement and suppression:'.

When the revolutionary guerrilla units first came into existence, their leaders often failed to assess the enemy's situation and our own correctly. Because they had been successful in organizing sudden armed uprisings in certain places or mutinies among the White troops, they saw only the momentarily favourable circumstances, or failed to see the grave situation actually confronting them, and so usually underestimated the enemy. Moreover, they had no understanding of their own weaknesses (i.e., lack of experience and smallness of forces). It was an objective fact that the enemy was strong and we were weak, and yet some people refused to give it thought, talked only of attack but never of defence or retreat, thus mentally disarming themselves In the matter of defence, and hence misdirected their actions. Many guerrilla units were defeated on this account.

Examples in which the Red Army, for this reason, failed to break the enemy's "encirclement and suppression" campaigns were its defeat In 1928 in the Haifeng-Lufeng area of Kwangtung Province, [18] and its loss of freedom of action in 1932, in the fourth counter-campaign against the enemy's "encirclement and suppression" in the Hupeh-Honan-Anhwei border area, where the Red Army acted on the theory that the Kuomintang army was merely an auxiliary force.

There are many instances of setbacks which were due to being terrified of the enemy.

As against those who underestimated him, some people greatly overestimated him and also greatly underestimated our own strength, as a result of which they adopted an unwarranted policy of retreat and likewise disarmed themselves mentally in the matter of defence. This resulted in the defeat of some guerrilla units, or the failure of certain Red Army campaigns, or the loss of base areas.

The most striking example of the loss of a base area was that of the Central Base Area in Kiangsi during the fifth counter-campaign against "encirclement and suppression". The mistake here arose from a Rightist viewpoint. The leaders feared the enemy as if he were a tiger, set up defences everywhere, fought defensive actions at every step and did not dare to advance to the enemy's rear and attack him there, which would have been to our advantage, or boldly to lure the enemy troops in deep so as to herd them together and annihilate them. As a result, the whole base area was lost and the Red Army had to undertake the Long March of over 12,000 kilometres. However, this kind of mistake was usually preceded by a "Left" error of underestimating the enemy. The military adventurism of attacking the key cities in 1932 was the root cause of the line of passive defence subsequently adopted in coping with the enemy's fifth "encirclement and suppression" campaign.

The most extreme example of being terrified of the enemy was the retreatism of the "Chang Kuo-tao line". The defeat of the Western Column of the Fourth Front Red Army west of the Yellow River [19] marked the final bankruptcy of this line.

Active defence is also known as offensive defence, or defence through decisive engagements. Passive defence is also known as purely defensive defence or pure defence. Passive defence is actually a spurious kind of defence, and the only real defence is active defence, defence for the purpose of counter-attacking and taking the offensive. As far as I know, there is no military manual of value nor any sensible military expert, ancient or modern, Chinese or foreign, that does not oppose passive defence, whether in strategy or tactics. Only a complete fool or a madman would cherish passive defence as a talisman. However, there are people in this world who do such things.

That is an error in war, a manifestation of conservatism in military matters, which we must resolutely oppose.

The military experts of the newer and rapidly developing imperialist countries, namely, Germany and Japan, trumpet the advantages of the strategic offensive and come out against the strategic defensive. This kind of military thinking is absolutely unsuited to China's revolutionary war. These military experts assert that a serious weakness of the defensive is that it shakes popular morale, instead of inspiring it. This applies to countries where class contradictions are acute and the war benefits only the reactionary ruling strata or the reactionary political groups in power. But our situation is different. With the slogan of defending the revolutionary base areas and defending China, we can rally the overwhelming majority of the people to fight with one heart and one mind, because we are the oppressed and the victims of aggression. It was also by using the form of the defensive that the Red Army of the Soviet Union defeated its enemies during the civil war. When the imperialist countries organized the Whites for attack, the war was waged under the slogan of defending the Soviets, even when the October Uprising was being prepared, the military mobilization was carried out under the slogan of defending the capital. In every just war the defensive not only has a lulling effect on politically alien elements, it also makes possible the rallying of the backward sections of the masses to join in the war.

When Marx said that once an armed uprising is started there must not be a moment's pause in the attack, [20] he meant that the masses having taken the enemy unawares in an insurrection, must give the reactionary rulers no chance to retain or recover their political power must seize this moment to beat the nation's reactionary ruling forces when they are unprepared, and must not rest content with the victories already won, underestimate the enemy, slacken their attacks or hesitate to press forward, and so let slip the opportunity of destroying the enemy, bringing failure to the revolution. This is correct. It does not mean, however, that when we are already locked in battle with an enemy who enjoys superiority, we revolutionaries should not adopt defensive measures even when we are hard pressed. Only a prize idiot would think in this way.

Taken as a whole, our war has been an offensive against the Kuomintang, but militarily it has assumed the form of breaking the enemy's "encirclement and suppression".

Militarily speaking, our warfare consists of the alternate use of the defensive and the offensive. In our case it makes no difference whether the offensive is said to follow or to precede the defensive, because the crux of the matter is to break the "encirclement and suppression". The defensive continues until an "encirclement and suppression" campaign is broken, whereupon the offensive begins, these being but two stages of the same thing; and one such enemy campaign is closely followed by another. Of the two stages, the defensive is the more complicated and the more important. It involves numerous problems of how to break the "encirclement and suppression". The basic principle here is to stand for active defence and oppose passive defence.

In our civil war, when the strength of the Red Army surpasses that of the enemy, we shall, in general, no longer need the strategic defensive Our policy then will be the strategic offensive alone. This change will depend on an over-all change in the balance of forces. By that time the only remaining defensive measures will be of a partial character.

2. PREPARATIONS FOR COMBATING "ENCIRCLEMENT AND SUPPRESSION" CAMPAIGNS

Unless we have made necessary and sufficient preparations against a planned enemy "encirclement and suppression" campaign, we shall certainly be forced into a passive position. To accept battle in haste is to fight without being sure of victory. Therefore, when the enemy is preparing an "encirclement and suppression" campaign, it is absolutely necessary for us to prepare our counter-campaign. To be opposed to such preparations, as some people in our ranks were at one time, is childish and ridiculous.

There is a difficult problem here on which controversy may easily arise. When should we conclude our offensive and switch to the phase of preparing our counter-campaign against "encirclement and suppression"? When we are victoriously on the offensive and the enemy is on the defensive, his preparations for the next "encirclement and suppression" campaign are conducted in secret, and therefore it is difficult for us to know when his offensive will begin. If our work of preparing the counter-campaign begins too early, it is bound to reduce the gains from our offensive and will sometimes even have certain harmful effects on the Red Army and the people. For the chief measures in the preparatory phase are the military preparations for withdrawal and the political mobilization for them. Sometimes, if we start preparing too early, this will turn into waiting for the enemy; after waiting a long time without the enemy's appearing, we will have to renew our offensive. And sometimes, the enemy will start his offensive just as our new offensive is beginning, thus putting us in a difficult position. Hence the choice of the right moment to begin our preparations is an important problem. The right moment should be determined with due regard both to the enemy's situation and our own and to the relation between the two. In order to know the enemy's situation, we should collect information on his political, military and financial position and the state of public opinion in his territory. In analysing such information we must take the total strength of the enemy into full account and must not exaggerate the extent of his past defeats, but on the other hand we must not fail to take into account his internal contradictions, his financial difficulties, the effect of his past defeats, etc. As for our side, we must not exaggerate the extent of our past victories, but neither should we fail to take full account of their effect. \

Generally speaking, however, the question of timing the preparations, it is preferable to start them too early rather than too late. For the former involves smaller losses and has the advantage that preparedness averts peril and puts us in a fundamentally invincible position.

The essential problems during the preparatory phase are the preparations for the withdrawal of the Red Army, political mobilization, recruitment, arrangements for finance and provisions, and the handling of politically alien elements.

By preparations for the Red Army's withdrawal we mean taking care that it does not move in a direction jeopardizing the withdrawal or advance too far in its attacks or become too fatigued. These are the things the main forces of the Red Army must attend to on the eve of a large-scale enemy offensive. At such a time, the Red Army must devote its attention mainly to planning the selection and preparation of the battle areas, the acquisition of supplies, and the enlargement and training of its own forces.

Political mobilization is a problem of prime importance in the struggle against "encirclement and suppression". That is to say, we should tell the Red Army and the people in the base area clearly, resolutely and fully that the enemy's offensive is inevitable and imminent and will do serious harm to the people, but at the same time, we should tell them about his weaknesses, the factors favourable to the Red Army, our indomitable will to victory and our general plan of work. We should call upon the Red Army and the entire population to fight against the enemy's "encirclement and suppression" campaign and defend the base area. Except where military secrets are concerned, political mobilization must be carried out openly, and, what is more, every effort should be made to extend it to all who might possibly support the revolutionary cause. The key link here is to convince the cadres.

Recruitment of new soldiers should be based on two considerations, first, on the level of political consciousness of the people and the size of the population and, second, on the current state of the Red Army and the possible extent of its losses in the whole course of the counter-campaign.

Needless to say, the problems of finance and food are of great importance to the counter-campaign. We must take the possibility of a prolonged enemy campaign into account. It is necessary to make an estimate of the minimum material requirements -- chiefly of the Red Army but also of the people in the revolutionary base area -- for the entire struggle against the enemy's "encirclement and suppression" campaign.

With regard to politically alien elements we should not be off our guard, but neither should we be unduly apprehensive of treachery on their part and adopt excessive precautionary measures. Distinction should be made between the landlords, the merchants and the rich peasants, and the main point is to explain things to them politically and win their neutrality, while at the same time organizing the masses of the people to keep an eye on them. Only against the very few elements who are most dangerous should stern measures like arrest be taken.

The extent of success in a struggle against "encirclement and suppression" is closely related to the degree to which the tasks of the preparatory phase have been fulfilled. Relaxation of preparatory work which is due to underestimation of the enemy and panic which is due to being terrified of the enemy's attacks are harmful tendencies, and both should be resolutely opposed. What we need is an enthusiastic but calm state of mind and intense but orderly work.

3. STRATEGIC RETREAT

A strategic retreat is a planned strategic step taken by an inferior force for the purpose of conserving its strength and biding its time to defeat the enemy, when it finds itself confronted with a superior force whose offensive it is unable to smash quickly. But military adventurists stubbornly oppose such a step and advocate "engaging the enemy outside the gates".

We all know that when two boxers fight, the clever boxer usually gives a little ground at first, while the foolish one rushes in furiously and uses up all his resources at the very start, and in the end he is often beaten by the man who has given ground.

In the novel Shui Hu Chuan, [21] the drill master Hung, challenging Lin Chung to a fight on Chai Chin's estate, shouts, "Come on! Come on ! Come on !" In the end it is the retreating Lin Chung who spots Hung's weak point and floors him with one blow.

During the Spring and Autumn Era, when the states of Lu and Chi [22] were at war, Duke Chuang of Lu wanted to attack before the Chi troops had tired themselves out, but Tsao Kuei prevented him. When instead he adopted the tactic of "the enemy tires, we attack", he defeated the Chi army. This is a classic example from China's military history of a weak force defeating a strong force. Here is the account given by the historian Tsochiu Ming: [23]

In the spring the Chi troop' invaded us. The Duke was about to fight. Tsao Kuei requested an audience. His neighbours said,

"This is the business of meat-eating officials, why meddle with it?" Tsao replied, "Meat-eaters are fools, they cannot plan ahead." So he saw the Duke. And he asked, "What will you rely on when you fight?" The Duke answered, "I never dare to keep all my food and clothing for my own enjoyment, but always share them with others." Tsao said, "Such paltry charity cannot reach all The people will not follow you." The Duke said, "I never offer to the gods less sacrificial beasts, jade or silk than are due to them. I keep good faith." Tsao said, "Such paltry faith wins no trust. The gods will not bless you." The Duke said, "Though unable personally to attend to the details of all trials, big and small, I always demand the facts." Tsao said, "That shows your devotion to your people. You can give battle. When you do so, I beg to follow you." The Duke and he rode in the same chariot. The battle was joined at Changshao. When the Duke was about to sound the drum for the attack, Tsao said, "Not yet." When the men of Chi had drummed thrice, Tsao said, "Now we can drum" The army of Chi was routed. The Duke wanted to pursue. Again Tsao said, "Not yet." He got down from the chariot to examine the enemy's wheel-tracks, then mounted the arm-rest of the chariot to look afar. He said, "Now we can pursue!" So began the pursuit of the Chi troops. After the victory the Duke asked Tsao why he had given such advice. Tsao replied, "A battle depends upon courage. At the first drum courage is aroused, at the second it flags, and with the third it runs out. When the enemy's courage ran out, ours was still high and so we won. It is difficult to fathom the moves of a great state, and I feared an ambush. But when I examined the enemy's wheel-tracks and found them cries-crossing and looked afar and saw his banners drooping, I advised pursuit."

That was a case of a weak state resisting a strong state The story speaks of the political preparations before a battle -- winning the confidence of the people; it speaks of a battlefield favourable for switching over to the counter-offensive -- Changshao, it indicates the favourable time for starting the counter-offensive -- when the enemy's courage is running out and one's own is high; and it points to the moment for starting the pursuit -- when the enemy's tracks are crisscrossed and his banners are drooping. Though the battle was not a big one, it illustrates the principles of the strategic defensive. China's military history contains numerous instances of victories won on these principles. In such famous battles as the Battle of Chengkao between the states of Chu and Han, [24] the Battle of Kunyang between the states of Hsin and Han, [25] the Battle of Kuantu between Yuan Shao and Tsao Tsao, [26] the Battle of Chipi between the states of Wu and Wei, [27] the Battle of Yiling between the states of Wu and Shu, [28] and the Battle of Feishui between the states of Chin and Tsin, [29] in each case the contending sides were unequal, and the weaker side, yielding some ground at first, gained mastery by striking only after the enemy had struck and so defeated the stronger side.

Our war began in the autumn of 1927, and we then had no experience at all. The Nanchang Uprising [30] and the Canton Uprising [31] failed, and in the Autumn Harvest Uprising [32] the Red Army in the Hunan-Hupeh-Kiangsi border area also suffered several defeats and shifted to the Chingkang Mountains on the Hunan-Kiangsi border. In the following April the units which had survived the defeat of the Nanchang Uprising also moved to the Chingkang Mountains by way of southern Hunan. By May 1928 however, basic principles of guerrilla warfare, simple in nature and suited to the conditions of the time, had already been evolved, that is, the sixteen-character formula: "The enemy advances, we retreat; the enemy camps, we harass; the enemy tires, we attack; the enemy retreats, we pursue." This sixteen-character formulation of military principles was accepted by the Central Committee before the Li Li-san line. Later our operational principles were developed a step further. At the time of our first counter-campaign against "encirclement and suppression" in the Kiangsi base area, the principle of "luring the enemy in deep" was put forward and, moreover, successfully applied. By the time the enemy's third "encirclement and suppression" campaign was defeated, a complete set of operational principles for the Red Army had taken shape. This marked a new stage in the development of our military principles, which were greatly enriched in content and underwent many changes in form, mainly in the sense that although they basically remained the same as in the sixteen-character formula, they transcended their originally simple nature. The sixteen-character formula covered the basic principles for combating "encirclement and suppression"; it covered the two stages of the strategic defensive and the strategic offensive, and within the defensive, it covered the two stages of the strategic retreat and the strategic counter-offensive. What came later was only a development of this formula.

But beginning from January 1932, after the publication of the Party's resolution entitled "Struggle for Victory First in One or More Provinces After Smashing the Third 'Encirclement and Suppression' Campaign", which contained serious errors of principle, the "Left" opportunists attacked these correct principles, finally abrogated the whole set and instituted a complete set of contrary "new principles" or "regular principles". From then on, the old principles were no longer to be considered as regular but were to be rejected as "guerrilla-ism". The opposition to "guerrilla-ism" reigned for three whole years. Its first stage was military adventurism, in the second it turned into military conservatism and, finally, in the third stage it became flightism. It was not until the Central Committee held the enlarged meeting of the Political Bureau at Tsunyi,

Kweichow Province, in January 1935 that this wrong line was declared bankrupt and the correctness of the old line reaffirmed. But at what a cost!

Those comrades who vigorously opposed "guerrilla-ism" argued along the following lines. It was wrong to lure the enemy in deep because we had to abandon so much territory. Although battles had been won in this way, was not the situation different now? Moreover, was it not better to defeat the enemy without abandoning territory? And was it not better still to defeat the enemy in his own areas, or on the borders between his areas and ours? The old practices had nothing "regular" about them and were methods used only by guerrillas. Now our own state had been established and our Red Army had become a regular army. Our fight against Chiang Kai-shek had become a war between two states, between two great armies. History should not repeat itself, and everything pertaining to "guerrilla-ism" should be totally discarded. The new principles were "completely Marxist", while the old had been created by guerrilla units in the mountains, and there was no Marxism in the mountains. The new principles were the antithesis of the old. They were: "Pit one against ten, pit ten against a hundred, fight bravely and determinedly, and exploit victories by hot pursuit"; "Attack on all fronts"; "Seize key cities"; and "Strike with two 'fists' in two directions at the same time". When the enemy attacked, the methods of dealing with him were: "Engage the enemy outside the gates", "Gain mastery by striking first", "Don't let our pots and pans be smashed", "Don't give up an inch of territory" and "Divide the forces into six routes". The war was "the decisive battle between the road of revolution and the road of colonialism", a war of short swift thrusts, blockhouse warfare, war of attrition, "protracted war". There were, further, the policy of maintaining a great rear area and an absolutely centralized command. Finally there was a large-scale "house-moving". And anyone who did not accept these things was to be punished, labelled an opportunist, and so on and so forth.

Without a doubt these theories and practices were all wrong. They were nothing but subjectivism. Under favourable circumstances this subjectivism manifested itself in petty-bourgeois revolutionary fanaticism and impetuosity, but in times of adversity, as the situation worsened, it changed successively into desperate recklessness, conservatism and flightism. They were the theories and practices of hotheads and ignoramuses; they did not have the slightest flavour of Marxism about them; indeed they were anti-Marxist.

Here we shall discuss only strategic retreat, which in Kiangsi was called "luring the enemy in deep" and in Szechuan "contracting the front". No previous theorist or practitioner of war has ever denied that this is the policy a weak army fighting a strong army must adopt in the initial stage of a war. It has been said by a foreign military expert that in strategically defensive operations, decisive battles are usually avoided in the beginning, and are sought only when conditions have become favourable. That is entirely correct and we have nothing to add to it.

The object of strategic retreat is to conserve military strength and prepare for the counter-offensive. Retreat is necessary because not to retreat a step before the onset of a strong enemy inevitably means to jeopardize the preservation of one's own forces. In the past, however, many people were stubbornly opposed to retreat, considering it to be an "opportunist line of pure defence". Our history has proved that their opposition was entirely wrong.

To prepare for a counter-offensive, we must select or create conditions favourable to ourselves but unfavourable to the enemy, so as to bring about a change in the balance of forces, before we go on to the stage of the counter-offensive.

In the light of our past experience, during the stage of retreat we should in general secure at least two of the following conditions before we can consider the situation as being favourable to us and unfavourable to the enemy and before we can go over to the counter-offensive. These conditions are:

(1) The population actively supports the Red Army.

(2) The terrain is favourable for operations.

(3) All the main forces of the Red Army are concentrated.

(4) The enemy's weak spots have been discovered.

(5) The enemy has been reduced to a tired and demoralized state).

(6) The enemy has been induced to make mistakes.

The first condition, active support of the population, is the most important one for the Red Army. It means having a base area. Moreover, given this condition, it is easy to achieve conditions 4, 5 and 6. Therefore, when the enemy launches a full-scale offensive, the Red Army generally withdraws from the White area into the base area, because that is where the population is most active in supporting the Red Army against the White army. Also, there is a difference between the borders and the central district of a base area; in the latter the people are better at blocking the passage of information to the enemy, better at reconnaissance, transportation, joining in the fighting, and so on. Thus when we were combating the first, second and third "encirclement and suppression" campaigns in Kiangsi, all the places selected as "terminal points for the retreat" were situated where the first condition, popular support, was excellent or quite good. This characteristic of our base areas made the Red Army's operations very different from ordinary operations and was the main reason why the enemy subsequently had to resort to the policy of blockhouse warfare.

One advantage of operating on interior lines is that it makes it possible for the retreating army to choose terrain favourable to itself and force the attacking army to fight on its terms. In order to defeat a strong army, a weak army must carefully choose favourable terrain as a battleground. But this condition alone is not enough and must be accompanied by others. The first of these is popular support. The next is a vulnerable enemy, for instance, an enemy who is tired or has made mistakes, or an advancing enemy column that is comparatively poor in fighting capacity. In the absence of these conditions, even if we have found excellent terrain, we have to disregard it and continue to retreat in order to secure them. In the White areas there is no lack of good terrain, but we do not have the favourable condition of active popular support. If other conditions are not yet fulfilled, the Red Army has no alternative but to retreat towards its base area. Distinctions such as those between the White areas and the Red areas also usually exist between the borders and the central district of a base area.

Except for local units and containing forces, all our assault troops should, on principle, be concentrated. When attacking an enemy who is on the defensive strategically, the Red Army usually disperses its own forces. Once the enemy launches a full-scale offensive, the Red Army effects a "retreat towards the centre". The terminal point chosen for the retreat is usually in the central section of the base area, but sometimes it is in the frontal or rear sections, as circumstances require. By such a retreat towards the centre all the main forces of the Red Army can be concentrated.

Another essential condition for a weak army fighting a strong one is to pick out the enemy's weaker units for attack. But at the beginning of the enemy's offensive we usually do not know which of his advancing columns is the strongest and which the second strongest, which is the weakest and which the second weakest, and so a process of reconnaissance is required. This often takes a considerable time. That is another reason why strategic retreat is necessary.

If the attacking enemy is far more numerous and much stronger than we are, we can accomplish a change in the balance of forces only when the enemy has penetrated deeply into our base area and tasted all the bitterness it holds for him. As the chief of staff of one of Chiang Kai-shek's brigades remarked during the third "encirclement and suppression'! campaign, "Our stout men have worn themselves thin and our thin men have worn themselves to death." Or, in the words of Chen Ming-shu, Commander-in-Chief of the Western Route of the Kuomintang's "Encirclement and Suppression" Army, "Everywhere the National Army gropes in the dark, while the Red Army walks in broad daylight." By then the enemy army, although still strong, is much weakened, its soldiers are tired, its morale is sagging and many of its weak spots are revealed. But the Red Army, though weak, has conserved its strength and stored up its energy, and is waiting at its ease for the fatigued enemy. At such a time it is generally possible to attain a certain parity between the two sides, or to change the enemy's absolute superiority to relative superiority and our absolute inferiority to relative inferiority, and occasionally even to become superior to the enemy. When fighting against the third "encirclement and suppression" campaign in Kiangsi, the Red Army executed a retreat to the extreme limit (to concentrate in the rear section of the base area); if it had not done so, it could not have defeated the enemy because the enemy's "encirclement and suppression" forces were then over ten times the size of the Red Army. When Sun Wu Tzu said, "Avoid the enemy when he is full of vigour, strike when he is fatigued and withdraws", he was referring to tiring and demoralizing the enemy so as to reduce his superiority.

Finally, the object of retreat is to induce the enemy to make mistakes or to detect his mistakes. One must realize that an enemy commander, however wise, cannot avoid making some mistakes over a relatively long period of time, and hence it is always possible for us to exploit the openings he leaves us. The enemy is liable to make mistakes, just as we ourselves sometimes miscalculate and give him openings to exploit. In addition, we can induce the enemy to make mistakes by our own actions, for instance, by "counterfeiting an appearance", as Sun Wu Tzu called it, that is, by making a feint to the east but attacking in the west. If we are to do this, the terminal point for the retreat cannot be rigidly limited to a definite area. Sometimes when we have retreated to the predetermined area and not yet found openings to exploit, we have to retreat farther and wait for the enemy to give us an opening.

The favourable conditions which we seek by retreating are in general those stated above. But this does not mean that a counter-offensive cannot be launched until all these conditions are present. The presence of all of them at the same time is neither possible nor necessary. But a weak force operating on interior lines against a strong enemy should strive to secure such conditions as are necessary in the light of the enemy's actual situation. All views to the contrary are incorrect.

The decision on the terminal point for retreat should depend on the situation as a whole. It is wrong to decide on a place which, considered in relation to only part of the situation, appears to be favourable for our passing to the counter-offensive, if it is not also advantageous from the point of view of the situation as a whole. For at the start of our counter-offensive we must take subsequent developments into consideration, and our counter-offensives always begin on a partial scale. Sometimes the terminal point for retreat should be fixed in the frontal section of the base area, as it was during our second and fourth counter-campaigns against "encirclement and suppression" in Kiangsi and our third counter-campaign in the Shensi-Kansu area. At times it should be in the middle section of the base area, as in our first counter-campaign in Kiangsi. At other times, it should be fixed in the rear section of the base area, as in our third counter-campaign in Kiangsi. In all these cases the decision was taken by correlating the partial situation with the situation as a whole. But during the fifth counter-campaign in Kiangsi, our army gave no consideration whatsoever to retreat, because it did not take account of either the partial or the total situation, and this was really rash and foolhardy conduct. A situation is made up of a number of factors; in considering the relation between a part of the situation and the whole, we should base our judgements on whether the factors on the enemy's side and on ours, as manifested in both the partial and the whole situation, are to a certain extent favourable for our starting a counter-offensive.

The terminal points for retreat in a base area can be generally divided into three types, those in the frontal, those in the middle, and those in the rear section of the base area. Does this, however, mean refusing to fight in the White areas altogether? No. It is only when we have to deal with a large-scale campaign of enemy "encirclement and suppression" that we refuse to fight in the White areas. It is only when there is a wide disparity between the enemy's strength and ours that, acting on the principle of conserving our strength and biding our time to defeat the enemy, we advocate retreating to the base area and luring him in deep, for only by so doing can we create or find conditions favourable for our counter-offensive.

If the situation is not so serious, or if it is so serious that the Red Army cannot begin its counter-offensive even in the base area, or if the counter-offensive is not going well and a further retreat is necessary to bring about a change in the situation, then we should recognize, theoretically at least, that the terminal point for the retreat may be fixed in a White area, though we have had very little experience of this kind.

In general, the terminal points for retreat in a White area can also be divided into three types: (1) those in front of our base area, (2) those on its flanks, and (3) those behind it. Here is an example of the first type.

During our first counter-campaign against "encirclement and suppression" in Kiangsi, had it not been for the disunity inside the Red Army and the split in the local Party organization (the two difficult problems created by the Li Li-san line and the A-B Group), [33] it is conceivable that we might have concentrated our forces within the triangle formed by Kian, Nanfeng and Changshu and launched a counter-offensive. For the enemy force advancing from the area between the Kan and Fu Rivers was not very greatly superior to the Red Army in strength (100,000 against 40,000). Though the popular support there was not as active as in the base area, the terrain was favourable; moreover, it would have been possible to smash, one by one, the enemy forces advancing along separate routes.

Now for an example of the second type.

During our third counter-campaign in Kiangsi, if the enemy's offensive had not been on so large a scale, if one of the enemy's columns had advanced from Chienning, Lichuan and Taining on the Fukien-Kiangsi border, and if that column had not been too strong for us to attack, it is likewise conceivable that the Red Army might have massed its forces in the White area in western Fukien and crushed that column first, without having to make a thousand-li detour through Juichin to Hsingkuo.

Finally, an example of the third type.

During that same third counter-campaign in Kiangsi, if the enemy's main force had headed south instead of west, we might have been compelled to withdraw to the Huichang-Hsunwu-Anyuan area (a White area), in order to induce the enemy to move further south; the Red Army could have then driven northward into the interior of the base area, by which time the enemy force in the north of the base area would not have been very large.

The above, however, are all hypothetical examples not based on actual experience; they should be regarded as exceptional and not treated as general principles. When the enemy launches a large-scale "encirclement and suppression" campaign, our general principle is to lure him in deep, withdraw into the base area and fight him there, because this is our surest method of smashing his offensive.

Those who advocate "engaging the enemy outside the gates" oppose strategic retreat, arguing that to retreat means to lose territory, to bring harm on the people ("to let our pots and pans be smashed", as they call it), and to give rise to unfavourable repercussions outside. During our fifth counter-campaign, they argued that every time we retreated a step the enemy would push his blockhouses forward a step, so that our base areas would continuously shrink and we would have no way of recovering lost ground. Even though luring the enemy deep into our territory might have been useful in the past, it would be useless against the enemy's fifth "encirclement and suppression" campaign in which he adopted the policy of blockhouse warfare. The only way to deal with this campaign, they said, was to divide up our forces for resistance and make short swift thrusts at the enemy.

It is easy to give an answer to such views, and our history has already done so. As for loss of territory, it often happens that only by loss can loss be avoided; this is the principle of "Give in order to take". If what we lose is territory and what we gain is victory over the enemy, plus recovery and also expansion of our territory, then it is a paying proposition. In a business transaction, if a buyer does not "lose" some money, he cannot obtain goods; if a seller does not "lose" some goods, he cannot obtain money. The losses incurred in a revolutionary movement involve destruction, and what is gained is construction of a progressive character. Sleep and rest involve loss of time, but energy is gained for tomorrow's work. If any fool does not understand this and refuses to sleep, he will have no energy the next day, and that is a losing proposition. We lost out in the fifth counter-campaign for precisely such reasons. Reluctance to give up part of our territory resulted in the loss of it all. Abyssinia, too, lost all her territory when she fought the enemy head-on, though that was not the sole cause of her defeat.

The same holds true on the question of bringing damage on the people. If you refuse to let the pots and pans of some households be smashed over a short period of time, you will cause the smashing of the pots and pans of all the people to go on over a long period of time. If you are afraid of unfavourable short-term political repercussions, you will have to pay the price in unfavourable long-term political repercussions. After the October Revolution, if the Russian Bolsheviks had acted on the opinions of the "Left Communists" and refused to sign the peace treaty with Germany, the new-born Soviets would have been in danger of early death. [34]

Such seemingly revolutionary "Left" opinions originate from the revolutionary impetuosity of the petty-bourgeois intellectuals as well as from the narrow conservatism of the peasant small producers. People holding such opinions look at problems only one-sidedly and are unable to take a comprehensive view of the situation as a whole; they are unwilling to link the interests of today with those of tomorrow or the interests of the part with those of the whole, but cling like grim death to the partial and the temporary. Certainly, we should cling tenaciously to the partial and the temporary when, in the concrete circumstances of the time, they are favourable -- and especially when they are decisive -- for the whole current situation and the whole period, or otherwise we shall become advocates of letting things slide and doing nothing about them. That is why a retreat must have a terminal point. We must not go by the short-sightedness of the small producer. We should learn the wisdom of the Bolsheviks. The naked eye is not enough, we must have the aid of the telescope and the microscope The Marxist method is our telescope and microscope in political and military matters.

Of course, strategic retreat has its difficulties. To pick the time for beginning the retreat, to select the terminal point, to convince the cadres and the people politically -- these are difficult problems demanding solution.

The problem of timing the beginning of the retreat is very important. If in the course of our first counter-campaign against "encirclement and suppression" in Kiangsi Province our retreat had not been carried out just when it was, that is, if it had been delayed, then at the very least the extent of our victory would have been affected. Both a premature and a belated retreat, of course, bring losses. But generally speaking, a belated retreat brings more losses than a premature one. A well-timed retreat, which enables us to keep all the initiative, is of great assistance to us in switching to the counter-offensive when, having reached the terminal point for our retreat, we have regrouped our forces and are waiting at our ease for the fatigued enemy. When smashing the enemy's first, second and fourth campaigns of "encirclement and suppression" in Kiangsi, we were able to handle him confidently and without haste. It was only during the third campaign that the Red Army was very fatigued by the detour it had hastily had to make m order to reassemble, because we had not expected the enemy to launch a new offensive so quickly after suffering such a crushing defeat in the second campaign (we ended our second counter-campaign on May 29, 1931, and Chiang Kai-shek began his third "encirclement and suppression" campaign on July 1). The timing of the retreat is decided in the same way as the timing of the preparatory phase of a counter-campaign which we discussed earlier, that is, entirely on the basis of the requisite information we have collected and of the appraisal of the general situation on the enemy side and on our own.

It is extremely difficult to convince the cadres and the people of the necessity of strategic retreat when they have had no experience of it, and when the prestige of the army leadership is not yet such that it can concentrate the authority for deciding on strategic retreat in the hands of a few persons or of a single person and at the same time enjoy the confidence of the cadres. Because the cadres lacked experience and had no faith in strategic retreat, great difficulties were encountered at the beginning of our first and fourth counter-campaigns and during the whole of the fifth. During the first counter-campaign the cadres, under the influence of the Li Li-san line, were in favour not of retreat but of attack until they were convinced otherwise. In the fourth counter-campaign the cadres, under the influence of military adventurism, objected to making preparations for retreat. In the fifth, they at first persisted in the military adventurist view, which opposed luring the enemy in deep, but later turned to military conservatism. Another case is that of the adherents of the Chang Kuo-tao line, who did not admit the impossibility of establishing our bases in the regions of the Tibetan and the Hui peoples [35] until they ran up against a brick wall. Experience is essential for the cadres, and failure is indeed the mother of success. But it is also necessary to learn with an open mind from other people's experience, and it is sheer "narrow empiricism" to insist on one's own personal experience in all matters and, in its absence, to adhere stubbornly to one's own opinions and reject other people's experience. Our war has suffered in no small measure on this account.

The people's lack of faith in the need for a strategic retreat, which was due to their inexperience, was never greater than in our first counter-campaign in Kiangsi. At that time the local Party organizations and the masses of the people in the counties of Kian, Hsingkuo and Yungfeng were all opposed to the Red Army's withdrawal. But after the experience of the first counter-campaign, no such problem occurred in the subsequent ones. Everyone was convinced that the loss of territory in the base area and the sufferings of the people were temporary and was confident that the Red Army could smash the enemy's "encirclement and suppression". However, whether or not the people have faith is closely tied up with whether or not the cadres have faith, and hence the first and foremost task is to convince the cadres.

Strategic retreat is aimed solely at switching over to the counteroffensive and is merely the first stage of the strategic defensive. The decisive link in the entire strategy is whether victory can be won in the stage of the counter-offensive which follows.

4. STRATEGIC COUNTER-OFFENSIVE

To defeat the offensive of an enemy who enjoys absolute superiority we rely on the situation created during the stage of our strategic retreat, a situation which is favourable to ourselves, unfavourable to the enemy and different from that at the beginning of his offensive. It takes many elements to make up such a situation. All this has been dealt with above.

However, the presence of these conditions and of a situation favourable to ourselves and unfavourable to the enemy does not mean that we have already defeated him. Such conditions and such a situation provide the possibility for our victory and his defeat, but do not constitute the reality of victory or defeat; they have not yet brought actual victory or defeat to either army. To bring about victory or defeat a decisive battle between the two armies is necessary. Only a decisive battle can settle the question as to which army is the victor and which the vanquished. This is the sole task in the stage of strategic counter-offensive. The counter-offensive is a long process, the most fascinating, the most dynamic, and also the final stage of a defensive campaign. What is called active defence refers chiefly to this strategic counter-offensive, which is in the nature of a decisive engagement.

Conditions and situation are created not only in the stage of the strategic retreat, but continue to be created in that of the counter-offensive. Whether in form or in nature, they are not exactly the same in the latter stage as in the former.

What might remain the same in form and in nature, for example, is the fact that the enemy troops will be even more fatigued and depleted, which is simply a continuation of their fatigue and depletion in the previous stage.

But wholly new conditions and a wholly new situation are bound to emerge. Thus, when the enemy has suffered one or more defeats, the conditions advantageous to us and disadvantageous to him will not be confined to his fatigue, etc., but a new factor will have been added, namely, that he has suffered defeats. New changes will take place in the situation, too. When the enemy begins to manoeuvre his troops in a disorderly way and to make false moves, the relative strengths of the two opposing armies will naturally no longer be the same as before.

But if it is not the enemy's forces but ours that have suffered one or more defeats, then both the conditions and the situation will change in the opposite direction. That is to say, the enemy's disadvantages will be reduced, while on our side disadvantages will emerge and even grow. That again will be something entirely new and different.

A defeat for either side will lead directly and speedily to a new effort by the defeated side to avert disaster, to extricate itself from the new conditions and the new situation unfavourable to it and favourable to the enemy and to re-create such conditions and such a situation as are favourable to it and unfavourable to its opponent, in order to bring pressure to bear on the latter.

The effort of the winning side will be exactly the opposite. It will strive to exploit its victory and inflict still greater damage on the enemy, add to the conditions that are in its favour and further improve its situation, and prevent the enemy from succeeding in extricating himself from his unfavourable conditions and unfavourable situation and averting disaster.

Thus, for either side, the struggle at the stage of the decisive battle is the most intense, the most complicated and the most changeful as well as the most difficult and trying in the whole war or the whole campaign; it is the most exacting time of all from the point of view of command.

In the stage of counter-offensive, there are many problems, the chief of which are the starting of the counter-offensive, the concentration of troops, mobile warfare, war of quick decision and war of annihilation.

Whether in a counter-offensive or in an offensive, the principles with regard to these problems do not differ in their basic character. In this sense we may say that a counter-offensive is an offensive.

Still, it is not exactly an offensive. The principles of the counter-offensive are applied when the enemy is on the offensive. The principles of the offensive are applied when the enemy is on the defensive. In this sense, there are certain differences between a counter-offensive and an offensive.

For this reason, although the various operational problems are all included in the discussion of the counter-offensive in the present chapter on the strategic defensive, and although the chapter on the strategic offensive will deal only with other problems in order to avoid repetition, we should not overlook either the similarities or the differences between the counter-offensive and the offensive when it comes to actual application.

5. STARTING THE COUNTER-OFFENSIVE

The problem of starting a counter-offensive is the problem of the "initial battle" or "prelude".

Many bourgeois military experts advise caution in the initial battle, whether one is on the strategic defensive or on the strategic offensive, but more especially when on the defensive. In the past we, too, have stressed this as a serious point. Our operations against the five enemy campaigns of "encirclement and suppression" in Kiangsi Province have given us rich experience, a study of which will not be without benefit.

In his first campaign, the enemy employed about 100,000 men, divided Into eight columns, to advance southward from the Kian-Chienning line against the Red Army's base area. The Red Army had about 40,000 men and was concentrated in the area of Huangpi and Hsiaopu in Ningtu County, Kiangsi Province.

The situation was as follows:

(1) The "suppression" forces did not exceed 100,000 men, none of whom were Chiang Kai-shek's own troops, and the general situation was not very grave.

(2) The enemy division under Lo Lin, defending Kian, was located across the Kan River to the west.

(3) The three enemy divisions under Kung Ping-fan, Chang Hui-tsan and Tan Tao-yuan had advanced and occupied the Futien-Tungku-Lungkang-Yuantou sector southeast of Kian and northwest of Ningtu. The main body of Chang Hui-tsan's division was at Lungkang and that of Tan Tao-yuan's division at Yuantou. It was not advisable to select Futien and Tungku as the battleground, as the inhabitants, misled by the A-B Group, were for a time mistrustful of and opposed to the Red Army.

(4) The enemy division under Liu Ho-ting was far away in Chienning in the White area of Fukien, and was unlikely to cross into Kiangsi.

(5) The two enemy divisions under Mao Ping-wen and Hsu Keh-hsiang had entered the Toupi-Lokou-Tungshao sector lying between Kuangchang and Ningtu. Toupi was a White area, Lokou a guerrilla zone, and Tungshao, where there were A-B Group elements, was a place from which information was liable to leak out. Furthermore, if we were to attack Mao Ping-

wen and Hsu Keh-hsiang and then drive westward, the three enemy divisions m the west under Chang Hui-tsan, Tan Tao-yuan and Kung Ping-fan might join forces, thus making it difficult for us to win victory and impossible to bring the issue to a final solution.

(6) The two divisions under Chang Hui-tsan and Tan Tao-yuan, which made up the enemy's main force, were troops belonging to Lu Ti-ping, who was commander-in-chief of this "encirclement and suppression" campaign and governor of Kiangsi Province, and Chang Hui-tsan was the field commander. To wipe out these two divisions would be practically to smash the campaign. Each division had about fourteen thousand men and Chang's was divided between two places, so that if we attacked one division at a time we would enjoy absolute superiority.

(7) The Lungkang-Yuantou sector, where the main forces of the Chang and Tan divisions were located, was close to our concentrations, and there was good popular support to cover our approach.

(8) The terrain in Lungkang was good. Yuantou was not easy to attack. But were the enemy to advance to Hsiaopu to attack us, we would have good terrain there too.

(9) We could mass the largest number of troops in the Lungkang sector. In Hsingkuo, less than a hundred li to the southwest of Lungkang, we had an independent division of over one thousand men, which could manoeuvre in the enemy's rear.

(10) If our troops made a breakthrough at the centre and breached the enemy's front, his columns to the east and west would be cut into two widely separated groups.

For the above reasons, we decided that our first battle should be against Chang Hui-tsan's main force, and we successfully hit two of his brigades and his divisional headquarters, capturing the entire force of nine thousand men and the divisional commander himself, without letting a single man or horse escape. This one victory scared Tan's division into fleeing towards Tungshao and Hsu's division into fleeing towards Toupi. Our troops then pursued Tan's division and wiped out half of it. We fought two battles in five days (December 27, 1930 to January 1, 1931), and, fearing defeat, the enemy forces in Futien, Tungku and Toupi retreated in disorder. So ended the first campaign of "encirclement and suppression".

The situation in the second campaign was as follows:

(1) The "suppression" forces numbering 200,000 were under the command of Ho Ying-chin with headquarters at Nanchang.

(2) As in the first enemy campaign, none of the forces were Chiang Kai-shek's own troops. Among them the 18th Route Army under Tsai Ting-kai, the 26th under Sun Lien-chung and the 8th under Chu Shao-liang were strong, or fairly strong, while all the rest were rather weak.

(3) The A-B Group had been cleaned up, and the entire population of the base area supported the Red Army.

(4) The 5th Route Army under Wang Chin-yu, newly arrived from the north, was afraid of us, and, generally speaking, so were the two divisions on its left flank under Kuo Hua-tsung and Hao Meng-ling.

(5) If our troops attacked Futien first and then swept across to the east, we could expand the base area to the

Chienning-Lichuan-Taining sector on the Pukien-Kiangsi border and acquire supplies to help smash the next "encirclement and suppression" campaign. But if we were to thrust westward, we would come up against the Kan River and have no room for expansion after the battle. To turn east again after the battle would tire our troops and waste time.

(6) Though our army (numbering over 30,000 men) was somewhat smaller than in the first campaign, it had had four months in which to recuperate and build up energy.

For these reasons, we decided, for our first battle, to engage the forces of Wang Chin-yu and of Kung Ping-fan (totalling 11 regiments) in the Futien sector. After winning this battle we attacked Kuo Huatsung, Sun Lien-chung, Chu Shao-liang and Liu Ho-ting in succession. In fifteen days (from May 16 to May 30, 1931) we marched seven hundred li, fought five battles, captured more than twenty thousand rifles and roundly smashed the enemy's "encirclement and suppression" campaign. When fighting Wang Chin-yu, we were between the two enemy forces under Tsai Ting-kai and Kuo Hua-tsung, some ten li from the latter and forty li from the former, and some people said we were "getting into a blind alley", but we got through all the same. This was mainly due to the popular support we enjoyed in the base area and to the lack of co-ordination among the enemy units. After Kuo Hua-tsung's division was defeated, Hao Meng-ling's division fled by night back to Yungfeng, and so avoided disaster.

The situation in the third "encirclement and suppression" campaign was as follows:

(1) Chiang Kai-shek personally took the held as commander-in-chief. Under him there were three subordinate commanders, each in charge of a column -- the left, the right and the centre. The central column was commanded by Ho

Ying-chin, who, like Chiang Kai-shek, had his headquarters in Nanchang, the right was commanded by Chen Ming-shu with headquarters at Kian, and the left by Chu Shao-liang with headquarters at Nanfeng.

(2) The "suppression" forces numbered 300,000. The main forces, totalling about 100,000 men, were Chiang Kai-shek's own troops and consisted of 5 divisions (of 9 regiments each), commanded by Chen Cheng, Lo Cho-ying, Chao Kuan-tao, Wei Lihuang and Chiang Ting-wen respectively. Besides these, there were 3 divisions (totalling 40,000 men) under Chiang Kuang-nai, Tsai Ting-kai and Han Teh-chin. Then there was Sun Lien-chung's army of 20,000. In addition, there were other, weaker forces that were likewise not Chiang's own troops.

(3) The enemy's strategy in this "suppression" campaign was to "drive straight in", which was vastly different from the strategy of "consolidating at every step" he used in the second campaign. The aim was to press the Red Army back against the Kan River and annihilate it there.

(4) There was an interval of only one month between the end of the second enemy campaign and the beginning of the third. The Red Army (then about 30,000 strong) had had neither rest nor replenishments after much hard fighting and had just made a detour of a thousand li to concentrate at Hsingkuo in the western part of the southern Kiangsi base area, when the enemy pressed it hard from several directions.

In this situation the plan we hrst decided on was to move from Hsingkuo by way of Wanan, make a breakthrough at Futien, and then sweep from west to east across the enemy's rear communication lines, thus letting the enemy's main forces make a deep but useless penetration into our base area in southern Kiangsi; this was to be the first phase of our operation. Then when the enemy turned back northward, inevitably very fatigued, we were to seize the opportunity to strike at his vulnerable units; that was to be the second phase of our operation. The heart of this plan was to avoid the enemy's main forces and strike at his weak spots. But when our forces were advancing on Futien, we were detected by the enemy, who rushed the two divisions under Chen Cheng and Lo Cho-ying to the scene. We had to change our plan and fall back to Kaohsinghsu in the western part of Hsingkuo County, which, together with its environs of less than a hundred square li, was then the only place for our troops to concentrate in. The day after our concentration we decided to make a thrust eastward towards Lientang in eastern Hsingkuo County, Liangtsun in southern Yungfeng County and Huangpi in northern Ningtu County. That same night, under covet of darkness, we passed through the forty-li gap between Chiang Ting-wen's division and the forces of Chiang Kuang-nai, Tsai Ting-kai and Han Teh-chin, and swung to Lientang. On the second day we skirmished with the forward units under Shangkuan Yun-hsiang (who was in command of Hao Meng-ling's division as well as his own). The first battle was fought on the third day with Shangkuan Yun-hsiang's division and the second battle on the fourth day with Hao Meng-ling's division; after a three day march we reached Huangpi and fought our third battle against Mao Ping-wen's division. We won all three battles and captured over ten thousand rifles. At this point all the main enemy forces, which had been advancing westward and southward, turned eastward. Focusing on Huangpi, they converged at furious speed to seek battle and closed in on us in a major compact encirclement. We slipped through in the high mountains that lay in the twenty-li gap between the forces of Chiang Kuang-nai, Tsai Ting-kai and Han Teh-chin on the one side and Chen Cheng and Lo Cho-ying on the other, and thus, returning from the east to the west, reassembled within the borders of Hsingkuo County. By the time the enemy discovered this fact and began advancing west again, our forces had already had a fortnight's rest, whereas the enemy forces, hungry, exhausted and demoralized, were no good for fighting and so decided to retreat. Taking advantage of their retreat, we attacked the forces of Chiang Kuang-nai, Tsai Ting-kai, Chiang Ting-wen and Han Teh-chin, wiping out one of Chiang Ting-wen's brigades and Han Tehchin's entire division. As for the divisions under Chiang Kuang-nai and Tsai Ting-kai, the fight resulted in a stalemate and they got away.

The situation in the fourth "encirclement and suppression" campaign was as follows. The enemy was advancing on Kuangchang in three columns; the eastern one was his main force, while the two divisions forming his western column were exposed to us and were also very close to the area where our forces were concentrated. Thus we had the opportunity to attack his western column in southern Yihuang County first, and at one stroke we annihilated the two divisions under Li Ming and Chen Shih-chi. As the enemy then sent two divisions from the eastern column to give support to his central column and advanced further, we were again able to wipe out a division in southern Yihuang County. In these two battles we captured more than ten thousand rifles and, in the main, smashed this campaign of "encirclement and suppression".

In his fifth campaign the enemy advanced by means of his new strategy of building blockhouses and first occupied Lichuan. But, in attempting to recover Lichuan and engage the enemy outside the base area, we made an attack north of Lichuan at Hsiaoshih, which was an enemy strong point and was situated, moreover, in the White area. Failing to win the battle, we shifted our attack to Tzehsichiao, which was also an enemy strongpoint situated in the White area southeast of Hsiaoshih, and again we failed. Then in seeking battle we milled around between the enemy's main forces and his blockhouses and were reduced to complete passivity. All through our fifth counter-campaign against "encirclement and suppression", which lasted a whole year, we showed not the slightest initiative or drive. In the end we had to withdraw from our Kiangsi base area.

Our army's experience in these five counter-campaigns against "encirclement and suppression" proves that the first battle in the counter-offensive is of the greatest importance for the Red Army, which is on the defensive, if it is to smash a large and powerful enemy "suppression" force. Victory or defeat in the first battle has a tremendous effect upon the entire situation, all the way to the final engagement. Hence we arrive at the following conclusions.

First, the first battle must be won. We should strike only when positively certain that the enemy's situation, the terrain and popular support are all in our favour and not in his. Otherwise we should rather fall back and carefully bide our time. There will always be opportunities; we should not rashly accept battle. In our first counter-campaign we originally planned to strike at Tan Tao-yuan's troops; we advanced twice but each time had to restrain ourselves and pull back, because they would not budge from their commanding position on the Yuantou heights. A few days later we sought out Chang Huitsan's troops, which were more vulnerable to our attack. In our second counter-campaign our army advanced to Tungku where, for the sole purpose of waiting for Wang Chin-yu's men to leave their strongpoint at Futien, we encamped close to the enemy for twenty-five days even at the risk of leakage of information; we rejected all impatient suggestions for a quick attack and finally attained our aim. In our third counter-campaign, although the storm was breaking all around us and we had made a detour of a thousand li, and although the enemy had discovered our plan to outflank him, we nevertheless exercised patience, turned back, changed our tactics to a breakthrough in the centre, and finally fought the first battle successfully at Lientang. In our fourth counter-campaign, after our attack on Nanfeng had failed, we unhesitatingly withdrew, wheeled round to the enemy's right flank, and reassembled our forces in the area of Tungshao, whereupon we launched our great and victorious battle in southern Yihuang County. It was only in the fifth counter-campaign that the importance of the first battle was not recognized at all. Taking alarm at the loss of the single county town of Lichuan, our forces marched north to meet the enemy in an attempt to recover it. Then, the unexpected encounter at Hsunkou, which had resulted in a victory (with the annihilation of an enemy division), was not treated as the first battle, nor were the changes that were bound to ensue foreseen, but instead Hsiaoshih was rashly attacked with no assurance of success. Thus the initiative was lost at the very first move, and that is really the worst and most stupid way to fight.

Second, the plan for the first battle must be the prelude to, and an organic part of, the plan for the whole campaign. Without a good plan for the whole campaign it is absolutely impossible to fight a really good first battle. That is to say, even though victory is won in the first battle, if the battle harms rather than helps the campaign as a whole, such a victory can only be reckoned a defeat (as in the case of the battle of Hsunkou in the fifth campaign). Hence, before fighting the first battle one must have a general idea of how the second, third, fourth, and even the final battle will be fought, and consider what changes will ensue in the enemy's situation as a whole if we win, or lose, each of the succeeding battles. Although the result may not -- and, in fact, definitely will not -- turn out exactly as we expect, we must think everything out carefully and realistically in the light of the general situation on both sides. Without a grasp of the situation as a whole, it is impossible to make any really good move on the chessboard.

Third, one must also consider what will happen in the next strategic stage of the war. Whoever directs strategy will not be doing his duty if he occupies himself only with the counter-offensive and neglects the measures to be taken after it succeeds, or in case it fails. In a particular strategic stage, he should take into consideration the succeeding stages, or, at the very least, the following one. Even though future changes are difficult to foresee and the farther ahead one looks the more blurred things seem, a general calculation is possible and an appraisal of distant prospects is necessary. In war as well as in politics, planning only one step at a time as one goes along is a harmful way of directing matters. After each step, it is necessary to examine the ensuing concrete changes and to modify or develop one's strategic and operational plans accordingly, or otherwise one is liable to make the mistake of rushing straight ahead regardless of danger. However, it is absolutely essential to have a long-term plan which has been thought out in its general outline and which covers an entire strategic stage or even several strategic stages. Failure to make such a plan will lead to the mistake of hesitating and allowing oneself to be tied down, which in fact serves the enemy's strategic objects and reduces one to a passive position. It must be borne in mind that the enemy's supreme command is not lacking in strategic insight. Only when we have trained ourselves to be a head taller than the enemy will strategic victories be possible. During the enemy's fifth "encirclement and suppression" campaign, failure to do so was the main reason for the errors in strategic direction under the "Left" opportunist and the Chang Kuo-tao lines. In short, in the stage of retreat we must see ahead to the stage of the counter-offensive, in the stage of the counter-offensive we must see ahead to that of the offensive, and in the stage of the offensive we must again see ahead to a stage of retreat. Not to do so but to confine ourselves to considerations of the moment is to court defeat.

The first battle must be won. The plan for the whole campaign must be taken into account. And the strategic stage that comes next must be taken into account. These are the three principles we must never forget when we begin a counter-offensive, that is, when we fight the first battle.

6. CONCENTRATION OF TROOPS

The concentration of troops seems easy but is quite hard in practice. Everybody knows that the best way is to use a large force to defeat a small one, and yet many people fail to do so and on the contrary often divide their forces up. The reason is that such military leaders have no head for strategy and are confused by complicated circumstances; hence, they are at the mercy of these circumstances, lose their initiative and have recourse to passive response.

No matter how complicated, grave and harsh the circumstances, what a military leader needs most of all is the ability to function independently in organizing and employing the forces under his command. He may often be forced into a passive position by the enemy, but the important thing is to regain the initiative quickly. Failure to do so spells defeat.

The initiative is not something imaginary but is concrete and material. Here the most important thing is to conserve and mass an armed force that is as large as possible and full of fighting spirit.

It is easy to fall into a passive position in defensive warfare, which gives far less scope for the full exercise of initiative than does offensive warfare. However, defensive warfare, which is passive in form, can be active in content, and can be switched from the stage in which it is passive in form to the stage in which it is active both in form and in content. In appearance a fully planned strategic retreat is made under compulsion, but in reality it is effected in order to conserve our strength and bide our time to defeat the enemy, to lure him in deep and prepare for our counter-offensive. On the other hand, refusal to retreat and hasty acceptance of battle (as in the battle of Hsiaoshih) may appear a serious effort to gain the initiative, while in reality it is passive. Not only is a strategic counter-offensive active in content, but in form, too, it discards the passive posture of the period of retreat. In relation to the enemy, our counter-offensive represents our effort to make him relinquish the initiative and put him in a passive position.

Concentration of troops, mobile warfare, war of quick decision and war of annihilation are all necessary conditions for the full achievement of this aim. And of these, concentration of troops is the first and most essential.

This concentration is necessary for the purpose of reversing the situation as between the enemy and ourselves. First, its purpose is to reverse the situation as regards advance and retreat. Previously it was the enemy who was advancing and we who were retreating; now we seek a situation in which we advance and he retreats. When we concentrate our troops and win a battle, then in that battle we gain the above purpose, and this influences the whole campaign.

Second, its purpose is to reverse the situation with regard to attack and defence. In defensive warfare the retreat to the prescribed terminal point belongs basically to the passive, or "defence", stage. The counter-offensive belongs to the active, or "attack", stage. Although the strategic defensive retains its defensive character throughout its duration, still as compared with the retreat the counter-offensive already represents a change not only in form but in content. The counter-offensive is transitional between the strategic defensive and the strategic offensive, and in the nature of a prelude to the strategic offensive; it is precisely for the purpose of the counter-offensive that troops are concentrated.

Third, its purpose is to reverse the situation with regard to interior and exterior lines. An army operating on strategically interior lines suffers from many disadvantages, and this is especially so in the case of the Red Army, confronted as it is with "encirclement and suppression". But in campaigns and battles we can and absolutely must change this situation. We can turn a big "encirclement and suppression" campaign waged by the enemy against us into a number of small, separate campaigns of encirclement and suppression waged by us against the enemy. We can change the converging attack directed by the enemy against us on the plane of strategy into converging attacks directed by us against the enemy on the plane of campaigns and battles. We can change the enemy's strategic superiority over us into our superiority over him in campaigns and battles. We can put the enemy who is in a strong position strategically into a weak position in campaigns and battles. At the same time we can change our own strategically weak position into a strong position in campaigns and battles. This is what we call exterior-line operations within interior-line operations, encirclement and suppression within "encirclement and suppression", blockade within blockade, the offensive within the defensive, superiority within inferiority, strength within weakness, advantage within disadvantage, and initiative within passivity. The winning of victory in the strategic defensive depends basically on this measure -- concentration of troops.

In the war annals of the Chinese Red Army, this has often been an important controversial issue. In the battle of Kian on October 4, 1930, our advance and attack were begun before our forces were fully concentrated, but fortunately the enemy force (Teng Ying's division) fled of its own accord; by itself our attack was ineffective.

Beginning from 1932, there was the slogan "Attack on all fronts", which called for attacks from the base area in all directions -- north, south, east and west. This is wrong not only for the strategic defensive but even for the strategic offensive. As long as there is no fundamental change in the over-all balance of forces, both strategy and tactics involve the defensive and the offensive, containing actions and assaults, and "attacks on all fronts" are in fact extremely rare. This slogan expresses the military equalitarianism which accompanies military adventurism.

In 1933 the exponents of military equalitarianism put forward the theory of "striking with two 'fists'" and splitting the main force of the Red Army in two, to seek victories simultaneously in two strategic directions. As a result, one fist remained idle while the other was tired out with fighting, and we failed to win the greatest victory possible at the time. In my opinion, when we face a powerful enemy, we should employ our army, whatever its size, in only one main direction at a time, not two. I am not objecting to operations in two or more directions, but at any given time there ought to be only one main direction. The Chinese Red Army, which entered the arena of the civil war as a small and weak force, has since repeatedly defeated its powerful antagonist and won victories that have astonished the world, and it has done so by relying largely on the employment of concentrated strength. Any one of its great victories can prove this point. When we say, "Pit one against ten, pit ten against a hundred", we are speaking of strategy, of the whole war and the over-all balance of forces, and in the strategic sense that is just what we have been doing. However, we are not speaking of campaigns and tactics, in which we must never do so. Whether in counter-offensives or offensives, we should always concentrate a big force to strike at one part of the enemy forces. We suffered every time we did not concentrate our troops, as in the battles against Tan Tao-yuan in the Tungshao area of Ningtu County in Kiangsi

Province in January 1931, against the 19th Route Army in the Kaohsinghsu area of Hsingkuo County in Kiangsi in August 1931, against Chen Chi-tang in the Shuikouhsu area of Nanhsiung County in Kwangtung Province in July 1932, and against Chen Cheng in the Tuantsun area of Lichuan County in Kiangsi in March 1934. In the past, battles such as those of Shuikouhsu and Tuantsun were generally deemed victories or even big victories (in the former we routed twenty regiments under Chen Chi-tang, in the latter twelve regiments under Chen Cheng), but we never welcomed such victories and in a certain sense even regarded them as defeats. For, in our opinion, a battle has little significance when there are no prisoners or war booty, or when they do not outweigh the losses.

Our strategy is "pit one against ten" and our tactics are "pit ten against one" -- this is one of our fundamental principles for gaining mastery over the enemy.

Military equalitarianism reached its extreme point in our fifth counter-campaign against "encirclement and suppression" in 1934. It was thought that we could beat the enemy by "dividing the forces into six routes" and "resisting on all fronts", but instead we were beaten by the enemy, and the reason was fear of losing territory. Naturally one can scarcely avoid loss of territory when concentrating the main forces in one direction while leaving only containing forces in others. But this loss is temporary and partial and is compensated for by victory in the place where the assault is made. After such a victory is won, territory lost in the area of the containing forces can be recovered. The enemy's first, second, third and fourth campaigns of "encirclement and suppression" all entailed the loss of territory -- particularly the third campaign, in which the Kiangsi base area of the Red Army was almost completely lost -- but in the end we not only recovered but extended our territory.

Failure to appreciate the strength of the people in the base area has often given rise to unwarranted fear of moving the Red Army too far away from the base area. This happened when the Red Army in Kiangsi made a long drive to attack Changchow in Fukien Province in 1932, and also when it wheeled around to attack Fukien after the victory in our fourth counter-campaign in 1933. There was fear in the first case that the enemy would seize the entire base area, and in the second that he would seize part of it; consequently there was opposition to concentrating our forces and advocacy of dividing them up for defence, but in the end all this proved to be wrong. As far as the enemy is concerned, he is afraid to advance into our base area, but the main danger in his eyes is a Red Army that has driven into the White area. His attention is always fixed on the whereabouts of the main force of the Red Army, and he rarely takes his eyes off it to concentrate on the base area. Even when the Red Army is on the defensive, it is still the centre of the enemy's attention. Part of his over-all plan is to reduce the size of our base area, but if the Red Army concentrates its main force to annihilate one of his columns, the enemy's supreme command will be compelled to focus greater attention on the Red Army and concentrate larger forces against it. Hence it is possible to wreck an enemy plan for reducing the size of a base area.

Also, it was wrong to say, "In the fifth 'encirclement and suppression' campaign which is being carried on by means of blockhouse warfare, it is impossible for us to operate with concentrated forces, and all we can do is to divide them up for defence and for short swift thrusts." The enemy's tactics of pushing forward 3, 5, 8, or 10 li at a time and building blockhouses at each halt were entirely the result of the Red Army's practice of fighting defensive actions at every successive point. The situation would certainly have been different if our army had abandoned the tactics of point-by-point defence on interior lines and, when possible and necessary, had turned and driven into the enemy's interior lines. The principle of concentration of forces is precisely the means for defeating the enemy's blockhouse warfare.

The kind of concentration of forces we advocate does not mean the abandonment of people's guerrilla warfare. To abandon small-scale guerrilla warfare and "concentrate every single rifle in the Red Army", as advocated by the Li Li-san line, has long since been proved wrong. Considering the revolutionary war as a whole, the operations of the people's guerrillas and those of the main forces of the Red Army complement each other like a man's right arm and left arm, and if we had only the main forces of the Red Army without the people's guerrillas, we would be like a warrior with only one arm. In concrete terms, and especially with regard to military operations, when we talk of the people in the base area as a factor, we mean that we have an armed people. That is the main reason why the enemy is afraid to approach our base area.

It is also necessary to employ Red Army detachments for operations in secondary directions; not all the forces of the Red Army should be concentrated. The kind of concentration we advocate is based on the principle of guaranteeing absolute or relative superiority on the battlefield. To cope with a strong enemy or to fight on a battlefield of vital importance, we must have an absolutely superior force; for instance, a force of 40,000 was concentrated to fight the 9,000 men under Chang Hui-tsan on December 30, 1930, in the first battle of our first counter-campaign. To cope with a weaker enemy or to fight on a battlefield of no great importance, a relatively superior force is sufficient; for instance, only some 10,000 Red Army men were employed to fight Liu Ho-ting's division of 7,000 men in Chienning on May 29, 1931, in the last battle of our second counter-campaign.

That is not to say we must have numerical superiority on every occasion. In certain circumstances, we may go into battle with a relatively or absolutely inferior force. Take the case of going into battle with a relatively inferior force when we have only a rather small Red Army force in a certain area (it is not that we have more troops and have not concentrated them). Then, in order to smash the attack of the stronger enemy in conditions where popular support, terrain and weather are greatly in our favour, it is of course necessary to concentrate the main part of our Red Army force for a surprise attack on a segment of one flank of the enemy while containing his centre and his other flank with guerrillas or small detachments, and in this way victory can be won. In our surprise attack on this segment of the enemy flank, the principle of using a superior force against an inferior force, of using the many to defeat the few, still applies. The same principle also applies when we go into battle with an absolutely inferior force, for example, when a guerrilla force makes a surprise attack on a large White army force, but is attacking only a small part of it.

As for the argument that the concentration of a large force for action in a single battle area is subject to the limitations of terrain, roads, supplies and billeting facilities, it should be evaluated according to the circumstances. There is a difference in the degree to which these limitations affect the Red Army and the White army, as the Red Army can stand greater hardships than the White army.

We use the few to defeat the many -- this we say to the rulers of China as a whole. We use the many to defeat the few -- this we say to each separate enemy force on the battlefield. That is no longer a secret, and in general the enemy is by now well acquainted with our way. However, he can neither prevent our victories nor avoid his own losses, because he does not know when and where we shall act. This we keep secret. The Red Army generally operates by surprise attacks.

7. MOBILE WARFARE

Mobile warfare or positional warfare? Our answer is mobile warfare. So long as we lack a large army or reserves of ammunition, and so long as there is only a single Red Army force to do the fighting in each base area, positional warfare is generally useless to us. For us, positional warfare is generally inapplicable in attack as well as in defence.

One of the outstanding characteristics of the Red Army's operations, which follows from the fact that the enemy is powerful while the Red Army is deficient in technical equipment, is the absence of fixed battle lines.

The Red Army's battle lines are determined by the direction in which it is operating. As its operational direction often shifts, its battle lines are fluid. Though the main direction does not change in a given period of time, within its ambit the secondary directions may shift at any moment; when we find ourselves checked in one direction, we must turn to another. If, after a time, we also find ourselves checked in the main direction, then we must change it too.

In a revolutionary civil war, there cannot be fixed battle lines, which was also the case in the Soviet Union. The difference between the Soviet Army and ours is that its battle lines were not so fluid as ours. There cannot be absolutely fixed battle lines in any war, because the vicissitudes of victory and defeat, advance and retreat, preclude it. But relatively fixed battle lines are often to be found in the general run of wars. Exceptions occur only where an army faces a much stronger enemy, as is the case with the Chinese Red Army in its present stage.

Fluidity of battle lines leads to fluidity in the size of our base areas. Our base areas are constantly expanding and contracting, and often as one base area falls another rises. This fluidity of territory is entirely a result of the fluidity of the war.

Fluidity in the war and in our territory produces fluidity in all fields of construction in our base areas. Construction plans covering several years are out of the question. Frequent changes of plan are all in the day's work.

It is to our advantage to recognize this characteristic. We must base our planning on it and must not have illusions about a war of advance without any retreats, take alarm at any temporary fluidity of our territory or of the rear areas of our army, or endeavour to draw up detailed long-term plans. We must adapt our thinking and our work to the circumstances, be ready to sit down as well as to march on, and always have our marching rations handy. It is only by exerting ourselves in today's fluid way of life that tomorrow we can secure relative stability, and eventually full stability.

The exponents of the strategy of "regular warfare" which dominated our fifth counter-campaign denied this fluidity and opposed| what they called "guerrilla-ism". Those comrades who opposed fluidity managed affairs as though they were the rulers of a big state, and the result was an extraordinary and immense fluidity -- the 25,000-li Long March.

Our workers' and peasants' democratic republic is a state, but today it is not yet a full-fledged one. Today we are still in the period of strategic defensive in the civil war, the form of our political power is still far from that of a full-fledged state, our army is still much inferior to the enemy both in numbers and technical equipment, our territory is still very small, and our enemy is constantly out to destroy us and will never rest content till he has done so. In defining our policy on the basis of these facts, we should not repudiate guerrilla-ism in general terms but should honestly admit the guerrilla character of the Red Army. It is no use being ashamed of this. On the contrary, this guerrilla character is precisely our distinguishing feature, our strong point, and our means of defeating the enemy. We should be prepared to discard it, but we cannot do so today. In the future this guerrilla character will definitely become something to be ashamed of and to be discarded, but today it is invaluable and we must stick to it.

"Fight when you can win, move away when you can't win" -- this is the popular way of describing our mobile warfare today. There is no military expert anywhere in the world who approves only of fighting and never of moving, though few people do as much moving as we do. We generally spend more time in moving than in fighting and would be doing well if we fought an average of one sizable battle a month. All our "moving" is for the purpose of "fighting", and all our strategy and tactics are built on "fighting". Nevertheless, there are times when it is inadvisable for us to fight. In the first place, it is inadvisable to fight when the force confronting us is too large; second, it is sometimes inadvisable to fight when the force confronting us, though not so large, is very dose to other enemy forces; third, it is generally inadvisable to fight an enemy force that is not isolated and is strongly entrenched; fourth, it is inadvisable to continue an engagement in which there is no prospect of victory. In any one of these situations we are prepared to move away. Such moving away is both permissible and necessary. For our recognition of the necessity of moving away is based on our recognition of the necessity of fighting. Herein lies the fundamental characteristic of the Red Army's mobile warfare.

Mobile warfare is primary, but we do not reject positional warfare where it is possible and necessary. It should be admitted that positional warfare should be employed for the tenacious defence of particular key points in a containing action during the strategic defensive, and when, during the strategic offensive, we encounter an enemy force that is isolated and cut off from help. We have had considerable experience in defeating the enemy by such positional warfare; we have cracked open many enemy cities, blockhouses and forts and broken through fairly well-fortified enemy field positions. In future we shall increase our efforts and remedy our inadequacies in this respect. We should by all means advocate positional attack or defence when circumstances require and permit it. At the present time, what we are opposed to is the general use of positional warfare or putting it on an equal footing with mobile` warfare; that is impermissible.

During the ten years' civil war, have there been no changes whatsoever in the guerrilla character of the Red Army, its lack of fixed battle lines, the fluidity of its base areas, or the fluidity of construction work in its base areas? Yes, there have been changes. The period from the days in the Chingkang Mountains to our first counter-campaign against "encirclement and suppression" in Kiangsi was the first stage, the stage in which the guerrilla character and fluidity were very pronounced, the Red Army being in its infancy and the base areas still being guerrilla zones. In the second stage, comprising the period from the first to the third counter-campaign, both the guerrilla character and the fluidity were considerably reduced, front armies having been formed and base areas with a population of several millions established. In the third stage, which comprised the period from the end of the third to the fifth counter-campaign, the guerrilla character and the fluidity were further reduced, and a central government and a revolutionary military commission had already been set up. The fourth stage was the Long March. The mistaken rejection of guerrilla warfare and fluidity on a small scale had led to guerrilla warfare and fluidity on a great scale. Now we are in the fifth stage. Because of our failure to smash the fifth "encirclement and suppression" campaign and because of this great fluidity, the Red Army and the base areas have been greatly reduced, but we have planted our feet in the Northwest and consolidated and developed the Shensi-Kansu-Ningsia Border Region, our base area here. The three front armies which form the main forces of the Red Army have been brought under a unified command, which is unprecedented.

Going by the nature of our strategy, we may also say the period from the days in the Chingkang Mountains to our fourth counter-campaign was one stage, the period of the fifth counter-campaign was another, and the period from the Long March to the present is the third. During the fifth counter-campaign the correct policy of the past was wrongly discarded; today we have correctly discarded the wrong policy adopted during the fifth counter-campaign and revived the earlier and correct policy. However, we have not thrown out everything in the fifth counter-campaign, nor revived everything that preceded it. We have revived only what was good in the past, and discarded only the mistakes of the period of the fifth counter-campaign.

Guerrilla-ism has two aspects. One is irregularity, that is, decentralization, lack of uniformity, absence of strict discipline, and simple methods of work. These features stemmed from the Red Army's infancy, and some of them were just what was needed at the time. As the Red Army reaches a higher stage, we must gradually and consciously eliminate them so as to make the Red Army more centralized, more unified, more disciplined and more thorough in its work -- in short, more regular in character. In the directing of operations we should also gradually and consciously reduce such guerrilla characteristics as are no longer required at a higher stage. Refusal to make progress in this respect and obstinate adherence to the old stage are impermissible and harmful, and are detrimental to large-scale operations.

The other aspect of guerrilla-ism consists of the principle of mobile warfare, the guerrilla character of both strategic and tactical operations which is still necessary at present, the inevitable fluidity of our base areas, flexibility in planning the development of the base areas, and the rejection of premature regularization in building the Red Army. In this connection, it is equally impermissible, disadvantageous and harmful to our present operations to deny the facts of history, oppose the retention of what is useful, and rashly leave the present stage in order to rush blindly towards a "new stage", which as yet is beyond reach and has no real significance.

We are now on the eve of a new stage with respect to the Red Army's technical equipment and organization. We must be prepared to go over to this new stage. Not to prepare ourselves would be wrong and harmful to our future warfare. In the future, when the technical and organizational conditions in the Red Army have changed and the building of the Red Army has entered a new stage, its operational directions and battle lines will become more stable; there will be more positional warfare; the fluidity of the war, of our territory and of our construction work will be greatly reduced and finally disappear; and we will no longer be handicapped by present limitations, such as the enemy's superiority and his strongly entrenched positions.

At present we oppose both the wrong measures of the period of the domination of "Left" opportunism and the revival of many of the irregular features which the Red Army had in its infancy but which are now unnecessary. But we should be resolute in restoring the many valuable principles of army building and of strategy and tactics by which the Red Army has consistently won its victories. We must sum up all that is good from the past in a systematic, more highly developed and richer military line, in order to win victories over the enemy today and prepare to go over to the new stage in the future.

The waging of mobile warfare involves many problems, such as reconnaissance, judgement, decision, combat disposition, command, concealment, concentration, advance, deployment, attack, pursuit, surprise attack, positional attack, positional defence, encounter action, retreat, night fighting, special operations, evading the strong and attacking the weak, besieging the enemy in order to strike at his reinforcements, feint attack, defence against aircraft, operating amongst several enemy forces, by-passing operations, consecutive operations, operating without a rear, the need for rest and building up energy. These problems exhibited many specific features in the history of the Red Army, features which should be methodically dealt with and summed up in the science of campaigns, and I shall not go into them here.

8. WAR OF QUICK DECISION

A strategically protracted war and campaigns or battles of quick decision are two aspects of the same thing, two principles which should receive equal and simultaneous emphasis in civil wars and which are also applicable in anti-imperialist wars.

Because the reactionary forces are very strong, revolutionary forces grow only gradually, and this fact determines the protracted nature of our war. Here impatience is harmful and advocacy of "quick decision" incorrect. To wage a revolutionary war for ten years, as we have done, might be surprising in other countries, but for us it is like the opening sections in an "eight-legged essay" -- the "presentation, amplification and preliminary exposition of the theme" [36] -- and many exciting parts are yet to follow. No doubt developments in the future will be greatly accelerated under the influence of domestic and international conditions. As changes have already taken place in the international and domestic situation and greater changes are coming, it can be said that we have outgrown the past state of slow development and fighting in isolation. But we should not expect successes overnight. The aspiration to "wipe out the enemy before breakfast" is admirable, but it is bad to make concrete plans to do so. As China's reactionary forces are backed by many imperialist powers, our revolutionary war will continue to be a protracted one until China's revolutionary forces have built up enough strength to breach the main positions of our internal and external enemies, and until the international revolutionary forces have crushed or contained most of the international reactionary forces. To proceed from this point in formulating our strategy of long-term warfare is one of the important principles guiding our strategy.

The reverse is true of campaigns and battles -- here the principle is not protractedness but quick decision. Quick decision is sought in campaigns and battles, and this is true at all times and in all countries. In a war as a whole, too, quick decision is sought at all times and in all countries, and a long drawn-out war is considered harmful. China's war, however, must be handled with the greatest patience and treated as a protracted war. During the period of the Li Li-san line, some people ridiculed our way of doing things as "shadowboxing tactics" (meaning our tactics of fighting many battles back and forth before going on to seize the big cities), and said that we would not see the victory of the revolution until our hair turned white. Such impatience was proved wrong long ago. But if their criticism had been applied not to strategy but to campaigns and battles, they would have been perfectly right, and for the following reasons. First, the Red Army has no sources from which to replenish its arms and especially its ammunition; second, the White forces consist of many armies while there is only one Red Army, which must be prepared to fight one operation after another in quick succession in order to smash each campaign of "encirclement and suppression"; and third, though the White armies advance separately, most of them keep fairly close to one another, and if we fail to gain a quick decision in attacking one of them, all the others will converge upon us. For these reasons we have to fight battles of quick decision. It is usual for us to conclude a battle in a few hours, or in a day or two. It is only when our plan is to "besiege the enemy in order to strike at his reinforcements" and our purpose is to strike not at the besieged enemy but at his reinforcements that we are prepared for a certain degree of protractedness in our besieging operations; but even then we seek a quick decision against the reinforcements. A plan of protracted operations is often applied in campaigns or battles when we are strategically on the defensive and are tenaciously defending positions on a holding front, or when, in a strategic offensive, we are attacking isolated enemy forces cut off from help, or are eliminating White strongholds within our base areas. But protracted operations of this kind help rather than hinder the main Red Army force in its battles of quick decision.

A quick decision cannot be achieved simply by wanting it, but requires many specific conditions. The main requirements are: adequate preparations, seizing the opportune moment, concentration of superior forces, encircling and outflanking tactics, favourable terrain, and striking at the enemy when he is on the move, or when he is stationary but has not yet consolidated his positions. Unless these requirements are satisfied, it is impossible to achieve quick decision in a campaign or battle.

The smashing of an enemy "encirclement and suppression" is a major campaign, but the principle of quick decision and not that of protractedness still applies. For the manpower, financial resources and military strength of a base area do not allow protractedness.

While quick-decision is the general principle, we must oppose undue impatience. It is altogether necessary that the highest military and political leading body of a revolutionary base area, having taken into account the circumstances in its base area and the situation of the enemy, should not be overawed by his truculence, dispirited by hardships that can be endured, or dejected by setbacks, but should have the requisite patience and stamina. The smashing of the first enemy "encirclement and suppression" campaign in Kiangsi Province | took only one week from the first battle to the last; the second was smashed in barely a fortnight; the third dragged on for three months; before it was smashed; the fourth took three weeks; and the fifth taxed our endurance for a whole year. When we were compelled to break through the enemy's encirclement after the failure to smash his fifth campaign, we showed an unjustifiable haste. In the circumstances then obtaining, we could well have held out for another two or three months, giving the troops some time for rest and reorganization. If that had been done, and if the leadership had been a little wiser after our breakthrough, the outcome would have been very different.

For all that, the principle of shortening the duration of a campaign by every possible means remains valid. Campaign and battle plans should call for our maximum effort in concentration of troops, mobile warfare, and so on, so as to ensure the destruction of the enemy's effective strength on the interior lines (that is, in the base area) and the quick defeat of his "encirclement and suppression" campaign, but where it is evident that the campaign cannot be terminated on our interior lines, we should employ the main Red Army force to break through the enemy's encirclement and switch to our exterior lines (that is, the enemy's interior lines) in order to defeat him there. Now that the enemy has developed his blockhouse warfare to a high degree, this will become our usual method of operation. At the time of the Fukien Incident, [37] two months after the commencement of our fifth counter-campaign, the main forces of the Red Army should undoubtedly have thrust into the Kiangsu-Chekiang-Anhwei-Kiangsi region, with Chekiang as the centre, and swept over the length and breadth of the area between Hangchow, Soochow, Nanking, Wuhu, Nanchang and Foochow, turning our strategic defensive into a strategic offensive, menacing the enemy's vital centres and seeking battles in the vast areas where there were no blockhouses. By such means we could have compelled the enemy, who was attacking southern Kiangsi and western Fukien, to turn back to defend his vital centres, broken his attack on the base area in Kiangsi and rendered aid to Fukien People's Government -- we certainly could have aided it by this means. As this plan was rejected, the enemy's fifth "encirclement and suppression" campaign could not be broken, and the People's Government in Fukien inevitably collapsed. Even after a year's fighting, though it had become inopportune for us to advance on Chekiang, we could still have turned to the strategic offensive in another direction by moving our main forces towards Hunan, that is, by driving into central Hunan instead of going through Hunan to Kweichow, and in this way we could have manoeuvred the enemy from Kiangsi into Hunan and destroyed him there. As this plan, too, was rejected, all hope of breaking the enemy's fifth campaign was finally dashed, and we had no alternative but to set out on the Long March.

9. WAR OF ANNIHILATION

It is inappropriate to advocate a "contest of attrition" for the Chinese Red Army today. A "contest of treasures" not between Dragon Kings but between a Dragon King and a beggar would be rather ludicrous. For the Red Army which gets almost all its supplies from the enemy, war of annihilation is the basic policy. Only by annihilating the enemy's effective strength can we smash his "encirclement and suppression" campaigns and expand our revolutionary base areas. Inflicting casualties is a means of annihilating the enemy, or otherwise there would be no sense to it. We incur losses ourselves in inflicting casualties on the enemy, but we replenish ourselves by annihilating his units, thereby not only making good our losses but adding to the strength of our army. A battle in which the enemy is routed is not basically decisive in a contest with a foe of great strength. A battle of annihilation, on the other hand, produces a great and immediate impact on any enemy. Injuring all of a man's ten fingers is not as effective as chopping off one, and routing ten enemy divisions is not as effective as annihilating one of them.

Our policy for dealing with the enemy's first, second, third and fourth "encirclement and suppression" campaigns was war of annihilation. The forces annihilated in each campaign constituted only part of his total strength', and yet all these "encirclement and suppression" campaigns were smashed. In our fifth counter-campaign, however, the opposite policy was pursued, which in fact helped the enemy to attain his aims.

War of annihilation entails the concentration of superior forces and the adoption of encircling or outflanking tactics. We cannot have the former without the latter. Conditions such as popular support, favourable terrain, a vulnerable enemy force and the advantage of surprise are all indispensable for the purpose of annihilation.

Merely routing one enemy force or permitting it to escape has meaning only if, in the battle or campaign as a whole, our main force is concentrating its operations of annihilation against another enemy force, or otherwise it is meaningless. Here the losses are justified by the gains.

In establishing our own war industry we must not allow ourselves to become dependent on it. Our basic policy is to rely on the war industries of the imperialist countries and of our domestic enemy. We have a claim on the output of the arsenals of London as well as of Hanyang, and, what is more, it is delivered to us by the enemy's transport corps. This is the sober truth, it is not a jest.

NOTES

[1] The science of strategy, the science of campaigns and the science of tactics are all components of Chinese military science. The science of strategy deals with the laws that govern the war situation as a whole. The science of campaigns deals with the laws that govern campaigns and is applied in directing campaigns. The science of tactics deals with the laws that govern battles and is applied in directing battles.

[2] Sun Wu Tzu, or Sun Wu, was a famous Chinese military scientist in the 5th century B.C., who wrote Sun Tzu, a treatise on war containing thirteen chapters. This quotation is from Chapter 3, "The Strategy of Attack".

[3] When Comrade Mao Tse-tung wrote this article in 1936, it was exactly fifteen years since the founding of the Chinese Communist Party in July 1921.

[4] Chen Tu-hsiu was originally a professor at Peking University and became famous as an editor of New Youth. He was one of the founders of the Communist Party of China. Owing to his reputation at the time of the May 4th Movement and owing to the Party's immaturity in its initial period, he became General Secretary of the Party. In the last period of the

revolution of 1924-27, the Rightist thinking in the Party represented by Chen Tu-hsiu developed into a line of capitulationism. Comrade Mao Tse-tung has observed that the capitulationists at that time "voluntarily gave up the Party's leadership of the peasant masses, urban petty bourgeoisie and middle bourgeoisie, and in particular gave up the Party's leadership of the armed forces, thus causing the defeat of the revolution" ("The Present Situation and Our Tasks", Selected Works of Mao Tse-tung, Eng. ed., FLP, Peking, 1961, Vol. IV, p. 171). After the defeat of 1927 Chen Tu-hsiu and a handful of other capitulationists lost faith in the future of the revolution and became liquidationists. They took the reactionary Trotskyist stand and together with the Trotskyites formed a small anti-Party group. Consequently Chen Tu-hsiu was expelled from the Party in November 1929. He died in 1942.

[5] The "Left" opportunism of Li Li-san, generally known as the "Li Li-san line", refers to the "Left" opportunist line which existed in the Party for about four months beginning from June 1930 and which was represented by Comrade Li Li-san, then the most influential leader of the Central Committee of the Communist Party of China. The Li Li-san line had the following characteristics: It violated the policy of the Party's Sixth National Congress; it denied that mass strength had to be built up for the revolution and denied that the development of the revolution was uneven; it regarded as "extremely erroneous... localism and conservatism characteristic of peasant mentality" the ideas of Comrade Mao Tse-tung that for a long time we should devote our attention mainly to creating rural base areas, use the rural areas to encircle the cities and use these bases to advance a high tide of country-wide revolution; and it held that preparations should be made for immediate insurrections in all parts of the country. On the basis of this erroneous line, Comrade Li Li-san drew up an adventurist plan for organizing immediate armed insurrections in the key cities throughout the country. At the same time, he refused to

recognize the uneven development of the world revolution, holding that the general outbreak of the Chinese revolution would inevitably lead to a general outbreak of world revolution, without which the Chinese revolution could not be successful; he also refused to recognize the protracted nature of China's bourgeois-democratic revolution, holding that the beginnings of victory in one or more provinces would mark the beginning of the transition to socialist revolution, and thus formulated a number of inappropriate "Left" adventurist policies. Comrade Mao Tse-tung opposed this erroneous line, and the broad masses of cadres and members in the Party also demanded its rectification. At the Third Plenary Session of the Party's Sixth Central Committee in September 1930 Comrade Li Li-san admitted the mistakes that had been pointed out and then relinquished his leading position in the Central Committee. Over a long period of time Comrade Li Li-san corrected his wrong views, and so he was re-elected to the Central Committee at the Seventh National Congress of the Party.

[6] The Third Plenary Session of the Sixth Central Committee of the Party held in September 1930, and the subsequent central leading body adopted many positive measures to put an end to the Li Li-san line. But later a number of Party comrades who were inexperienced in practical revolutionary struggle, with Chen Shao-yu (Wang Ming) and Chin Pang-hsien (Po Ku) in the lead, came out against the Central Committee's measures. In the pamphlet, The Two Lines or The Struggle for the Further Bolshevization of the Communist Party of China, they most emphatically declared that the main danger then existing in the Party was not "Left" opportunism but "Right opportunism" and, to justify their own activities, they "criticized" the Li Li-san line as "Rightist". They put forward a new political programme which continued, revived or developed the Li Li-san line and other "Left" ideas and policies in a new guise, and set themselves against the

correct line of Comrade Mao Tse-tung. It was mainly to criticize the military mistakes of this new "Left" opportunist line that Comrade Mao Tse-tung wrote the present article "Problems of Strategy in China's Revolutionary War". This line was dominant in the Party from the Fourth Plenary Session of the Sixth Central Committee in January 1931 to the meeting of the Political Bureau convened by the Central Committee at Tsunyi, Kweichow Province, in January 1935, which ended the dominance of this erroneous line and established the new central leadership headed by Comrade Mao Tse-tung. The erroneous "Left" line dominated the Party for a particularly long time (four years) and brought extremely heavy losses, with disastrous consequences, to the Party and the revolution. A loss of go per cent was inflicted on the Chinese Communist Party, the Chinese Red Army and its base areas tens of millions of people in the revolutionary base areas were made to suffer the cruel oppression of the Kuomintang, and the progress of the Chinese revolution was retarded. The overwhelming majority of the errant comrades have realized and corrected their mistakes through a long process of learning from experience and have done much good work for the Party and the people. Under Comrade Mao Tse-tung's leadership they are now united with the masses of other comrades in the Party on the basis of a common political understanding.

[7] For the Right opportunism of Chang Kuo-tao, see "On Tactics Against Japanese Imperialism".

[8] The Officers' Training Corps at Lushan was an organization set up by Chiang Kai-shek in July 1933 on Lushan Mountain in Kiukiang, Kiangsi Province, for training anti-Communist military cadres. Officers of Chiang Kai-shek's armed forces were sent there in rotation to receive fascist military and political training from German, Italian and American instructors.

[9] These new military principles largely constituted the Chiang Kai-shek gang's policy of "blockhouse warfare" in accordance with which it advanced gradually and entrenched itself at every step.

[10] See V. I. Lenin, " 'Communism' ", in which Lenin, criticizing the Hungarian Communist Bela Kun, said that he "gives up the most essential thing in Marxism, the living soul of Marxism, the concrete analysis of concrete conditions" (Collected Works. Russ. ed., Moscow, 1950, Vol. XXXI, p. 143).

[11] The First Party Congress of the Hunan-Kiangsi Border Area was held on May 20, 1928 at Maoping, Ningkang County.

[12] For an explanation, see pp. 236-37 of this volume.

[13] For roving rebels, see "On Correcting Mistaken Ideas in the Party", Notes 4 and 5, pp. 115-16 of this volume.

[14] "Bandit ways" refers to plundering and looting resulting from lack of discipline, organization and clear political direction.

[15] The Long March of 25,000 li (12,500 kilometres) was made by the Red Army from Kiangsi Province to northern Shensi Province. For further reference, see "On Tactics Against Japanese Imperialism", Note 20, p. 175 of this volume.

[16] The period after the December uprising of 1905 was defeated, in which the revolutionary tide in Russia gradually receded. See History of the Communist Party of the Soviet Union (Bolsheviks), Short Course, Chapter 3, Sections 5 and 6.

[17] The peace treaty of Brest-Litovsk was concluded between Soviet Russia and Germany in March 1918. Confronted with obviously superior enemy forces, the revolutionary forces had to make a temporary retreat in order to prevent the German imperialists from launching an attack on the new-born Soviet Republic, which as yet had no army of its own. The conclusion of this treaty gained time for the Soviet Republic to consolidate the political power of the proletariat, reorganize its economy and build up the Red Army. It enabled the proletariat to maintain its leadership over the peasantry and build up sufficient strength to defeat the White Guards and the armed intervention of Britain, the United States, France, Japan, Poland and other countries in 1918-20.

[18] On October 30, 1927 the peasants of the Haifeng-Lufeng area of Kwangtung Province launched their third insurrection under the leadership of the Communist Party of China. They occupied Haifeng and Lufeng and the surrounding area, organized a Red Army and established the democratic political power of the workers and peasants. They were later defeated because they made the mistake of underestimating the enemy.

[19] The Fourth Front Army and the Second Front Army of the Red Army joined forces in the autumn of 1936 and shifted northward from the northeastern part of Sikang. Chang Kuo-tao was then still persisting in his anti-Party stand and in his policy of retreat and liquidation. In October of the same year, when the Second and Fourth Front Armies arrived in Kansu, he ordered the advance units of the Fourth Front Army, numbering more than ~20,000, to organize the Western Column for crossing the Yellow River and advancing westward to Chinghai. This Column was practically defeated after suffering blows in battles in December 1936 and was completely defeated in March 1937.

[20] See letter from Karl Marx to L. Kugelmann on the Paris Commune.

[21] Shui Hu Chuan (Heroes of the Marshes) is a celebrated Chinese novel describing a peasant war. The novel is attributed to Shih Nai-an who lived around the end of the Yuan Dynasty and the beginning of the Ming Dynasty (14th century). Lin Chung and Chai Chin are both heroes in this novel. Hung is the drill master on Chai Chin's estate.

[22] Lu and Chi were two feudal states in the Spring and Autumn Era (722-481 B.C.). Chi was a big state in the central part of the present Shantung Province, nod Lu was a smaller one in the southern part. Duke Chuang reigned over Lu from 693 to 662 B.C.

[23] Tsochiu Ming was the author of Tso Chuan, a classical chronicle of the Chou Dynasty. For the passage quoted, see the section in Tso Chuan enticed "The loth Year of Duke Chuang" (684 B.C.).

[24] The ancient town of Chengkao, in the northwest of the present Chengkao County, Honan Province, was of great military importance. It was the scene of battles fought in 203 B.C. between Liu Pang, King of Han, and Hsiang Yu, King of Chu. At first Hsiang Yu captured Hsingyang and Chengkao and Liu Pang's troops were almost routed. Liu Pang waited until the opportune moment when Hsiang Yu's troops were in midstream «crossing the Szeshui River, and then crushed them and recaptured Chengkao.

[25] The ancient town of Kunyang, in the north of the present Yehhsien County, Honan Province, was the place where Liu Hsiu, founder of the Eastern Han Dynasty, defeated the troops of Wang Mang, Emperor of the Hsin Dynasty, in A.D. 23. There was a huge numerical disparity between the

two sides, Liu Hsiu's forces totalling 8,000 to 9,000 men as against Wang Mang's 400,000. But taking advantage of the negligence of Wang Mang's generals, Wang Hsun and Wang Yi, who underestimated the enemy, Liu Hsiu with only 3,000 picked troops put Wang Mang's main forces to rout. He followed up this victory by crushing the rest of the enemy troops.

[26] Kuantu was in the northeast of the present Chungmou County, Honan Province, and the scene of the battle between the armies of Tsao Tsao and Yuan Shao in A.D. 200. Yuan Shao had an army of 100,000 while Tsao Tsao had only a meagre force and was short of supplies. Taking advantage of lack of vigilance on the part of Yuan Shao's troops, who belittled the enemy, Tsao Tsao dispatched his light-footed soldiers to spring a surprise attack on them and set their supplies on fire. Yuan Shao's army was thrown into confusion and its main force wiped out.

[27] The state of Wu was ruled by Sun Chuan, and the state of Wei by Tsao Tsao. Chihpi is situated on the south bank of the Yangtse River, to the northeast of Chinyni Hupeh Province. In A.D. 208 Tsao Tsao led an army of over 500,000 men, which he proclaimed to be 800,000 strong, to launch an attack on Sun Chuan. The latter, in alliance with Tsao Tsao's antagonist Liu Pei, mustered a force of 30,000. Knowing that Tsao Tsao's army was plagued by epidemics and was unaccustomed to action afloat, the allied forces of Sun Chuan and Liu Pei set fire to Tsao Tsao's fleet and crushed his army.

[28] Yiling, to the east of the present Ichang, Hupeh Province, was the place where Lu Hsun, a general of the state of Wu, defeated the army of Liu Pei, ruler of Shu, in A.D. 222. Liu Pei's troops scored successive victories at the beginning of the war and penetrated five or six hundred li into the territory of Wu as far as Yiling. Lu Hsun, who was defending Yiling,

avoided battle for over seven months until Liu Pei "was at his wits' end and his troops were exhausted and demoralized". Then he crushed Liu Pei's troops by taking advantage of a favourable wind to set fire to their tents.

[29] Hsieh Hsuan, a general of Eastern Tsin Dynasty, defeated Pu Chien, ruler of the state of Chin, in A.D. 383 at the Peishui River in Anhwei Province. Pu Chien had an infantry force of more than 600,000, a cavalry force of 270,000 and a guards corps of more than 30,000, while the land and river forces of Eastern Tsin numbered only 80,000. When the armies lined up on opposite banks of the Peishui River, Hsieh Hsuan, taking advantage of the overconfidence and conceit of the enemy troops, requested Pu Chien to move his troops back so as to leave room for the Eastern Tsin troops to cross the river and fight it out. Pu Chien complied, but when he ordered withdrawal, his troops got into a panic and could not be stopped. Seizing the opportunity, the Eastern Tsin troops crossed the river, launched an offensive and crushed the enemy.

[30] Nanchang, capital of Kiangsi Province, was the scene of the famous uprising on August 1, 1927 led by the Communist Party of China in order to combat the counterrevolution of Chiang Kai-shek and Wang Ching-wei and to continue the revolution of 1924-27. More than thirty thousand troops took part in the uprising which was led by Comrades Chou En-lai, Chu The, Ho Lung and Yeh Ting. The insurrectionary army withdrew from Nanchang on August 5 as planned, but suffered a defeat when approaching Chaochow and Swatow in Kwangtung Province. Led by Comrades Chu Teh, Chen Yi and Lin Piao, part of the troops later fought their way to the Chingkang Mountains and joined forces with the 1st Division of the First Workers' and Peasants' Revolutionary Army under Comrade Mao Tse-tung.

[31] See "Why Is It That Red Political Power Can Exist in China?", Note 8, p. 72 of this volume.

[32] The famous Autumn Harvest Uprising under the leadership of Comrade Mao Tse-tung was launched in September 1927 by the people's armed forces of Hsiushui, Pinghsiang, Pingkiang and Liuyang Counties on the Hunan-Kiangd border, who formed the 1st Division of the Pirst Workers' and Peasants' Revolutionary Army. Comrade Mao Tse-tung led this force to the Chingkang Mountains where a revolutionary base was established.

[33] The A-B (initials for "Anti-Bolshevik") Group was a counter-revolutionary organization of undercover Kuomintang agents in the Red areas.

[34] See V. I. Lenin, "Theses on the Question of the Immediate Conclusion of a Separate and Annexationist Peace", "Strange and Monstrous", "A Serious Lesson and a Serious Responsibility", "Report on War and Peace", Selected Works, in two volumes, Eng. ed., FLPH, Moscow, 1952, Vol. II, Part I, and also History of the Communist Party of the Soviet Union (Bolsheviks), Short Course, Chapter 7, Section 7.

[35] The regions referred to here are those inhabited by the Tibetans in Sikang and the Hui people in Kansu, Chinghai and Sinkiang Provinces.

[36] The "eight-legged essay" was the prescribed form in the imperial competitive examinations in feudal China from the 15th to the 19th century. The main body of the essay was made up of the inceptive paragraph, the middle paragraph, the rear paragraph and the concluding paragraph, with each paragraph comprising two parts. Here Comrade Mao Tse-tung is using the development of the theme in this kind of essay as a metaphor to illustrate the development of the revolution through its various

stages. However, Comrade Mao Tse-tung generally uses the term "eight-legged essay" to ridicule dogmatism.

[37] In November 1933, under the influence of the people's anti-Japanese upsurge throughout China, the leaders of the Kuomintang's 19th Route Army, in alliance with the Kuomintang forces under Li Chi-shen, publicly renounced Chiang Kai-shek and established the "People's Revolutionary Government of the Republic of China" in Fukien, concluding an agreement with the Red Army to attack Chiang Kai-shek and resist Japan. This episode was referred to as the Fukien Incident. The 19th Route Army and Fukien People's Government, however, collapsed under the attacks of Chiang Kai-shek's troops.

THE ART OF WAR

PART 2

PROBLEMS OF STRATEGY

IN GUERRILLA WAR

AGAINST JAPAN

by

Mao Tse-tung

May 1938

Mao Tse-tung

Preface

In the early days of the War of Resistance Against Japan, many people inside and outside the Party belittled the important strategic role of guerrilla warfare and pinned their hopes on regular warfare alone, and particularly on the operations of the Kuomintang forces. Comrade Mao Tse-tung refuted this view and wrote this article to show the correct road of development for anti-Japanese guerrilla warfare.

As a result, the Eighth Route Army and the New Fourth Army, which had just over 40,000 men when the War of Resistance began in 1937, grew to a great army of one million by the time Japan surrendered in 1945, established many revolutionary base areas, played a great part in the war and thus, throughout this period, made Chiang Kai-shek afraid to capitulate to Japan or launch a nation-wide civil war.

In 1946, when Chiang Kai-shek did launch a nation-wide civil war, the People's Liberation Army, formed out of the Eighth Route and New Fourth Armies, was strong enough to deal with his attacks.

Mao Tse-tung

Chapter I

WHY RAISE THE QUESTION OF STRATEGY
IN GUERRILLA WAR?

In the War of Resistance Against Japan, regular warfare is primary and guerrilla warfare supplementary. This point has already been correctly settled. Thus, it seems there are only tactical problems in guerrilla warfare. Why then raise the question of strategy?

If China were a small country in which the role of guerrilla warfare was only to render direct support over short distances to the campaigns of the regular army, there would, of course, be only tactical problems but no strategic ones. On the other hand, if China were a country as strong as the Soviet Union and the invading enemy could either be quickly expelled, or, even though his expulsion were to take some time, he could not occupy extensive areas, then again guerrilla warfare would simply play a supporting role in campaigns, and would naturally involve only tactical but not strategic problems.

The question of strategy in guerrilla war does arise, however, in the case of China, which is neither small nor like the Soviet Union, but which is both a large and a weak country. This large and weak country is being attacked by a small and strong country, but the large and weak country is in an era of progress; this is the source of the whole problem. It is in these circumstances that vast areas have come under enemy occupation and that the war has become a protracted one. The enemy is occupying vast areas of this large country of ours, but Japan is a small country, she does not have sufficient soldiers and has to leave many gaps in the occupied areas, so that our anti Japanese guerrilla warfare consists primarily not in interior-line operations in support of the campaigns of the regular troops but in independent operations on exterior lines;

furthermore, China is progressive, that is to say, she has a staunch army and broad masses of people, both led by the Communist Party, so that, far from being small-scale, our anti-Japanese guerrilla warfare is in fact large-scale warfare. Hence the emergence of a whole series of problems, such as the strategic defensive, the strategic offensive, etc. The protracted nature of the war and its attendant ruthlessness have made it imperative for guerrilla warfare to undertake many unusual tasks; hence such problems as those of the base areas, the development of guerrilla warfare into mobile warfare, and so on. For all these reasons, China's guerrilla warfare against Japan has broken out of the bounds of tactics to knock at the gates of strategy, and it demands examination from the viewpoint of strategy. The point that merits our particular attention is that such extensive as well as protracted guerrilla warfare is quite new in the entire history of war. This is bound up with the fact that we are now in the Nineteen Thirties and Nineteen Forties and that we now have the Communist Party and the Red Army. Herein lies the heart of the matter. Our enemy is probably still cherishing fond dreams of emulating the Mongol conquest of the Sung Dynasty, the Manchu conquest of the Ming Dynasty, the British occupation of North America and India, the Latin occupation of Cen tral and South America, etc. But such dreams have no practical value in present-day China because there are certain factors present in the China of today which were absent in those historical instances, and one of them is guerrilla warfare, which is quite a new phenomenon. If our enemy overlooks this fact, he will certainly come to grief.

These are the reasons why our anti-Japanese guerrilla warfare, though occupying only a supplementary place in the War of Resistance as a whole, must nevertheless be examined from the viewpoint of strategy.

Why not, then, apply to guerrilla warfare the general strategic principles of the War of Resistance?

The question of strategy in our anti-Japanese guerrilla warfare is indeed closely linked with the question of strategy in the War of Resistance as a whole, because they have much in common. On the other hand, guerrilla warfare is different from regular warfare and has its own peculiarities, and consequently many peculiar elements are involved in the question of strategy in guerrilla warfare. With out modification it is impossible to apply the strategic principles of the War of Resistance in general to guerrilla warfare with its own peculiarities.

Chapter II

THE BASIC PRINCIPLE OF WAR IS TO PRESERVE ONESELF AND DESTROY THE ENEMY

Before discussing the question of strategy in guerrilla warfare in concrete terms, a few words are needed on the fundamental problem of war. All the guiding principles of military operations grow out of the one basic principle: to strive to the utmost to preserve one's own strength and destroy that of the enemy. In a revolutionary war, this principle is directly linked with basic political principles. For instance, the basic political principle of China's War of Resistance Against Japan, i.e., its political aim, is to drive out Japanese imperialism and build an independent, free and happy new China.

In terms of military action this principle means the use of armed force to defend our motherland and to drive out the Japanese invaders. To attain this end, the operations of the armed units take the form of doing their utmost to preserve their own strength on the one hand and destroy the enemy's on the other. How then do we justify the encouragement of heroic sacrifice in war? Every war exacts a price, sometimes an extremely high one. Is this not in contradiction with "preserving oneself"? In fact, there is no contradiction at all; to put it more exactly, sacrifice and self-preservation are both opposite and complementary to each other. For such sacrifice is essential not only for destroying the enemy but also for preserving oneself -- partial and temporary "non-preservation" (sacrifice, or paying the price) is necessary for the sake of general and permanent preservation. From this basic principle stems the series of principles guiding military operations, all of which -- from the principles of shooting (taking cover to preserve oneself, and making full use of fire-power to destroy the enemy) to the principles of strategy -- are permeated with the spirit of this basic principle. All technical, tactical and strategic principles represent applications of this basic principle. The principle of preserving one self and destroying the enemy is the basis of all military principles.

Chapter III

SIX SPECIFIC PROBLEMS OF STRATEGY IN
GUERRILLA WAR AGAINST JAPAN

Now let us see what policies or principles have to be
adopted in guerrilla operations against Japan before we can
attain the object of preserving ourselves and destroying the
enemy. Since the guerrilla units in the War of Resistance (and
in all other revolutionary wars) generally grow out of nothing
and expand from a small to a large force, they must preserve
themselves and, moreover, they must expand. Hence the
question is, what policies or principles have to be adopted
before we can attain the object of preserving and expanding
ourselves and destroying the enemy?

Generally speaking, the main principles are as follows: (1)
the use of initiative, flexibility and planning in conducting
offensives within the defensive, battles of quick decision
within protracted war, and exterior-line operations within
interior-line operations; (2) co-ordination with regular warfare;
(3) establishment of base areas; (4) the strategic defensive and
the strategic offensive; (5) the development of guerrilla warfare
into mobile warfare; and (6) correct relationship of command.
These six items constitute the whole of the strategic
programme for guerrilla war against Japan and are the means
necessary for the preservation and expansion of our forces, for
the destruction and expulsion of the enemy, for co-ordination
with regular warfare and the winning of final victory.

Chapter IV

INITIATIVE, FLEXIBILITY AND PLANNING IN
CONDUCTING OFFENSIVES WITHIN THE DEFENSIVE,
BATTLES OF QUICK DECISION WITHIN PROTRACTED
WAR, AND EXTERIOR-LINE OPERATIONS WITHIN
INTERIOR-LINE OPERATIONS

Here the subject may be dealt with under four headings: (1)
the relationship between the defensive and the offensive,
between protractedness and quick decision, and between the
interior and exterior lines; (2) the initiative in all operations; (3)
flexible employment of forces; and (4) planning in all
operations.

To start with the first.

If we take the War of Resistance as a whole, the fact that
Japan is a strong country and is attacking while China is a
weak country and is defending herself makes our war
strategically a defensive and protracted war. As far as the
operational lines are concerned, the Japanese are operating on
exterior and we on interior lines. This is one aspect of the
situation. But there is another aspect which is just the reverse.
The enemy forces, though strong (in arms, in certain qualities
of their men, and certain other factors), are numerically small,
whereas our forces, though weak (likewise, in arms, in certain
qualities of our men, and certain other factors), are numerically
very large. Added to the fact that the enemy is an alien nation
invading our country while we are resisting his invasion on our
own soil, this determines the following strategy. It is possible
and necessary to use tactical offensives within the strategic
defensive, to fight campaigns and battles of quick decision
within a strategically protracted war and to fight campaigns
and battles on exterior lines within strategically interior lines.
Such is the strategy to be adopted in the War of Resistance as a

whole. It holds true both for regular and for guerrilla warfare. Guerrilla warfare is different only in degree and form. Offensives in guerrilla warfare generally take the form of surprise attacks. Although surprise attacks can and should be employed in regular warfare too, the degree of surprise is less. In guerrilla warfare, the need to bring operations to a quick decision is very great, and our exterior-line ring of encirclement of the enemy in campaigns and battles is very small All these distinguish it from regular warfare.

Thus it can be seen that in their operations guerrilla units have to concentrate the maximum forces, act secretly and swiftly, attack the enemy by surprise and bring battles to a quick decision, and that they must strictly avoid passive defence, procrastination and the dis persal of forces before engagements. Of course, guerrilla warfare includes not only the strategic but also the tactical defensive. The latter embraces, among other things, containing and outpost actions during battles; the disposition of forces for resistance at narrow passes, strategic points, rivers or villages in order to deplete and exhaust the enemy; and action to cover withdrawal. But the basic principle of guerrilla warfare must be the offensive, and guerrilla warfare is more offensive in its character than regular warfare. The offensive, moreover, must take the form of surprise attacks, and to expose our selves by ostentatiously parading our forces is even less permissible in guerrilla warfare than in regular warfare. From the fact that the enemy is strong and we are weak it necessarily follows that, in guerrilla operations in general even more than in regular warfare, battles must be decided quickly, though on some occasions guerrilla fighting may be kept up for several days, as in an assault on a small and isolated enemy force cut off from help. Because of its dispersed character, guerrilla warfare can spread everywhere, and in many of its tasks, as in harassing, containing and disrupting the enemy and in mass work, its principle is dispersal of forces; but a guerrilla unit, or a guerrilla formation, must concentrate its main forces when it is engaged in destroying the enemy, and especially when it is striving to smash an enemy attack. "Concentrate a big force to strike at a small section of the enemy force" remains a principle of field operations in guerrilla warfare.

Thus it can also be seen that, if we take the War of Resistance as a whole, we can attain the aim of our strategic defensive and finally defeat Japanese imperialism only through the cumulative effect of many offensive campaigns and battles in both regular and guerrilla warfare, namely, through the cumulative effect of many victories in offensive actions. Only through the cumulative effect of many campaigns and battles of quick decision, namely, the cumulative effect of many victories achieved through quick decision in offensive campaigns and battles, can we attain our goal of strategic protractedness, which means gaining time to increase our capacity to resist while hastening or awaiting changes in the international situation and the internal collapse of the enemy, in order to be able to launch a strategic counter-offensive and drive the Japanese invaders out of China. We must concentrate superior forces and fight exterior-line operations in every campaign or battle, whether in the stage of strategic defensive or in that of strategic counter-offensive, in order to encircle and destroy the enemy forces, encircling part if not all of them, destroying part if not all of the forces we have encircled, and inflicting heavy casualties on the encircled forces if we cannot capture them in large numbers. Only through the cumulative effect of many such battles of annihilation can we change the relative position as between the enemy and ourselves, thoroughly smash his strategic encirclement -- that is, his scheme of exterior-line operations -- and finally, in co-ordination with international forces and the revolutionary struggles of the Japanese people, surround the Japanese imperialists and deal them the coup de grace. These results are to be achieved mainly through regular warfare, with guerrilla warfare making a secondary contribution. What is common to both, however, is the accumulation of many minor victories to make a major victory. Herein lies the great strategic role of guerrilla warfare in the War of Resistance.

Now let us discuss initiative, flexibility and planning in guerrilla warfare.

What is initiative in guerrilla warfare?

In any war, the opponents contend for the initiative, whether on a battlefield, in a battle area, in a war zone or in the whole war, for the initiative means freedom of action for an army. Any army which, losing the initiative, is forced into a passive position and ceases to have freedom of action, faces the danger of defeat or extermination. Naturally, gaining the initiative is harder in strategic defensive and interior-line operations and easier in offensive exterior-line operations. However, Japanese imperialism has two basic weaknesses, namely, its shortage of troops and the fact that it is fighting on foreign soil. Moreover, its underestimation of China's strength and the internal contradictions among the Japanese militarists have given rise to many mistakes in command, such as piecemeal reinforcement, lack of strategic co-ordination, occasional absence of a main direction for attack, failure to grasp opportunities in some operations and failure to wipe out encircled forces, all of which may be considered the third weakness of Japanese imperialism. Thus, despite the advantage of being on the offensive and operating on exterior lines, the Japanese militarists are gradually losing the initiative, because of their shortage of troops (their small territory, small population, inadequate resources, feudalistic imperialism, etc.), because of the fact that they are fighting on foreign soil (their war is imperialist and barbarous) and because of their stupidities in command. Japan is neither willing nor able to conclude the war at present, nor has her strategic offensive yet come to an end, but, as the general trend shows, her offensive is confined within certain limits, which is the inevitable consequence of her three weaknesses; she cannot go on indefinitely till she swallows the whole of China. Already there are signs that Japan will one day hnd herself in an utterly passive position. China, on the other hand, was in a rather passive position at the beginning of the war, but, having gained experience, she is now turning to the new policy of mobile warfare, the policy of taking the offensive, seeking quick decisions and operating on exterior lines in campaigns and battles, which, together with the policy of developing widespread guerrilla warfare, is helping China to build up a position of initiative day by day.

The question of the initiative is even more vital in guerrilla warfare. For most guerrilla units operate in very difficult circumstances, fighting without a rear, with their own weak forces facing the enemy's strong forces, lacking experience (when the units are newly organized), being separated, etc. Nevertheless, it is possible to build up the initiative in guerrilla warfare, the essential condition being to seize on the enemy's three weaknesses. Taking advantage of the enemy's shortage of troops (from the viewpoint of the war as a whole), the guerrilla units can boldly use vast areas as their fields of operation; taking advantage of the fact that the enemy is an alien invader and is pursuing a most barbarous policy, the guerrilla units can boldly enlist the support of millions upon millions of people; and taking advantage of the stupidities in the enemy's command, the guerrilla units can give full scope to their resourcefulness. While the regular army must seize on all these weaknesses of the enemy and turn them to good account in order to defeat him, it is even more important for the guerrilla units to do so. As for the guerrilla units' own weaknesses, they can be gradually reduced in the course of the struggle. Moreover, these weaknesses sometimes constitute the very condition for gaining the initiative. For example, it is precisely because the guerrilla units are small that they can mysteriously appear and disappear in their operations behind enemy lines, without the enemy's being able to do anything about them, and thus enjoy a freedom of action such as massive regular armies never can.

When the enemy is making a converging attack from several directions, a guerrilla unit can exercise initiative only with difficulty and can lose it all too easily. In such a case, if its appraisals and dispositions are wrong, it is liable to get into a passive position and consequently fail to smash the converging enemy attack. This may occur even when the enemy is on the defensive and we are on the offensive. For the initiative results from making a correct appraisal of the situation (both our own and that of the enemy) and from making the correct military and political dispositions. A pessimistic appraisal out of accord with the objective conditions and the passive dispositions ensuing from it will undoubtedly result in the loss of the initiative and throw one into a passive position. On the other hand, an over-optimistic appraisal out of accord with the objective conditions and the risky (unjustifiably risky) dispositions ensuing from it will also result in the loss of the initiative and eventually land one in a position similar to that of the pessimists. The initiative is not an innate attribute of genius, but is something an intelligent leader attains through open-minded study and correct appraisal of the objective conditions and through correct military and political dispositions. It follows that the initiative is not ready-made but is something that requires conscious effort.

When forced into a passive position through some incorrect appraisal and disposition or through overwhelming pressure, a guerrilla unit must strive to extricate itself. How this can be done depends on the circumstances. In many cases it is necessary to "move away". The ability to move is the distinctive feature of a guerrilla unit. To move away is the principal method for getting out of a passive position and regaining the initiative. But it is not the sole method. The moment when the enemy is most energetic and we are in the greatest difficulties is often the very moment when things begin to turn against him and in our favour. Frequently a favourable situation recurs and the initiative is regained as a result of "holding out a little longer".

Next, let us deal with flexibility.

Flexibility is a concrete expression of the initiative. The flexible employment of forces is more essential in guerrilla warfare than in regular warfare.

A guerrilla commander must understand that the flexible employment of his forces is the most important means of changing the situation as between the enemy and ourselves and of gaining the initiative. The nature of guerrilla warfare is such that guerrilla forces must be employed flexibly in accordance with the task in hand and with such circumstances as the state of the enemy, the terrain and the local population, and the chief ways of employing the forces are dispersal, concentration and shifting of position. In employing his forces, a guerrilla commander is like a fisherman casting his net, which he should be able to spread wide as well as draw in tight. When casting his net, the fisherman has to ascertain the depth of the water, the speed of the current and the presence or absence of obstructions; similarly, when dispersing his units, a guerrilla commander must take care not to incur losses through ignorance of the situation or through miscalculated action. Just as the fisherman must keep a grip on the cord in order to draw his net in tight, so the guerrilla commander must maintain liaison and communication with all his forces and keep enough of his main forces at hand. Just as a frequent change of position is necessary in fishing, so a frequent shift of position is necessary for a guerrilla unit. Dispersal, concentration and shifting of position are the three ways of flexibly employing forces in guerrilla warfare. Generally speaking, the dispersal of guerrilla units, or "breaking up the whole into parts", is employed chiefly: (1) when we want to threaten the enemy with a wide frontal attack because he is on the defensive, and there is temporarily no chance to mass our forces for action; (2) when we want to harass and disrupt the enemy throughout an area where his forces are weak; (3) when we are unable to break through the enemy's encirclement and try to slip away by making ourselves less conspicuous; (4) when we are restricted by terrain or supplies; or (5) when we are carrying on mass work over a wide area. But whatever the circumstances, when dispersing for action we should pay attention to the following: 1) we should never make an absolutely even dispersal of forces, but should keep a fairly large part in an area convenient for manoeuvre, so that any possible exigency can be met and there is a centre of gravity for the task being carried out in dispersion; and (2) we should assign to the dispersed units clearly defined tasks, fields of operation, time limits for actions, places for reassembly and ways and means of liaison.

Concentration of forces, or "assembling the parts into a whole", is the method usually applied to destroy an enemy when he is on the offensive and sometimes to destroy some of his stationary forces when he is on the defensive. Concentration of forces does not mean absolute concentration, but the massing of the main forces for use in one important direction while retaining or dispatching part of the forces for use in other directions to contain, harass or disrupt the enemy, or to carry on mass work.

Although the flexible dispersal or concentration of forces according to circumstances is the principal method in guerrilla warfare, we must also know how to shift (or transfer) our forces flexibly. When the enemy feels seriously threatened by guerrillas, he will send troops to attack or suppress them. Hence the guerrilla units will have to take stock of the situation. If advisable, they should fight where they are; if not, they should lose no time in shifting elsewhere. Sometimes, in order to crush the enemy units one by one, guerrilla units which have destroyed an enemy force in one place may immediately shift to another so as to wipe out a second enemy force; sometimes, finding it inadvisable to fight in one place, they may have to disengage quickly and fight the enemy elsewhere. If the enemy's forces in a certain place present a particularly serious threat, the guerrilla units should not linger, but should move off with lightning speed. In general, shifts of position should be made with secrecy and speed. In order to mislead, decoy and confuse the enemy, they should constantly use stratagems, such as making a feint to the east but attacking in the west, appearing now in the south and now in the north, hit-and-run attacks, and night actions.

Flexibility in dispersal, concentration and shifts of position is a concrete expression of the initiative in guerrilla warfare, whereas rigidness and inertia inevitably lead to passivity and cause unnecessary losses. But a commander proves himself wise not just by recognition of the importance of employing his forces flexibly but by skill in dispersing, concentrating or shifting them in good time according to the specific circumstances. This wisdom in sensing changes and choosing the right moment to act is not easily acquired; it can be gained only by those who study with a receptive mind and investigate and ponder diligently. Prudent consideration of the circumstances is essential to prevent flexibility from turning into impulsive action.

Lastly, we come to planning.

Without planning, victories in guerrilla warfare are impossible. Any idea that guerrilla warfare can be conducted in haphazard fashion indicates either a flippant attitude or ignorance of guerrilla warfare. The operations in a guerrilla zone as a whole, or those of a guerrilla unit or formation, must be preceded by as thorough planning as possible, by preparation in advance for every action. Grasping the situation, setting the tasks, disposing the forces, giving military and political training, securing supplies, putting the equipment in good order, making proper use of the people's help, etc. -- all these are part of the work of the guerrilla commanders, which they must carefully consider and conscientiously perform and check up on. There can be no initiative, no flexibility, and no offensive unless they do so. True, guerrilla conditions do not allow as high a degree of planning as do those of regular warfare, and it would be a mistake to attempt very thorough planning in guerrilla warfare. But it is necessary to plan as thoroughly as the objective conditions permit, for it should be understood that fighting the enemy is no joke.

The above points serve to explain the first of the strategic principles of guerrilla warfare, the principle of using initiative, flexibility and planning in conducting offensives within the defensive, battles of quick decision within protracted war, and exterior-line operations within interior-line operations. It is the key problem in the strategy of guerrilla warfare. The solution of this problem provides the major guarantee of victory in guerrilla warfare so far as military command is concerned.

Although a variety of matters have been dealt with here, they all revolve around the offensive in campaigns and battles. The initiative can be decisively grasped only after victory in an offensive. Every offensive operation must be organized on our initiative and not launched under compulsion. Flexibility in the employment of forces revolves around the effort to take the offensive, and planning likewise is necessary chiefly in order to ensure success in offensive operations. Measures of tactical defence are meaningless if they are divorced from their role of giving either direct or indirect support to an offensive. Quick decision refers to the tempo of an offensive, and exterior lines refer to its scope. The offensive is the only means of destroying the enemy and is also the principal means of self-preservation, while pure defence and retreat can play only a temporary and partial role in self-preservation and are quite useless for destroying the enemy.

The principle stated above is basically the same for both regular and guerrilla war; it differs to some degree only in its form of expression. But in guerrilla war it is both important and necessary to note this difference. It is precisely this difference in form which distinguishes the operational methods of guerrilla war from those of regular war. If we confuse the two different forms in which the principle is expressed, victory in guerrilla war will be impossible.

Chapter V

CO-ORDINATION WITH REGULAR WARFARE

The second problem of strategy in guerrilla warfare is its co-ordination with regular warfare. It is a matter of clarifying the relation between guerrilla and regular warfare on the operational level, in the light of the nature of actual guerrilla operations. An understanding of this relation is very important for effectiveness in defeating the enemy.

There are three kinds of co-ordination between guerrilla and regular warfare, co-ordination in strategy, in campaigns and in battles.

Taken as a whole, guerrilla warfare behind the enemy lines, which cripples the enemy, pins him down, disrupts his supply lines and inspires the regular forces and the people throughout the country, is co-ordinated with regular warfare in strategy. Take the case of the guerrilla warfare in the three northeastern provinces. Of course, the question of co-ordination did not arise before the nation-wide War of Resistance, but since the war began the significance of such co-ordination has become obvious. Every enemy soldier the guerrillas kill there, every bullet they make the enemy expend, every enemy soldier they stop from advancing south of the Great Wall, can be reckoned a contribution to the total strength of the resistance. It is, moreover, clear that they are having a demoralizing effect on the whole enemy army and all Japan and a heartening effect on our whole army and people. Still clearer is the role in strategic co-ordination played by the guerrilla warfare along the Peiping-Suiyuan, Peiping-Hankow, Tientsin-Pukow, Tatung-Puchow, Chengting-Taiyuan and Shanghai-Hangchow Railways. Not only are the guerrilla units performing the function of co-ordination with the regular forces in our present strategic defensive, when the enemy is on the strategic offensive; not only will they co-ordinate with the regular forces in disrupting the enemy's hold on the occupied territory, after he concludes his strategic offensive and switches to the safeguarding of his gains; they will also co-ordinate with the regular forces in driving out the enemy forces and recovering all the lost territories, when the regular forces launch the strategic counter-offensive. The great role of guerrilla warfare in strategic co-ordination must not be overlooked. The commanders both of the guerrilla units and of the regular forces must clearly understand this role.

In addition, guerrilla warfare performs the function of co-ordination with regular warfare in campaigns. For instance, in the campaign at Hsinkou, north of Taiyuan, the guerrillas played a remarkable role in co-ordination both north and south of Yenmenkuan by wrecking the Tatung-Puchow Railway and the motor roads running through Pinghsingkuan and Yangfangkou. Or take another instance. After the enemy occupied Fenglingtu, guerrilla warfare, which was already widespread throughout Shansi Province and was conducted mainly by the regular forces, played an even greater role through co-ordination with the defensive campaigns west of the Yellow River in Shensi Province and south of the Yellow River in Honan Province. Again, when the enemy attacked southern Shantung, the guerrilla warfare in the five provinces of northern China contributed a great deal through co-ordination with the campaigns of our army. In performing a task of this sort, the leaders of each guerrilla base behind the enemy lines, or the commanders of a guerrilla formation temporarily dispatched there, must dispose their forces well and, by adopting different tactics suited to the time and place, move energetically against the enemy's most vital and vulnerable spots in order to cripple him, pin him down, disrupt his supply lines, inspire our armies campaigning on the interior lines, and so fulfil their duty of co-ordinating with the campaign. If each guerrilla zone or unit goes it alone without giving any attention to co-ordinating with the campaigns of the regular forces, its role in strategic co-ordination will lose a great deal of its significance, although it will still play some such role in the general strategy. All guerrilla commanders should give this point serious attention. To achieve co-ordination in campaigns, it is absolutely necessary for all larger guerrilla units and guerrilla formations to have radio equipment.

Finally, co-ordination with the regular forces in battles, in actual fighting on the battlefield, is the task of all guerrilla units in the vicinity of an interior-line battlefield. Of course, this applies only to guerrilla units operating close to the regular forces or to units of regulars dispatched on temporary guerrilla missions. In such cases, a guerrilla unit has to perform whatever task it is assigned by the commander of the regular forces, which is usually to pin down some of the enemy's forces, disrupt his supply lines, conduct reconnaissance, or act as guides for the regular forces. Even without such an assignment, the guerrilla unit should carry out these tasks on its own initiative. To sit by idly, neither moving nor fighting, or to move about without fighting, would be an intolerable attitude for a guerrilla unit.

Chapter VI

THE ESTABLISHMENT OF BASE AREAS

The third problem of strategy in anti-Japanese guerrilla warfare is the establishment of base areas, which is important and essential because of the protracted nature and ruthlessness of the war. The recovery of our lost territories will have to await the nation-wide strategic counter-offensive; by then the enemy's front will have extended deep into central China and cut it in two from north to south, and a part or even a greater part of our territory will have fallen into the hands of the enemy and become his rear. We shall have to extend guerrilla warfare all over this vast enemy-occupied area, make a front out of the enemy's rear, and force him to fight ceaselessly throughout the territory he occupies. Until such time as our strategic counter-offensive is launched and so long as our lost territories are not recovered, it will be necessary to persist in guerrilla warfare in the enemy's rear, certainly for a fairly long time, though one cannot say definitely for how long. This is why the war will be a protracted one. And in order to safeguard his gains in the occupied areas, the enemy is bound to step up his anti-guerrilla measures and, especially after the halting of his strategic offensive, to embark on relentless suppression of the guerrillas. With ruthlessness thus added to protractedness, it will be impossible to sustain guerrilla warfare behind the enemy lines without base areas.

What, then, are these base areas? They are the strategic bases on which the guerrilla forces rely in performing their strategic tasks and achieving the object of preserving and expanding themselves and destroying and driving out the enemy. Without such strategic bases, there will be nothing to depend on in carrying out any of our strategic tasks or achieving the aim of the war. It is a characteristic of guerrilla warfare behind the enemy lines that it is fought without a rear, for the guerrilla forces are severed from the country's general rear. But guerrilla warfare could not last long or grow without base areas. The base areas, indeed, are its rear.

History knows many peasant wars of the "roving rebel" type, but none of them ever succeeded. In the present age of advanced communications and technology, it would be all the more groundless to imagine that one can win victory by fighting in the manner of roving rebels. However, this roving-rebel idea still exists among impoverished peasants, and in the minds of guerrilla commanders it becomes the view that base areas are neither necessary nor important. Therefore, ridding the minds of guerrilla commanders of this idea is a prerequisite for deciding on a policy of establishing base areas. The question of whether or not to have base areas and of whether or not to regard them as important, in other words, the conflict between the idea of establishing base areas and that of fighting like roving rebels, arises in all guerrilla warfare, and, to a certain extent, our anti-Japanese guerrilla warfare is no exception. Therefore the struggle against the roving-rebel ideology is an inevitable process. Only when this ideology is thoroughly overcome and the policy of establishing base areas is initiated and applied will there be conditions favourable for the maintenance of guerrilla warfare over a long period.

Now that the necessity and importance of base areas have been made clear, let us pass on to the following problems which must be understood and solved when it comes to establishing the base areas. These problems are the types of base areas, the guerrilla zones and the base areas, the conditions for establishing base areas, their consolidation and expansion, and the forms in which we and the enemy encircle one another.

1. THE TYPES OF BASE AREAS

Base areas in anti-Japanese guerrilla warfare are mainly of three types, those in the mountains, those on the plains and those in the river-lake-estuary regions.

The advantage of setting up base areas in mountainous regions is obvious, and those which have been, are being or will be established in the Changpai,[1] Wutai,[2] Taihang,[3] Taishan,[4] Yenshan [5] and Maoshan [6] Mountains all belong to this type. They are all places where anti-Japanese guerrilla warfare can be maintained for the longest time and are important strongholds for the War of Resistance. We must develop guerrilla warfare and set up base areas in all the mountainous regions behind the enemy lines.

Of course, the plains are less suitable than the mountains, but it is by no means impossible to develop guerrilla warfare or establish any base areas there. Indeed, the widespread guerrilla warfare in the plains of Hopei and of northern and northwestern Shantung proves that it is possible to develop guerrilla warfare in the plains. While there is as yet no evidence on the possibility of setting up base areas there and maintaining them for long, it has been proved that the setting up of temporary base areas is possible, and it should be possible to set up base areas for small units or for seasonal use. On the one hand, the enemy does not have enough troops at his disposal and is pursuing a policy of unparalleled brutality, and on the other hand, China has a vast territory and vast numbers of people who are resisting Japan; the objective conditions for spreading guerrilla warfare and setting up temporary base areas in the plains are therefore fulfilled. Given competent military command, it should of course be possible to establish bases for small guerrilla units there, bases which are long-term but not fixed.[7] Broadly speaking, when the strategic offensive of the enemy is brought to a halt and he enters the stage of safeguarding his occupied areas, he will undoubtedly launch savage attacks on all the guerrilla base areas, and those in the plains will naturally be the first to bear the brunt. The large guerrilla formations operating on the plains will be unable to keep on fighting there for long and will gradually have to move up into the mountains as the circumstances require, as for instance, from the Hopei Plain to the Wutai and Taihang Mountains, or from the Shantung Plain to Taishan Mountain and the Shantung Peninsula in the east. But in the circumstances of our national war it is not impossible for numerous small guerrilla units to keep going in various counties over the vast plains and adopt a fluid way of fighting, i.e., by shifting their bases from place to place. It is definitely possible to conduct seasonal guerrilla warfare by taking advantage of the "green curtain" of tall crops in summer and of the frozen rivers in winter. As the enemy has no strength to spare now and will never be able to attend to everything even when he has the strength to spare, it is absolutely necessary for us to decide on the policy, for the present, of spreading guerrilla warfare far and wide and setting up temporary base areas in the plains and, for the future, of preparing to keep up guerrilla warfare by small units, if only seasonally, and of creating base areas which are not fixed.

Objectively speaking, the possibilities of developing guerrilla warfare and establishing base areas are greater in the river-lake-estuary regions than in the plains, though less than in the mountains. The dramatic battles fought by "pirates" and "water-bandits", of which our history is full, and the guerrilla warfare round the Hunghu Lake kept up for several years in the Red Army period, both testify to the possibility of developing guerrilla warfare and of establishing base areas in the river-lake-estuary regions. So far, however, the political parties and the masses who are resisting Japan have given this possibility little attention. Though the subjective conditions are as yet lacking, we should undoubtedly turn our attention to this possibility and start working on it. As one aspect in the development of our nation-wide guerrilla warfare, we should effectively organize guerrilla warfare in the Hungtse Lake region north of the Yangtse River, in the Taihu Lake region south of the Yangtse, and in all river-lake-estuary regions in the enemy-occupied areas along the rivers and on the seacoast, and we should create permanent base areas in and near such places. By overlooking this aspect we are virtually providing the enemy with water transport facilities; this is a gap in our strategic plan for the War of Resistance which must be filled in good time.

2. GUERRILLA ZONES AND BASE AREAS

In guerrilla warfare behind the enemy lines, there is a difference between guerrilla zones and base areas. Areas which are surrounded by the enemy but whose central parts are not occupied or have been recovered, like some counties in the Wutai mountain region (i.e., the Shansi-Chahar-Hopei border area) and also some places in the Taihang and Taishan mountain regions, are ready-made bases for the convenient use of guerrilla units in developing guerrilla warfare. But elsewhere in these areas the situation is different, as for instance in the eastern and northern sections of the Wutai mountain region, which include parts of western Hopei and southern Chahar, and in many places east of Paoting and west of Tsangchow. When guerrilla warfare began, the guerrillas could not completely occupy these places but could only make frequent raids; they are areas which are held by the guerrillas when they are there and by the puppet regime when they are gone, and are therefore not yet guerrilla bases but only what may be called guerrilla zones. Such guerrilla zones will be transformed into base areas when they have gone through the necessary processes of guerrilla warfare, that is, when large numbers of enemy troops have been annihilated or defeated there, the puppet regime has been destroyed, the masses have been roused to activity, anti-Japanese mass organizations have been formed, people's local armed forces have been developed, and anti-Japanese political power has been established. By the expansion of our base areas we mean the addition of areas such as these to the bases already established.

In some places, for example, eastern Hopei, the whole area of guerrilla operations has been a guerrilla zone from the very beginning. The puppet regime is of long standing there, and from the beginning the whole area of operations has been a guerrilla zone both for the people's armed forces that have grown out of local uprisings and for the guerrilla detachments dispatched from the Wutai Mountains. At the outset of their activities, all they could do was to choose some fairly good spots there as temporary rear or base areas. Such places will not be transformed from guerrilla zones into relatively stable base areas until the enemy forces are destroyed and the work of arousing the people is in full swing.

Thus the transformation of a guerrilla zone into a base area is an arduous creative process, and its accomplishment depends on the extent to which the enemy is destroyed and the masses are aroused.

Many regions will remain guerrilla zones for a long time. In these regions the enemy will not be able to set up stable puppet regimes, however much he tries to maintain control, while we, on our part, will not be able to achieve the aim of establishing anti-Japanese political power, however much we develop guerrilla warfare. Examples of this kind are to be found in the enemy-occupied regions along the railway lines, in the neighbourhood of big cities and in certain areas in the plains.

As for the big cities, the railway stops and the areas in the plains which are strongly garrisoned by the enemy, guerrilla warfare can only extend to the fringes and not right into these places which have relatively stable puppet regimes. This is another kind of situation.

Mistakes in our leadership or strong enemy pressure may cause a reversal of the state of affairs described above, i.e., a guerrilla base may turn into a guerrilla zone, and a guerrilla zone may turn into an area under relatively stable enemy occupation. Such changes are possible, and they deserve special vigilance on the part of guerrilla commanders.

Therefore, as a result of guerrilla warfare and the struggle between us and the enemy, the entire enemy-occupied territory will fall into the following three categories: first, anti-Japanese bases held by our guerrilla units and our organs of political power; second, areas held by Japanese imperialism and its puppet regimes; and third, intermediate zones contested by both sides, namely, guerrilla zones. Guerrilla commanders have the duty to expand the first and third categories to the maximum and to reduce the second category to the minimum. This is the strategic task of guerrilla warfare.

3. CONDITIONS FOR ESTABLISHING BASE AREAS

The fundamental conditions for establishing a base area are that there should be anti-Japanese armed forces, that these armed forces should be employed to inflict defeats on the enemy and that they should arouse the people to action. Thus the establishment of a base area is first and foremost a matter of building an armed force. Leaders in guerrilla war must devote their energy to building one or more guerrilla units, and must gradually develop them in the course of struggle into guerrilla formations or even into units and formations of regular troops. The building up of an armed force is the key to establishing a base area; if there is no armed force or if the armed force is weak, nothing can be done. This constitutes the first condition.

The second indispensable condition for establishing a base area is that the armed forces should be used in co-ordination with the people to defeat the enemy. All places under enemy control are enemy, and not guerrilla, base areas, and obviously cannot be transformed into guerrilla base areas unless the enemy is defeated. Unless we repulse the enemy's attacks and defeat him, even places held by the guerrillas will come under enemy control, and then it will be impossible to establish base areas.

The third indispensable condition for establishing a base area is the use of all our strength, including our armed forces, to arouse the masses for struggle against Japan. In the course of this struggle we must arm the people, i.e., organize self-defence corps and guerrilla units. In the course of this struggle, we must form mass organizations, we must organize the workers, peasants, youth, women, children, merchants and professional people -- according to the degree of their political consciousness and fighting enthusiasm -- into the varioug mass organizations necessary for the struggle against Japanese aggression, and we must gradually expand them. Without organization, the people cannot give effect to their anti-Japanese strength. In the course of this struggle, we must weed out the open and the hidden traitors a task which can be accomplished only by relying on the strength of the people. In this struggle, it is particularly important to arouse the people to establish, or to consolidate, their local organs of anti-Japanese political power. Where the original Chinese organs of political power have not been destroyed by the enemy, we must re-organize and strengthen them with the support of the broad masses, and where they have been destroyed by the enemy, we should rebuild them by the efforts of the masses. They are organs of political power for carrying out the policy of the Anti-Japanese National United Front and should unite all the forces of the people to fight against our sole enemy, Japanese imperialism, and its jackals, the traitors and reactionaries.

A base area for guerrilla war can be truly established only with the gradual fulfilment of the three basic conditions, i.e., only after the anti-Japanese armed forces are built up, the enemy has suffered defeats and the people are aroused.

Mention must also be made of geographical and economic conditions. As for the former, we have already discussed three different categories in the earlier section on the types of base areas, and here we need only mention one major requirement, namely, that the area must be extensive. In places surrounded by the enemy on all sides, or on three sides, the mountainous regions naturally offer the best conditions for setting up base areas which can hold out for a long time, but the main thing is that there must be enough room for the guerrillas to manoeuvre, namely, the areas have to be extensive. Given an extensive area, guerrilla warfare can be developed and sustained even in the plains, not to mention the river-lake-estuary regions. By and large, the vastness of China's territory and the enemy's shortage of troops provide guerrilla warfare in China with this condition. This is an important, even a primary condition, as far as the possibility of waging guerrilla warfare is concerned, and small countries like Belgium which lack this condition have few or no such possibilities.[8] In China, this condition is not something which has to be striven for, nor does it present a problem; it is there physically, waiting only to be exploited.

So far as their physical setting is concerned, the economic conditions resemble the geographical conditions. For now we are discussing the establishment of base areas not in a desert, where no enemy is to be found, but behind the enemy lines; every place the enemy can penetrate already has its Chinese inhabitants and an economic basis for subsistence, so that the question of choice of economic conditions in establishing base areas simply does not arise. Irrespective of the economic conditions, we should do our utmost to develop guerrilla warfare and set up permanent or temporary base areas in all places where Chinese inhabitants and enemy forces are to be found. In a political sense, however, the economic conditions do present a problem, a problem of economic policy which is of immense importance to the establishment of base areas. The economic policy of the guerrilla base areas must follow the principles of the Anti-Japanese National United Front by equitably distributing the financial burden and protecting commerce. Neither the local organs of political power nor the guerrilla units must violate these principles, or otherwise the establishment of base areas and the maintenance of guerrilla warfare would be adversely affected. The equitable distribution of the financial burden means that "those with money should contribute money", while the peasants should supply the guerrilla units with grain within certain limits. The protection of commerce means that the guerrilla units should be highly disciplined and that the confiscation of shops, except those owned by proved traitors, should be strictly prohibited. This is no easy matter, but the policy is set and must be put into effect.

4. THE CONSOLIDATION AND EXPANSION OF BASE AREAS

In order to confine the enemy invaders to a few strongholds, that is, to the big cities and along the main communication lines, the guerrillas must do all they can to extend guerrilla warfare from their base areas as widely as possible and hem in all the enemy's strongholds, thus threatening his existence and shaking his morale while expanding the base areas. This is essential. In this context, we must oppose conservatism in guerrilla warfare. Whether originating in the desire for an easy life or in overestimation of the enemy's strength, conservatism can only bring losses in the War of Resistance and is harmful to guerrilla warfare and to the base areas themselves. At the same time, we must not forget the consolidation of the base areas, the chief task being to arouse and organize the masses and to train guerrilla units and local armed forces. Such consolidation is needed for maintaining protracted warfare and also for expansion, and in its absence energetic expansion is impossible. If we attend only to expansion and forget about consolidation in our guerrilla warfare, we shall be unable to withstand the enemy's attacks, and consequently not only forfeit the possibility of expansion but also endanger the very existence of the base areas. The correct principle is expansion with consolidation, which is a good method and allows us to take the offensive or the defensive as we choose. Given a protracted war, the problem of consolidating and expanding base areas constantly arises for every guerrilla unit. The concrete solution depends, of course, on the circumstances. At one time, the emphasis may be on expansion, i.e., on expanding the guerrilla zones and increasing the number of guerrillas. At another, the emphasis may be on consolidation, i.e., on organizing the masses and training the troops. As expansion and consolidation differ in nature, and as the military dispositions and other tasks will differ accordingly, an effective solution of the problem is possible only if we alternate the emphasis according to time and circumstances.

5. FORMS IN WHICH WE AND THE ENEMY ENCIRCLE ONE ANOTHER

Taking the War of Resistance as a whole, there is no doubt that we are strategically encircled by the enemy, because he is on the strategic offensive and is operating on exterior lines while we are on the strategic defensive and are operating on interior lines. This is the first form of enemy encirclement. We on our part encircle each of the enemy columns advancing on us along separate routes, because we apply the policy of the offensive and of exterior-line operations in campaigns and battles by using numerically preponderant forces against these enemy columns advancing on us from exterior lines. This is the first form of our encirclement of the enemy. Next, if we consider the guerrilla base areas in the enemy's rear, each area taken singly is surrounded by the enemy on all sides, like the Wutai mountain region, or on three sides, like the northwestern Shansi area. This is the second form of enemy encirclement. However, if one considers all the guerrilla base areas together and in their relation to the battle fronts of the regular forces, one can see that we in turn surround a great many enemy forces. In Shansi Province, for instance, we have surrounded the Tatung-Puchow Railway on three sides (the east and west flanks and the southern end) and the city of Taiyuan on all sides; and there are many similar instances in Hopei and Shantung Provinces. This is the second form of our encirclement of the enemy. Thus there are two forms of encirclement by the enemy forces and two forms of encirclement by our own -- rather like a game of weicbi.[9] Campaigns and battles fought by the two sides resemble the capturing of each other's pieces, and the establishment of strongholds by the enemy and of guerrilla base areas by us resembles moves to dominate spaces on the board. It is in the matter of "dominating the spaces" that the great strategic role of guerrilla base areas in the rear of the enemy is revealed. We are raising this question in the War of Resistance in order that the nation's military authorities and the guerrilla com manders in all areas should place on the agenda the development of guerrilla warfare behind the enemy lines and the establishment of base areas wherever possible, and carry this out as a strategic task. If on the international plane we can create an anti-Japanese front in the Pacific region, with China as one strategic unit, and the Soviet Union and other countries which may join it as other strategic units, we shall then have one more form of encirclement against the enemy than he has against us and bring about exterior-line operations in the Pacific region by which to encircle and destroy fascist Japan. To be sure, this is of little practical significance at present, but such a prospect is not impossible.

Chapter VII

THE STRATEGIC DEFENSIVE AND THE STRATEGIC OFFENSIVE IN GUERRILLA WAR

The fourth problem of strategy in guerrilla war concerns the strategic defensive and the strategic offensive. This is the problem of how the policy of offensive warfare, which we mentioned in our discussion of the first problem, is to be carried out in practice, when we are on the defensive and when we are on the offensive in our guerrilla warfare against Japan.

Within the nation-wide strategic defensive or strategic offensive (to be more exact, the strategic counter-offensive), small-scale strategic defensives and offensives take place in and around each guerrilla base area. By strategic defensive we mean our strategic situation and policy when the enemy is on the offensive and we are on the defensive; by strategic offensive we mean our strategic situation and policy when the enemy is on the defensive and we are on the offensive.

1. THE STRATEGIC DEFENSIVE IN GUERRILLA WAR

After guerrilla warfare has broken out and grown to a considerable extent, the enemy will inevitably attack the guerrilla base areas, especially in the period when his strategic offensive against the country as a whole is brought to an end and he adopts the policy of safeguarding his occupied areas. It is essential to recognize the inevitability of such attacks, for otherwise the guerrilla commanders will be caught wholly unprepared, and in the face of heavy enemy attacks they will undoubtedly become alarmed and confused and their forces will be routed.

To wipe out the guerrillas and their base areas, the enemy frequently resorts to converging attacks. For instance, in each of the four or five "punitive expeditions" directed against the Wutai mountain region, the enemy made a planned advance in three, four or even six or seven columns simultaneously. The larger the scale of the guerrilla fighting, the more important the position of the base areas, and the greater the threat to the enemy's strategic centres and vital communication lines, the fiercer will be the enemy's attacks. Therefore, the fiercer the enemy's attacks on a guerrilla area, the greater the indication that the guerrilla warfare there is successful and is being effectively co-ordinated with the regular fighting.

When the enemy launches a converging attack in several columns, the guerrilla policy should be to smash it by counter-attack. It can be easily smashed if each advancing enemy column consists of only one unit, whether big or small, has no follow-up units and is unable to station troops along the route of advance, construct blockhouses or build motor roads. When the enemy launches a converging attack, he is on the offensive and operating on exterior lines, while we are on the defensive and operating on interior lines. As for our dispositions, we should use our secondary forces to pin down several enemy columns, while our main force should launch surprise attacks (chiefly in the form of ambushes) in a campaign or battle against a single enemy column, striking it when it is on the move. The enemy, though strong, will be weakened by repeated surprise attacks and will often withdraw when he is halfway; the guerrilla units can then make more surprise attacks during the pursuit and weaken him still further. The enemy generally occupies the county towns or other towns in our base areas before he stops his offensive or begins to withdraw, and we should encircle these towns, cutting off his grain supply and severing his communications, so that when he cannot hold out and begins to retreat, we can seize the opportunity to pursue and attack him. After smashing one column, we should shift our forces to smash another, and, by smashing them one by one, shatter the converging attack.

A big base area like the Wutai mountain region forms a military area, which is divided into four or five, or even more, military sub-areas, each with its own armed forces operating independently. By employing the tactics described above, these forces have often smashed the enemy's attacks simultaneously or successively.

In our plan of operations against a converging attack by the enemy, we generally place our main force on interior lines. But when we have the strength to spare, we should use our secondary forces (such as the county or the district guerrilla units, or even detachments of the main force) on exterior lines to disrupt the enemy's communications and pin down his reinforcements. Should the enemy stay put in our base area, we may reverse the tactics, namely, leave some of our forces in the base area to invest the enemy while employing the main force to attack the region whence he has come and to step up our activities there, in order to induce him to withdraw and attack our main force; this is the tactic of "relieving the state of Chao by besieging the state of Wei".[10]

In the course of operations against a converging attack, the local anti-Japanese self-defence corps and all the mass organizations should mobilize for action and in every way help our troops to fight the enemy. In fighting the enemy, it is important both to enforce local martial law and, as far as possible, to "strengthen our defence works and clear the fields". The purpose of the former is to suppress traitors and prevent the enemy from getting information, and of the latter to assist our own operations (by strengthening our defence works) and prevent the enemy from getting food (by clearing the fields). "Clearing the fields" means harvesting the crops as soon as they are ripe.

When the enemy retreats, he often burns down the houses in the cities and towns he has occupied and razes the villages along his route, with the purpose of destroying the guerrilla base areas; but in so doing he deprives himself of shelter and food in his next offensive, and the damage recoils upon his own head. This is a concrete illustration of what we mean by one and the same thing having two contradictory aspects.

A guerrilla commander should not think of abandoning his base area and shifting to another, unless it proves impossible, after repeated operations, to smash the enemy's heavy converging attacks. In these circumstances he must guard against pessimism. So long as the leaders do not blunder in matters of principle, it is generally possible to smash the converging attacks and hold on to the base areas in the mountainous regions. It is only in the plains that, when confronted by a heavy converging attack, the guerrilla commander should consider other measures in the light of the specific circumstances, namely, leaving many small units for scattered operations, while temporarily shifting large guerrilla formations to some mountainous region, so that they can return and resume their activities in the plains once the main forces of the enemy move away.

Generally speaking, the Japanese cannot adopt the principle of blockhouse warfare, which the Kuomintang employed in the days of the civil war, because their forces are inadequate in relation to China's vast territory. However, we should reckon with the possibility that they may use it to some extent against those guerrilla base areas which pose a particular threat to their vital positions, but even in such circumstances we should be prepared to keep up guerrilla warfare n those areas. Since we have had the experience of being able to maintain guerrilla warfare during the civil war, there is not the slightest doubt of our greater capacity to do so in a national war. Though, in point of relative military strength, the enemy can throw forces that are vastly superior in quantity as well as in quality against some of our base areas, there remain the insoluble national contradiction between us and the enemy and the unavoidable weaknesses of his command. Our victories are based on thorough work among the masses and flexible tactics in our operations.

2. THE STRATEGIC OFFENSIVE IN GUERRILLA WAR

After we have smashed an enemy offensive and before the enemy starts a new offensive, he is on the strategic defensive and we are on the strategic offensive.

At such times our operational policy is not to attack enemy forces which are entrenched in defensive positions and which we are not sure of defeating, but systematically to destroy or drive out the small enemy units and puppet forces in certain areas, which our guerrilla units are strong enough to deal with, and to expand our areas, arouse the masses for struggle against Japan, replenish and train our troops and organize new guerrilla units. If the enemy still remains on the defensive when these tasks are under way, we can expand our new areas still further and attack weakly garrisoned cities and communication lines and hold them for as long as circumstances permit. These are all tasks of the strategic offensive, and the purpose is to take advantage of the fact that the enemy is on the defensive so that we may effectively build up our own military and mass strength, effectively reduce the enemy's strength and prepare to smash the enemy methodically and vigorously when he mounts an offensive again.

It is essential to rest and train our troops, and the best time for doing so is when the enemy is on the defensive. It is not a question of shutting ourselves off from everything else for rest and training, but of finding time for rest and training while expanding our areas, mopping up small enemy units and arousing the people. This is usually also the time for tackling the difficult problem of getting food supplies, bedding, clothing, etc.

It is also the time for destroying the enemy's communication lines on a large scale, hampering his transport and giving direct support to the regular forces in their campaigns.

At such times the guerrilla base areas, guerrilla zones and guerrilla units are in high spirits, and the areas devastated by the enemy are gradually rehabilitated and revived. The people in the enemy-occupied territories are also delighted, and the fame of the guerrillas resounds everywhere. On the other hand, in the camp of the enemy and his running dogs, the traitors, panic and disintegration are mounting, while there is growing hatred of the guerrillas and their base areas and preparations to deal with them are intensified. During the strategic offensive, therefore, it is impermissible for the guerrilla commanders to become so elated as to underrate the enemy and forget to strengthen unity in their own ranks and to consolidate their base areas and their forces. At such times, they must skilfully watch the enemy's every move for signs of any new offensive against us, so that the moment it comes they can wind up their strategic offensive in good order, turn to the strategic defensive and thereby smash the enemy's offensive.

Chapter VIII

DEVELOPMENT OF GUERRILLA WAR
INTO MOBILE WAR

The fifth problem of strategy in guerrilla war against Japan is its development into mobile war, a development which is necessary and possible because the war is protracted and ruthless. If China could speedily defeat the Japanese invaders and recover her lost territories, and if the war were neither protracted nor ruthless, this would not be necessary. But as, on the contrary, the war is protracted and ruthless, guerrilla warfare cannot adapt itself to such a war except by developing into mobile warfare. Since the war is protracted and ruthless, it is possible for the guerrilla units to undergo the necessary steeling and gradually to transform themselves into regular forces, so that their mode of operations is gradually regularized and guerrilla warfare develops into mobile warfare. The necessity and possibility of this development must be clearly recognized by the guerrilla commanders if they are to persist in, and systematically carry out, the policy of turning guerrilla warfare into mobile warfare.

In many places, such as the Wutai mountain region, the present guerrilla warfare owes its growth to the strong detachments sent there by the regular forces. The operations there, though generally of a guerrilla character, have contained an element of mobile warfare from the very beginning. This element will gradually increase as the war goes on. Herein lies the advantage which makes possible the swift expansion of the present anti-Japanese guerrilla warfare and its rapid development to a higher level; thus the conditions for guerrilla warfare are far superior to what they were in the three northeastern provinces.

To transform guerrilla units waging guerrilla warfare into regular forces waging mobile warfare, two conditions are necessary -- an increase in numbers, and an improvement in quality. Apart from directly mobilizing the people to join the forces, increased numbers can be attained by amalgamating small units, while better quality depends on steeling the fighters and improving their weapons in the course of the war.

In amalgamating small units, we must, on the one hand, guard against localism, whereby attention is concentrated exclusively on local interests and centralization is impeded, and, on the other, guard against the purely military approach, whereby local interests are brushed aside.

Localism exists among the local guerrilla units and local governments, which are frequently preoccupied with local considerations to the neglect of the general interest, or which prefer to act each on its own because they are unaccustomed to acting in larger groups. The commanders of the main guerrilla units or of the guerrilla formations must take this into account and adopt the method of gradual amalgamation of part of the local units, allowing the localities to keep some of their forces and expand their guerrilla warfare; the commanders should draw these units into joint operations and then bring about their amalgamation without breaking up their original organization or reshuffling their cadres, so that the small groups may integrate smoothly into the larger group.

As against localism, the purely military approach represents the wrong viewpoint held in the main forces by those who are bent on expanding their own strength and who neglect to assist the local armed units. They do not realize that the development of guerrilla warfare into mobile warfare means not the abandonment of guerrilla warfare, but the gradual formation, in the midst of widespread guerrilla warfare, of a main force capable of conducting mobile warfare, a force around which there must still be numerous guerrilla units carrying on extensive guerrilla operations. These guerrilla units are powerful auxiliaries to the main force and serve as inexhaustible reserves for its continuous growth. Therefore, if a commander of a main force has made the mistake of neglecting the interests of the local population and the local government as a result of a purely military approach, he must correct it in order that the expansion of the main force and the multiplication of the local armed units may both receive due attention.

To raise the quality of the guerrilla units it is imperative to raise their political and organizational level and improve their equipment, military technique, tactics and discipline, so that they gradually pattern themselves on the regular forces and shed their guerrilla ways. Politically, it is imperative to get both the commanders and the fighters to realize the necessity of raising the guerrilla units to the level of the regular forces, to encourage them to strive towards this end, and to guarantee its attainment by means of political work. Organizationally, it is imperative gradually to fulfil all the requirements of a regular formation in the following respects -- military and political organs, staff and working methods, a regular supply system, a medical service, etc. In the matter of equipment, it is imperative to acquire: better and more varied weapons and increase the supply of the necessary communications equipment. In the matter of military technique and tactics, it is imperative to raise the guerrilla units to the level required of a regular formation. In the matter of discipline, it is imperative to raise the level so that uniform standards are observed, every order is executed without fail and all slackness is eliminated. To accomplish all these tasks requires a prolonged effort, and it cannot be done overnight; but that is the direction in which we must develop. Only thus can a main force be built up in each guerrilla base area and mobile warfare emerge for more effective attacks on the enemy. Where detachments or cadres have been sent in by the regular forces, the goal can be achieved more easily. Hence all the regular forces have the responsibility of helping the guerrilla units to develop into regular units.

Chapter IX

THE RELATIONSHIP OF COMMAND

The last problem of strategy in guerrilla war against Japan concerns the relationship of command. A correct solution of this problem is one of the prerequisites for the unhampered development of guerrilla warfare.

Since guerrilla units are a lower level of armed organization characterized by dispersed operations, the methods of command in guerrilla warfare do not allow as high a degree of centralization as in regular warfare. If any attempt is made to apply the methods of command in regular warfare to guerrilla warfare, its great flexibility will inevitably be restricted and its vitality sapped. A highly centralized command is in direct contradiction to the great flexibility of guerrilla warfare and must not and cannot be applied to it.

However, guerrilla warfare cannot be successfully developed without some centralized command. When extensive regular warfare and extensive guerrilla warfare are going on at the same time, their operations must be properly co-ordinated; hence the need for a command co-ordinating the two, i.e., for a unified strategic command by the national general staff and the war-zone commanders. In a guerrilla zone or guerrilla base area with many guerrilla units, there are usually one or more guerrilla formations (sometimes together with regular formations) which constitute the main force, a number of other guerrilla units, big and small, which represent the supplementary force, and many armed units composed of people not withdrawn from production; the enemy forces there usually form a unified complex to concert their operations against the guerrillas. Consequently, the problem arises of setting up a unified or centralized command in such guerrilla zones or base areas.

Hence, as opposed both to absolute centralization and to absolute decentralization, the principle of command in guerrilla war should be centralized strategic command and decentralized command in campaigns and battles.

Centralized strategic command includes the planning and direction of guerrilla warfare as a whole by the state, the co-ordination of guerrilla warfare with regular warfare in each war zone, and the unified direction of all the anti-Japanese armed forces in each guerrilla zone or base area. Here lack of harmony, unity and centralization is harmful, and every effort must be made to ensure all three. In general matters, that is, matters of strategy, the lower levels should report to the higher and follow their instructions so as to ensure concerted action. Centralization, however, stops at this point, and it would likewise be harmful to go beyond it and interfere with the lower levels in matters of detail like the specific dispositions for a campaign or battle. For such details must be settled in the light of specific conditions, which change from time to time and from place to place and are quite beyond the knowledge of the distant higher levels of command. This is what is meant by the principle of decentralized command in campaigns and battles. The same principle generally applies in regular operations, especially when communications are inadequate. In a word, it means guerrilla warfare waged independently and with the initiative in our hands within the framework of a unified strategy.

Where a guerrilla base area constitutes a military area divided into sub-areas, each comprising several counties, each of which is again divided into districts, the relationship between the various levels, from the headquarters of the military area and sub-areas down to the county and district governments, is one of consecutive subordination, and every armed force must, according to its nature, be under the direct command of one of these. On the principle that has been enunciated, in the relationship of command at these levels matters of general policy should be centralized in the higher levels, while actual operations should be carried out in the light of the specific circumstances by the lower levels, which should have the right of independent action. If a higher level has something to say about the actual operations undertaken at a lower level, it can and should advance its views as "instructions" but must not issue hard and fast "commands". The more extensive the area, the more complex the situation and the greater the distance between the higher and the lower levels, the more advisable it becomes to allow greater independence to the lower levels in their actual operations and thus give those operations a character conforming more closely to the local requirements, so that the lower levels and the local personnel may develop the ability to work independently, cope with complicated situations, and successfully expand guerrilla warfare. For an armed unit or bigger formation which is engaged in a concentrated operation, the principle to be applied is one of centralization in its internal relationship of command, since the situation is clear to the higher command but the moment this unit or formation breaks up for dispersed action, the principle of centralization in general matters and of decentralization in details should be applied, for then the specific situation cannot be clear to the higher command. Absence of centralization where it is needed means negligence by the higher levels or usurpation of authority by the lower levels, neither of which can be tolerated in the relationship between higher and lower levels, especially in the military sphere. If decentralization is not effected where it should be, that means monopolization of power by the higher levels and lack of initiative on the part of the lower levels, neither of which can be tolerated in the relationship between higher and lower levels, especially in the command of guerrilla war fare. The above principles constitute the only correct policy for solving the problem of the relationship of command.

NOTES

[1] The Changpai mountain range is situated on the northeastern border of China. After the Japancse invasion on September 18, 1931, the region became a base area for the anti-Japanae guerrillas led by thc Chinese Communist Party.

[2] The Wutai mountain range is situated on the borders between Shansi, Hopei and what was then Chahar Province. In October 1937 the Eighth Route Army led by the Chinese Communist Party started building the Shansi-Chahar-Hopei anti-Japanese base area with the Wutai mountain region as its centre.

[3] The Taihang mountain range is situated on the borders between Shansi, Hopei and Honan Provinces. In November 1937 the Eighth Route Army started building the southeastern Shansi anti-Japanese base area with the Taihang mountain region as its centre.

[4] The Taishan Mountain is one of the chief peaks of the Tai-Yi mountain range in central Shantung. In the winter of 1937 the guerrilla forces led by the Communist Party started building the central Shantung anti-Japanese base area with the Tai-Yi mountain region as its centre.

[5] The Yenshan mountain range is situated on the border of Hopei and what was then Jehol Province. In the summer of 1938 the Eighth Route Army started building the eastern Hopei anti-Japanese base area with the Yenshan mountain region as its centre.

[6] The Maoshan Mountains are in southern Kiangsu. In June 1938 the New Fourth Army led by the Communist Party started building the southern Kiangsu anti-Japanese base area with the Maoshan mountain tegion as its centre.

[7] Experience gained in the War of Resistance proved that it was possible to establish long-term and, in many places, stable base areas in the plains. This was due to their vastness and big populations, the correctness of the Communist Party's policies, the extensive mobilization of the people and the enemy's shortage of troops. Comrade Mao Tse-tung affirmed this possibility more definitely in later directives.

[8] Ever since the end of World War II, the national and democratic revolutionary movement has been surging forward in Asia, Africa and Latin America. In many countries the people, led by their own revolutionary and progressive forces, have carried on sustained armed struggles to overthrow the dark rule of imperialism and reaction. This demonstrates that in the new historical circumstances -- when the socialist camp, the revolutionary forces of the people in the colonial countries and the forces of the people striving for democracy and progress in all countries are taking giant strides forward, when the world capitalist system is weakening still further, and when the colonial rule of imperialism is heading for disintegration -- the conditions under which the people of various countries conduct guerrilla warfare today need not be quite the same as those which were necessary in the days of the guerrilla warfare waged by the Chinese people against Japan. In other words, guerrilla war can be victoriously waged in a country which is not large in territory, as for instance, in Cuba, Algeria, Laos and southern Viet Nam.

[9] Weichi is an old Chinese game, in which the two players try to encircle each other's pieces on the board. When a player's pieces are encircled, they are counted as "dead" (captured). But if there is a sufficient number of blank spaces among the encircled pieces, then the latter are still "alive" (not captured).

[10] In 353 B.C. the state of Wei laid siege to Hantan, capital of the state of Chao. The king of the state of Chi, an ally of Chao, ordered his generals Tien Chi and Sun Pin to aid Chao with their troops. Knowing that the crack forces of Wei had entered Chao and left their own territory weakly garrisoned, General Sun Pin attacked the state of Wei whose troops withdrew to defend their own country. Taking advantage of their exhaustion, the troops of Chi engaged and routed them at Kueiling (northeast of the present Hotse County in Shantung). The siege of Hantan, capital of Chao, was thus lifted. Since then Chinese strategists have referred to similar tactics as "relieving the state of Chao by besieging the state of Wei".

Mao Tse-tung

THE ART OF WAR

PART 3

ON PROTRACTED WAR

by

Mao Tse-tung

May 1938

Mao Tse-tung

Preface

This series of lectures was delivered by Mao Tse-tung from May 26 to June 3, 1938, at the Yenan Association for the Study of the War of Resistance Against Japan.

Mao Tse-tung

STATEMENT OF THE PROBLEM

1. It will soon be July 7, the first anniversary of the great War of Resistance Against Japan. Rallying in unity, persevering in resistance and persevering in the united front, the forces of the whole nation have been valiantly fighting the enemy for almost a year. The people of the whole world are attentively following this war, which has no precedent in the history of the East, and which will go down as a great war in world history too. Every Chinese suffering from the disasters of the war and fighting for the survival of his nation daily yearns for victory. But what actually will be the course of the war? Can we win? Can we win quickly? Many people are talking about a protracted war, but why is it a protracted war? How to carry on a protracted war? Many people are talking about final victory, but why will final victory be ours? How shall we strive for final victory? Not everyone has found answers to these questions; in fact, to this day most people have not done so. Therefore the defeatist exponents of the theory of national subjugation have come forward to tell people that China will be subjugated, that final victory will not be China's. On the other hand, some impetuous friends have come forward to tell people that China will win very quickly without having to exert any great effort. But are these views correct? We have said all along they are not. However, most people have not yet grasped what we have been saying. This is partly because we did not do enough propaganda and explanatory work, and partly because the development of objective events had not yet fully and clearly revealed their inherent nature and their features to the people, who were thus not in a position to foresee the over-all trend and the outcome and hence to decide on a complete set of policies and tactics. Now things are better; the experience of ten months of war has been quite sufficient to explode the utterly baseless theory of national subjugation and to dissuade our impetuous friends from their theory of quick victory. In these circumstances many people are asking for a

comprehensive explanation. All the more so with regard to protracted war, not only because of the opposing theories of national subjugation and quick victory but also because of the shallow understanding of its nature. "Our four hundred million people have been making a concerted effort since the Lukouchiao Incident, and the final victory will belong to China." This formula has a wide currency. It is a correct formula but needs to be given more content. Our perseverance in the War of Resistance and in the united front has been possible because of many factors. Internally, they comprise all the political parties in the country from the Communist Party to the Kuomintang, all the people from the workers and peasants to the bourgeoisie, and all the armed forces from the regular forces to the guerrillas; internationally, they range from the land of socialism to justice-loving people in all countries; in the camp of the enemy, they range from those people in Japan who are against the war to those Japanese soldiers at the front who are against the war. In short, all these forces have contributed in varying degrees to our War of Resistance. Every man with a conscience should salute them. We Communists, together with all the other anti-Japanese political parties and the whole people, have no other course than to strive to unite all forces for the defeat of the diabolical Japanese aggressors. July I this year will be the 17th anniversary of the founding of the Communist Party of China. A serious study of protracted war is necessary in order to enable every Communist to play a better and greater part in the War of Resistance. Therefore my lectures will be devoted to such a study. I shall try- to speak on all the problems relevant to the protracted war, but I cannot possibly go into everything in one series of lectures.

2. All the experience of the ten months of war proves the error both of the theory of China's inevitable subjugation and of the theory of China's quick victory. The former gives rise to the tendency to compromise and the latter to the tendency to

underestimate the enemy. Both approaches to the problem are subjective and one-sided, or, in a word, unscientific.

3. Before the War of Resistance, there was a great deal of talk about national subjugation. Some said, "China is inferior in arms and is bound to lose in a war." Others said, "If China offers armed resistance, she is sure to become another Abyssinia." Since the beginning of the war, open talk of national subjugation has disappeared, but secret talk, and quite a lot of it too, still continues. For instance, from time to time an atmosphere of compromise arises and the advocates of compromise argue that "the continuance of the war spells subjugation". [1] In a letter from Hunan a student has written:

In the countryside everything seems difficult. Doing propaganda work on my own, I have to talk to people when and where I find them. The people I have talked to are by no means ignoramuses; they all have some understanding of what is going on and are very interested in what I have to say. But when I run into my own relatives, they always say: "China cannot win; she is doomed." They make one sick! Fortunately, they do not go around spreading their views, otherwise things would really be bad. The peasants would naturally put more stock in what they say.

Such exponents of the theory of China's inevitable subjugation form the social basis of the tendency to compromise. They are to be found everywhere in China, and therefore the problem of compromise is liable to crop up within the anti-Japanese front at any time and will probably remain with us right until the end of the war. Now that Hsuchow has fallen and Wuhan is in danger, it will not be unprofitable, I think, to knock the bottom out of the theory of national subjugation.

4. During these ten months of war all kinds of views which are indicative of impetuosity have also appeared. For instance, at the outset of the war many people were groundlessly optimistic, underestimating Japan and even believing that the Japanese could not get as far as Shansi. Some belittled the strategic role of guerrilla warfare in the War of Resistance and doubted the proposition, "With regard to the whole, mobile warfare is primary and guerrilla warfare supplementary; with regard to the parts, guerrilla warfare is primary and mobile warfare supplementary." They disagreed with the Eighth Route Army's strategy, "Guerrilla warfare is basic, but lose no chance for mobile warfare under favourable conditions", which they regarded as a "mechanical" approach. [2] During the battle of Shanghai some people said: "If we can fight for just three months, the international situation is bound to change, the Soviet Union is bound to send troops, and the war will be over." They pinned their hopes for the future of the War of Resistance chiefly on foreign aid. [3] After the Taierhchuang victory, [4] some people maintained that the Hsuchow campaign should be fought as a "quasi-decisive campaign" and that the policy of protracted war should be changed. They said such things as, "This campaign marks the last desperate struggle of the enemy," or, "If we win, the Japanese warlords will be demoralized and able only to await their Day of Judgement." [5] The victory at Pinghsingkuan turned some people's heads, and further victory at Taierhchuang has turned more people's heads. Doubts have arisen as to whether the enemy will attack Wuhan. Many people think "probably not", and many others "definitely not". Such doubts may affect all major issues. For instance, is our anti-Japanese strength already sufficient? Some people may answer affirmatively, for our present strength is already sufficient to check the enemy's advance, so why increase it? Or, for instance, is the slogan "Consolidate and expand the Anti-Japanese National United Front" still correct? Some people may answer negatively, for the united front in its

present state is already strong enough to repulse the enemy, so why consolidate and expand it? Or, for instance, should our efforts in diplomacy and international propaganda be intensified? Here again the answer may be in the negative. Or, for instance, should we proceed in earnest to reform the army system and the system of government, develop the mass movement, enforce education for national defence, suppress traitors and Trotskyites, develop war industries and improve the people's livelihood? Or, for instance, are the slogans calling for the defence of Wuhan, of Canton and of the Northwest and for the vigorous development of guerrilla warfare in the enemy's rear still correct? The answers might all be in the negative. There are even some people who, the moment a slightly favourable turn occurs in the war situation, are prepared to intensify the "friction" between the Kuomintang and the Communist Party, diverting attention from external to internal matters. This almost invariably occurs whenever a comparatively big battle is won or the enemy's advance comes to a temporary halt. All the above can be termed political and military short-sightedness. Such talk, however plausible, is actually specious and groundless. To sweep away such verbiage should help the victorious prosecution of the War of Resistance.

5. The question now is: Will China be subjugated? The answer is, No, she will not be subjugated, but will win final victory. Can China win quickly? The answer is, No, she cannot win quickly, and the War of Resistance will be a protracted war.

6. As early as two years ago, we broadly indicated the main arguments on these questions. On July 16, 1936, five months before the Sian Incident and twelve months before the Lukouchiao Incident, in an interview with the American correspondent, Mr. Edgar Snow, I made a general estimate of the situation with regard to war between China and Japan and

advanced various principles for winning victory. The following excerpts may serve as a reminder:

Question: Under what conditions do you think China can defeat and destroy the forces of Japan?

Answer: Three conditions are required: first, the establishment of an anti-Japanese united front in China; second, the formation of an international anti-Japanese united front; third, the rise of the revolutionary movement of the people in Japan and the Japanese colonies. From the standpoint of the Chinese people, the unity of the people of China is the most important of the three conditions.

Question: How long do you think such a war would last?

Answer: That depends on the strength of China's anti-Japanese united front and many other conditioning factors involving China and Japan. That is to say, apart from China's own strength, which is the main thing, international help to China and the help rendered by the revolution in Japan are also important. If China's anti-Japanese united front is greatly expanded and effectively organized horizontally and vertically, if the necessary help is given to China by those governments and peoples which recognize the Japanese imperialist menace to their own interests and if revolution comes quickly in Japan, the war will speedily be brought to an end and China will speedily win victory. If these conditions are not realized quickly, the war will be prolonged. But in the end, just the same, Japan will certainly be defeated and China will certainly be victorious. Only the sacrifices will be great and there will be a very painful period.

Question: What is your opinion of the probable course of development of such a war, politically and militarily?

Answer: Japan's continental policy is already fixed, and those who think they can halt the Japanese advance by making compromises with Japan at the expense of more Chinese territory and sovereign rights are indulging in mere fantasy. We definitely know that the lower Yangtse valley and our southern seaports are already included in the continental programme of Japanese imperialism. Moreover, Japan wants to occupy the Philippines, Siam, Indo-China, the Malay Peninsula and the Dutch East Indies in order to cut off other countries from China and monopolize the southwestern Pacific. This is Japan's maritime policy. In such a period, China will undoubtedly be in an extremely difficult position. But the majority of the Chinese people believe that such difficulties can be overcome; only the rich in the big port cities are defeatists because they are afraid of losing their property. Many people think it would be impossible for China to continue the war, once her coastline is blockaded by Japan. This is nonsense. To refute them we need only cite the war history of the Red Army. In the present War of Resistance Against Japan, China's position is much superior to that of the Red Army in the civil war. China is a vast country, and even if Japan should succeed in occupying a section of China with as many as 100 to 200 million people, we would still be far from defeated. We would still have ample strength to fight against Japan, while the Japanese would have to fight defensive battles in their rear throughout the war. The heterogeneity and uneven development of China's economy are rather advantageous in the war of resistance. For example, to sever Shanghai from the rest of China would definitely not be as disastrous to China as would be the severance of New York from the rest of the United States. Even if Japan blockades the Chinese coastline, it is impossible for her to blockade China's Northwest, Southwest and West. Thus, once more the central point of the problem is the unity of the entire Chinese people and the building up of a nation-wide anti-Japanese front. This is what we have long been advocating.

Question: If the war drags on for a long time and Japan is not completely defeated, would the Communist Party agree to the negotiation of a peace with Japan and recognize her rule in northeastern China?

Answer: No. Like the people of the whole country, the Chinese Communist Party will not allow Japan to retain an inch of Chinese territory.

Question: What, in your opinion, should be the main strategy and tactics to be followed in this "war of liberation"?

Answer: Our strategy should be to employ our main forces to operate over an extended and fluid front. To achieve success, the Chinese troops must conduct their warfare with a high degree of mobility on extensive battlefields, making swift advances and withdrawals, swift concentrations and dispersals. This means largescale mobile warfare, and not positional warfare depending exclusively on defence works with deep trenches, high fortresses and successive rows of defensive positions. It does not mean the abandonment of all the vital strategic points, which should be defended by positional warfare as long as profitable. But the pivotal strategy must be mobile warfare. Positional warfare is also necessary, but strategically it is auxiliary and secondary. Geographically the theatre of the war is so vast that it is possible for us to conduct mobile warfare most effectively. In the face of the vigorous actions of our forces, the Japanese army will have to be cautious. Its war-machine is ponderous and slow-moving, with limited efficiency. If we concentrate our forces on a narrow front for a defensive war of attrition, we would be throwing away the advantages of our geography and economic organization and repeating the mistake of Abyssinia. In the early period of the war, we must avoid any major decisive battles, and must first employ mobile warfare gradually to break the morale and combat effectiveness of the enemy troops.

Besides employing trained armies to carry on mobile warfare, we must organize great numbers of guerrilla units among the peasants. One should know that the anti-Japanese volunteer units in the three northeastern provinces are only a minor demonstration of the latent power of resistance that can be mobilized from the peasants of the whole country. The Chinese peasants have very great latent power; properly organized and directed, they can keep the Japanese army busy twenty-four hours a day and worry it to death. It must be remembered that the war will be fought in China, that is to say, the Japanese army will be entirely surrounded by the hostile Chinese people, it will be forced to move in all its provisions and guard them, it must use large numbers of troops to protect its lines of communications and constantly guard against attacks, and it needs large forces to garrison Manchuria and Japan as well.

In the course of the war, China will be able to capture many Japanese soldiers and seize many weapons and munitions with which to arm herself; at the same time China will win foreign aid to reinforce the equipment of her troops gradually. Therefore China will be able to conduct positional warfare in the latter period of the war and make positional attacks on the Japanese-occupied areas. Thus Japan's economy will crack under the strain of China's long resistance and the morale of the Japanese forces will break under the trial of innumerable battles. On the Chinese side, however, the growing latent power of resistance will be constantly brought into play and large numbers of revolutionary people will be pouring into the front lines to fight for their freedom. The combination of all these and other factors will enable us to make the final and decisive attacks on the fortifications and bases in the Japanese-occupied areas and drive the Japanese forces of aggression out of China.

The above views have been proved correct in the light of the experience of the ten months of war and will also be borne out in the future.

7. As far back as August 25, 1937, less than two months after the Lukouchiao Incident, the Central Committee of the Chinese Communist Party clearly pointed out in its "Resolution on the Present Situation and the Tasks of the Party":

The military provocation by the Japanese aggressors at Lukouchiao and their occupation of Peiping and Tientsin represent only the beginning of their large-scale invasion of China south of the Great Wall. They have already begun their national mobilization for war. Their propaganda that they have "no desire to aggravate the situation" is only a smokescreen for further attacks.

The resistance at Lukouchiao on July 7 marked the starting point of China's national War of Resistance.

Thus a new stage has opened in China's political situation, the stage of actual resistance. The stage of preparation for resistance is over. In the present stage the central task is to mobilize all the nation's forces for victory in the War of Resistance.

The key to victory in the war now lies in developing the resistance that has already begun into a war of total resistance by the whole nation. Only through such a war of total resistance can final victory be won.

The existence of serious weaknesses in the War of Resistance may lead to many setbacks, retreats, internal splits, betrayals, temporary and partial compromises and other such reverses. Therefore it should be realized that the war will be an arduous and protracted war. But we are confident that, through the efforts of our Party and the whole people, the resistance already started will sweep aside all obstacles and continue to advance and develop.

The above thesis, too, has been proved correct in the light of the experience of the ten months of war and will also be borne out in the future.

8. Epistemologically speaking, the source of all erroneous views on war lies in idealist and mechanistic tendencies on the question. People with such tendencies are subjective and one-sided in their approach to problems. They either indulge in groundless and purely subjective talk, or, basing themselves upon a single aspect or a temporary manifestation, magnify it with similar subjectivity into the whole of the problem. But there are two categories of erroneous views, one comprising fundamental, and therefore consistent, errors which are hard to correct, and the other comprising accidental, and therefore temporary, errors which are easy to correct. Since both are wrong, both need to be corrected. Therefore, only by opposing idealist and mechanistic tendencies and taking an objective and all-sided view in making a study of war can we draw correct conclusions on the question of war.

THE BASIS OF THE PROBLEM

9.   Why is the War of Resistance Against Japan a protracted war? Why will the final victory be China's? What is the basis for these statements?

The war between China and Japan is not just any war, it is specifically a war of life and death between semi-colonial and semi-feudal China and imperialist Japan, fought in the Nineteen Thirties. Herein lies the basis of the whole problem. The two sides in the war have many contrasting features, which will be considered in turn below.

10.   The Japanese side. First, Japan is a powerful imperialist country, which ranks first in the East in military, economic and politicalorganizational power, and is one of the five or six foremost imperialist countries of the world. These are the basic factors in Japan's war of aggression. The inevitability of the war and the impossibility of quick victory for China are due to Japan's imperialist system and her great military, economic and political-organizational power. Secondly, however, the imperialist character of Japan's social economy determines the imperialist character of her war, a war that is retrogressive and barbarous. In the Nineteen Thirties, the internal and external contradictions of Japanese imperialism have driven her not only to embark on an adventurist war unparalleled in scale but also to approach her final collapse. In terms of social development, Japan is no longer a thriving country; the war will not lead to the prosperity sought by her ruling classes but to the very reverse, the doom of Japanese imperialism. This is what we mean by the retrogressive nature of Japan's war. It is this reactionary quality, coupled with the military-feudal character of Japanese imperialism, that gives rise to the peculiar barbarity of Japan's war. All of which will arouse to the utmost the class antagonisms within Japan, the antagonism between the Japanese and the Chinese nations, and

the antagonism between Japan and most other countries of the world. The reactionary and barbarous character of Japan's war constitutes the primary reason for her inevitable defeat. Thirdly, Japan's war is conducted on the basis of her great military, economic and political-organizational power, but at the same time it rests on an inadequate natural endowment. Japan's military, economic and political-organizational power is great but quantitatively inadequate. Japan is a comparatively small country, deficient in manpower and in military, financial and material resources, and she cannot stand a long war. Japan's rulers are endeavouring to resolve this difficulty through war, but again they will get the very reverse of what they desire; that is to say, the war they have launched to resolve this difficulty will eventually aggravate it and even exhaust Japan's original resources. Fourthly and lastly, while Japan can get international support from the fascist countries, the international opposition she is bound to encounter will be greater than her international support. This opposition will gradually grow and eventually not only cancel out the support but even bear down upon Japan herself. Such is the law that an unjust cause finds meagre support, and such is the consequence of the very nature of Japan's war. To sum up, Japan's advantage lies in her great capacity to wage war, and her disadvantages lie in the reactionary and barbarous nature of her war, in the inadequacy of her manpower and material resources, and in her meagre international support. These are the characteristics on the Japanese side.

11. The Chinese side. First, we are a semi-colonial and semi-feudal country. The Opium War, [6] the Taiping Revolution, [7] the Reform Movement of 1898, [8] the Revolution of 1911 [9] and the Northern Expedition [10] -- the revolutionary or reform movements which aimed at extricating China from her semi-colonial and semi-feudal state -- all met with serious setbacks, and China remains a semi-colonial and semi-feudal country. We are still a weak country and

manifestly inferior to the enemy in military, economic and political-organizational power. Here again one can find the basis for the inevitability of the war and the impossibility of quick victory for China. Secondly, however, China's liberation movement, with its cumulative development over the last hundred years, is now different from that of any previous period. Although the domestic and foreign forces opposing it have caused it serious setbacks, at the same time they have tempered the Chinese people. Although China today is not so strong as Japan militarily, economically, politically and culturally, yet there are factors in China more progressive than in any other period of her history. The Communist Party of China and the army under its leadership represent these progressive factors. It is on the basis of this progress that China's present war of liberation can be protracted and can achieve final victory. By contrast with Japanese imperialism, which is declining, China is a country rising like the morning sun. China's war is progressive, hence its just character. Because it is a just war, it is capable of arousing the nation to unity, of evoking the sympathy of the people in Japan and of winning the support of most countries in the world. Thirdly, and again by contrast with Japan, China is a very big country with vast territory, rich resources, a large population and plenty of soldiers, and is capable of sustaining a long war. Fourthly and lastly, there is broad international support for China stemming from the progressive and just character of her wet, which is again exactly the reverse of the meagre support for Japan's unjust cause. To sum up, China's disadvantage lies in her military weakness, and her advantages lie in the progressive and just character of her war, her great size and her abundant international support. These are China's characteristics.

12. Thus it can be seen that Japan has great military, economic and political-organizational power, but that her war is reactionary and barbarous, her manpower and material

resources are inadequate, and she is in an unfavourable position internationally. China, on the contrary, has less military, economic and political-organizational power, but she is in her era of progress, her war is progressive and just, she is moreover a big country, a factor which enables her to sustain a protracted war, and she will be supported by most countries. The above are the basic, mutually contradictory characteristics of the Sino-Japanese war. They have determined and are determining all the political policies and military strategies and tactics of the two sides; they have determined and are determining the protracted character of the war and its outcome, namely, that the final victory will go to China and not to Japan. The war is a contest between these characteristics. They will change in the course of the war, each according to its own nature; and from this everything else will follow. These characteristics exist objectively and are not invented to deceive people; they constitute all the basic elements of the war, and are not incomplete fragments; they permeate all major and minor problems on both sides and all stages of the war, and they are not matters of no consequence. If anyone forgets these characteristics in studying the Sino-Japanese war, he will surely go wrong; and even though some of his ideas win credence for a time and may seem right, they will inevitably be proved wrong by the course of the war. On the basis of these characteristics we shall now proceed to explain the problems to be dealt with.

REFUTATION OF THE THEORY OF
NATIONAL SUBJUGATION

13. The theorists of national subjugation, who see nothing but the contrast between the enemy's strength and our weakness, used to say, "Resistance will mean subjugation," and now they are saying: "The continuance of the war spells subjugation." We shall not be able to convince them merely by stating that Japan, though strong; is small, while China, though weak, is large. They can adduce historical instances, such as the destruction of the Sung Dynasty by the Yuan and the destruction of the Ming Dynasty by the Ching, to prove that a small but strong country can vanquish a large but weak one and, moreover, that a backward country can vanquish an advanced one. If we say these events occurred long ago and do not prove the point, they can cite the British subjugation of India to prove that a small but strong capitalist country can vanquish a large but weak and backward country. Therefore, we have to produce other grounds before we can silence and convince all the subjugationists, and supply everyone engaged in propaganda with adequate arguments to persuade those who are still confused or irresolute and so strengthen their faith in the War of Resistance.

14. What then are the grounds we should advance? The characteristics of the epoch. These characteristics are concretely reflected in Japan's retrogression and paucity of support and in China's progress and abundance of support.

15. Our war is not just any war, it is specifically a war between China and Japan fought in the Nineteen Thirties. Our enemy, Japan, is first of all a moribund imperialist power; she is already in her era of decline and is not only different from Britain at the time of the subjugation of India, when British capitalism was still in the era of its ascendancy, but also different from what she herself was at the time of World War I

twenty years ago. The present war was launched on the eve of the general collapse of world imperialism and, above all, of the fascist countries; that is the very reason the enemy has launched this adventurist war, which is in the nature of a last desperate struggle. Therefore, it is an inescapable certainty that it will not be China but the ruling circles of Japanese imperialism which will be destroyed as a result of the war. Moreover, Japan has undertaken this war at a time when many countries have been or are about to be embroiled in war, when we are all fighting or preparing to fight against barbarous aggression, and China's fortunes are linked with those of most of the countries and peoples of the world. This is the root cause of the opposition Japan has aroused and will increasingly arouse among those countries and peoples.

16.   What about China? The China of today cannot be compared with the China of any other historical period. She is a semi-colony and a semi-feudal society, and she is consequently considered a weak country. But at the same time, China is historically in her era of progress; this is the primary reason for her ability to defeat Japan.

When we say that the War of Resistance Against Japan is progressive, we do not mean progressive in the ordinary or general sense, nor do we mean progressive in the sense that the Abyssinian war against Italy, or the Taiping Revolution or the Revolution of 1911 were progressive, we mean progressive in the sense that China is progressive today. In what way is the China of today progressive? She is progressive because she is no longer a completely feudal country and because we already have some capitalism in China, we have a bourgeoisie and a proletariat, we have vast numbers of people who have awakened or are awakening, we have a Communist Party, we have a politically progressive army -- the Chinese Red Army led by the Communist Party -- and we have the tradition and the experience of many decades of revolution, and especially the experience of the seventeen years since the 'founding of the Chinese Communist Party. This experience has schooled the people and the political parties of China and forms the very basis for the present unity against Japan. If it is said that without the experience of 1905 the victory of 1917 would have been impossible in Russia, then we can also say that without the experience of the last seventeen years it would be impossible to win our War of Resistance. Such is the internal situation.

In the existing international situation, China is not isolated in the war, and this fact too is without precedent in history. In the past, China's wars, and India's too, were wars fought in isolation. It is only today that we meet with world-wide popular movements, extraordinary in breadth and depth, which have arisen or are arising and which are supporting China. The Russian Revolution of 1917 also received international support, and thus the Russian workers and peasants won; but that support was not so broad in scale and deep in nature as ours today. The popular movements in the world today are developing on a scale and with a depth that are unprecedented. The existence of the Soviet Union is a particularly vital factor in present-day international politics, and the Soviet Union will certainly support China with the greatest enthusiasm; there was nothing like this twenty years ago. All these factors have created and are creating important conditions indispensable to China's final victory Large-scale direct assistance is as yet lacking and will come only in the future, but China is progressive and is a big country, and these are the factors enabling her to protract the war and to promote as well as await international help.

17. There is the additional factor that while Japan is a small country with a small territory, few resources, a small population and a limited number of soldiers, China is a big country with vast territory, rich resources, a large population

and plenty of soldiers, so that, besides the contrast between strength and weakness, there is the contrast between a small country, retrogression and meagre support and a big country, progress and abundant support. This is the reason why China will never be subjugated. It follows from the contrast between strength and weakness that Japan can ride roughshod over China for a certain time and to a certain extent, that China must unavoidably travel a hard stretch of road, and that the War of Resistance will be a protracted war and not a war of quick decision; nevertheless, it follows from the other contrast -- a small country, retrogression and meagre support versus a big country, progress and abundant support -- that Japan cannot ride roughshod over China indefinitely but is sure to meet final defeat, while China can never be subjugated but is sure to win final victory.

18. Why was Abyssinia vanquished? First, she was not only weak but also small. Second, she was not as progressive as China; she was an old country passing from the slave to the serf system, a country without any capitalism or bourgeois political parties, let alone a Communist Party, and with no army such as the Chinese army, let alone one like the Eighth Route Army. Third, she was unable to hold out and wait for international assistance and had to fight her war in isolation. Fourth, and most important of all, there were mistakes in the direction of her war against Italy. Therefore Abyssinia was subjugated. But there is still quite extensive guerrilla warfare in Abyssinia, which, if persisted in, will enable the Abyssinians to recover their country when the world situation changes.

19. If the subjugationists quote the history of the failure of liberation movements in modern China to prove their assertions first that "resistance will mean subjugation", and then that "the continuance of the war spells subjugation", here again our answer is, "Times are different." China herself, the internal situation in Japan and the international environment

are all different now. It is a serious matter that Japan is stronger than before while China in her unchanged semi-colonial and semi-feudal position is still fairly weak. It is also a fact that for the time being Japan can still control her people at home and exploit international contradictions in order to invade China. But during a long war, these things are bound to change in the opposite direction. Such changes are not yet accomplished facts, but they will become so in future. The subjugationists dismiss this point. As for China, we already have new people, a new political party, a new army and a new policy of resistance to Japan, a situation very different from that of over a decade ago, and what is more, all these will inevitably make further progress. It is true that historically the liberation movements met with repeated setbacks with the result that China could not accumulate greater strength for the present War of Resistance -- this is a very painful historical lesson, and never again should we destroy any of our revolutionary forces. Yet even on the present basis, by exerting great efforts we can certainly forge ahead gradually and increase the strength of our resistance. All such efforts should converge on the great Anti-Japanese National United Front. As for international support, though direct and large-scale assistance is not yet in sight, it is in the making, the international situation being fundamentally different from before. The countless failures in the liberation movement of modern China had their subjective and objective causes, but the situation today is entirely different. Today, although there are many difficulties which make the War of Resistance arduous -- such as the enemy's strength and our weakness, and the fact that his difficulties are just starting, while our own progress is far from sufficient -- nevertheless many favourable conditions exist for defeating the enemy; we need only add our subjective efforts, and we shall be able to overcome the difficulties and win through to victory. These are favourable conditions such as never existed before in any period of our history, and that is why the War of Resistance

Against Japan, unlike the liberation movements of the past, will not end in failure.

COMPROMISE OR RESISTANCE?
CORRUPTION OR PROGRESS?

20. It has been fully explained above that the theory of national subjugation is groundless. But there are many people who do not subscribe to this theory; they are honest patriots, who are nevertheless deeply worried about the present situation. Two things are worrying them, fear of a compromise with Japan and doubts about the possibility of political progress. These two vexing questions are being widely discussed and no key has been found to their solution. Let us now examine them.

21. As previously explained, the question of compromise has its social roots, and as long as these roots exist the question is bound to arise. But compromise will not avail. To prove the point, again we need only look for substantiation to Japan, China, and the international situation. First take Japan. At the very beginning of the War of Resistance, we estimated that the time would come when an atmosphere conducive to compromise would arise, in other words, that after occupying northern China, Kiangsu and Chekiang, Japan would probably resort to the scheme of inducing China to capitulate. True enough, she did resort to the scheme, but the crisis soon passed, one reason being that the enemy everywhere pursued a barbarous policy and practiced naked plunder. Had China capitulated, every Chinese would have become a slave without a country. The enemy's predatory policy, the policy of subjugating China, has two aspects, the material and the spiritual, both of which are being applied universally to all Chinese, not only to the people of the lower strata but also to members of the upper strata; of course the latter are treated a little more politely, but the difference is only one of degree, not of principle. In the main the enemy is transplanting into the interior of China the same old measures he adopted in the three northeastern provinces. Materially, he is robbing the common

people even of their food and clothing, making them cry out in hunger and cold; he is plundering the means of production, thus ruining and enslaving China's national industries. Spiritually, he is working to destroy the national consciousness of the Chinese people. Under the flag of the "Rising Sun" all Chinese are forced to be docile subjects, beasts of burden forbidden to show the slightest trace of Chinese national spirit. This barbarous enemy policy will be carried deeper into the interior of China. Japan with her voracious appetite is unwilling to stop the war. As was inevitable, the policy set forth in the Japanese cabinet's statement of January 6, 1938 [11] is still being obstinately carried out, which has enraged all strata of the Chinese people. This rage is engendered by the reactionary and barbarous character of Japan's war -- "there is no escape from fate", and hence an absolute hostility has crystallized. It is to be expected that on some future occasion the enemy will once again resort to the scheme of inducing China to capitulate and that certain subjugationists will again crawl out and most probably collude with certain foreign elements (to be found in Britain, the United States and France, and especially among the upper strata in Britain) as partners in crime. But the general trend of events will not permit capitulation; the obstinate and peculiarly barbarous character of Japan's war has decided this aspect of the question.

22. Second, let us take China. There are three factors contributing to China's perseverance in the War of Resistance. In the first place, the Communist Party, which is the reliable force leading the people to resist Japan. Next, the Kuomintang, which depends on Britain and the United States and hence will not capitulate to Japan unless they tell it to. Finally, the other political parties and groups, most of which oppose compromise and support the War of Resistance. With unity among these three, whoever compromises will be standing with the traitors, and anybody will have the right to punish him. All those unwilling to be traitors have no choice but to unite and carry on

the War of Resistance to the end; therefore compromise can hardly succeed.

23. Third, take the international aspect. Except for Japan's allies and certain elements in the upper strata of other capitalist countries, the whole world is in favour of resistance, and not of compromise by China. This factor reinforces China's hopes. Today the people throughout the country cherish the hope that international forces will gradually give China increasing help. It is not a vain hope; the existence of the Soviet Union in particular encourages China in her War of Resistance. The socialist Soviet Union, now strong as never before; has always shared China's joys and sorrows. In direct contrast to all the members of the upper strata in the capitalist countries who seek nothing but profits, the Soviet Union considers it its duty to help all weak nations and all revolutionary wars. That China is not fighting! her war in isolation has its basis not only in international support in general but in Soviet support in particular. China and the Soviet Union are in close geographical proximity, which aggravates Japan's crisis and facilitates China's War of Resistance. Geographical proximity to Japan increases the difficulties of China's resistance. Proximity to the Soviet Union, on the other hand, is a favourable condition for the War of Resistance.

24. Hence we may conclude that the danger of compromise exists but can be overcome. Even if the enemy can modify his policy to some extent, he cannot alter it fundamentally. In China the social roots of compromise are present, but the opponents of compromise are in the majority. Internationally, also, some forces favour compromise, but the main forces favour resistance. The combination of these three factors makes it possible to overcome the danger of compromise and persist to the end in the War of Resistance.

25.   Let us now answer the second question. Political progress at home and perseverance in the War of Resistance are inseparable. The greater the political progress, the more we can persevere in the war, and the more we persevere in the war, the greater the political progress. But, fundamentally, everything depends on our perseverance in the War of Resistance. The unhealthy phenomena in various fields under the Kuomintang regime are very serious, and the accumulation of these undesirable factors over the years has caused great anxiety and vexation among the broad ranks of our patriots. But there is no ground for pessimism, since experience in the War of Resistance has already proved that the Chinese people have made as much progress in the last ten months as in many years in the past. Although the cumulative effects of long years of corruption are seriously retarding the growth of the people's strength to resist Japan, thus reducing the extent of our victories and causing us losses in the war, yet the over-all situation in China, in Japan and in the world is such that the Chinese people cannot but make progress. This progress will be slow because of the factor of corruption, which impedes progress. Progress and the slow pace of progress are two characteristics of the present situation, and the second ill accords with the urgent needs of the war, which is a source of great concern to patriots. But we are in the midst of a revolutionary war, and revolutionary war is an antitoxin which not only eliminates the enemy's poison but also purges us of our own filth. Every just, revolutionary war is endowed with tremendous power, which can transform many things or clear the way for their transformation. The Sino-Japanese war will transform both China and Japan; provided China perseveres in the War of Resistance and in the united front, the old Japan will surely be transformed into a new Japan and the old China into a new China, and people and everything else in both China and Japan will be transformed during and after the war. It is proper for us to regard the anti-Japanese war and our national reconstruction as interconnected. To say that Japan can also be

transformed is to say that the war of aggression by her rulers will end in defeat and may lead to a revolution by the Japanese people. The day of triumph of the Japanese people's revolution will be the day Japan is transformed. All this is closely linked with China's War of Resistance and is a prospect we should take into account.

THE THEORY OF NATIONAL SUBJUGATION
IS WRONG
AND THE THEORY OF QUICK VICTORY
IS LIKEWISE WRONG

26. In our comparative study of the enemy and ourselves with respect to the basic contradictory characteristics, such as relative strength, relative size, progress or reaction, and the relative extent of support, we have already refuted the theory of national subjugation, and we have explained why compromise is unlikely and why political progress is possible. The subjugationists stress the contradiction between strength and weakness and puff it up until it becomes the basis of their whole argument on the question, neglecting all the other contradictions. Their preoccupation with the contrast in strength shows their one-sidedness, and their exaggeration of this one side of the matter into the whole shows their subjectivism. Thus, if one looks at the matter as a whole, it will be seen that they have no ground to stand on and are wrong. As for those who are neither subjugationists nor confirmed pessimists, but who are in a pessimistic frame of mind for the moment simply because they are confused by the disparity between our strength and that of the enemy at a given time and in certain respects or by the corruption in the country, we should point out to them that their approach also tends to be one-sided and subjective. But in their case correction is relatively easy; once they are alerted, they will understand, for they are patriots and their error is only momentary.

27. The exponents of quick victory are likewise wrong. Either they completely forget the contradiction between strength and weakness, remembering only the other contradictions, or they exaggerate China's advantages beyond all semblance of reality and beyond recognition, or they presumptuously take the balance of forces at one time and place for the whole situation, as in the old saying, "A leaf

before the eye shuts out Mount Tail" In a word, they lack the courage to admit that the enemy is strong while we are weak. They often deny this point and consequently deny one aspect of the truth. Nor do they have the courage to admit the limitations of our advantages, and thus they deny another aspect of the truth. The result is that they make mistakes, big and small, and here again it is subjectivism and one-sidedness that are doing the mischief. These friends have their hearts in the right place, and they, too, are patriots. But while "the gentlemen's aspirations are indeed lofty", their views are wrong, and to act according to them would certainly be to run into a brick wall. For if appraisal does not conform to reality, action cannot attain its objective; and to act notwithstanding would mean the army's defeat and the nation's subjugation, so that the result would be the same as with the defeatists. Hence this theory of quick victory will not do either.

28. Do we deny the danger of national subjugation? No, we do not. We recognize that China faces two possible prospects, liberation or subjugation, and that the two are in violent conflict. Our task is to achieve liberation and to avert subjugation. The conditions for liberation are China's progress, which is basic, the enemy's difficulties, and international support. We differ from the subjugationists. Taking an objective and all-sided view, we recognize the two possibilities of national subjugation and liberation, stress that liberation is the dominant possibility, point out the conditions for its achievement, and strive to secure them. The subjugationists, on the other hand, taking a subjective and one-sided view, recognize only one possibility, that of subjugation; they do not admit the possibility of liberation, and still less point out the conditions necessary for liberation or strive to secure them. Moreover, while acknowledging the tendency to compromise and the corruption, we see other tendencies and phenomena which, we indicate, will gradually prevail and are already in violent conflict with the former; in addition, we point out the

conditions necessary for the healthy tendencies and phenomena to prevail, and we strive to overcome the tendency to compromise and to change the state of corruption. Therefore, contrary to the pessimists, we are not at all down-hearted.

29. Not that we would not like a quick victory; everybody would be in favour of driving the "devils" out overnight. But we point out that, in the absence of certain definite conditions, quick victory is something that exists only in one's mind and not in objective reality, and that it is a mere illusion, a false theory. Accordingly, having made an objective and comprehensive appraisal of all the circumstances concerning both the enemy and ourselves, we point out that the only way to final victory is the strategy of protracted war, and we reject the groundless theory of quick victory. We maintain that we must strive to secure all the conditions indispensable to final victory, and the more fully and the earlier these conditions are secured, the surer we shall be of victory and the earlier we shall win it. We believe that only in this way can the course of the war be shortened, and we reject the theory of quick victory, which is just idle talk and an effort to get things on the cheap.

WHY A PROTRACTED WAR?

30. Let us now examine the problem of protracted war. A correct answer to the question "Why a protracted war?" can be arrived at only on the basis of all the fundamental contrasts between China and Japan. For instance, if we say merely that the enemy is a strong imperialist power while we are a weak semi-colonial and semi-feudal country, we are in danger of falling into the theory of national subjugation. For neither in theory nor in practice can a struggle become protracted by simply pitting the weak against the strong. Nor can it become protracted by simply pitting the big against the small, the progressive against the reactionary, or abundant support against meagre support. The annexation of a small country by a big one or of a big country by a small one is a common occurrence. It often happens that a progressive country which is not strong is destroyed by a big, reactionary country, and the same holds for everything that is progressive but not strong. Abundant or meagre support is an important but a subsidiary factor, and the degree of its effect depends upon the fundamental factors on both sides. Therefore when we say that the War of Resistance Against Japan is a protracted war, our conclusion is derived from the interrelations of all the factors at work on both sides. The enemy is strong and we are weak, and the danger of subjugation is there. But in other respects the enemy has shortcomings and we have advantages. The enemy's advantage can be reduced and his shortcomings aggravated by our efforts. On the other hand, our advantages can be enhanced and our shortcoming remedied by our efforts. Hence, we can win final victory and avert subjugation, while the enemy will ultimately be defeated and will be unable to avert the collapse of his whole imperialist system.

31. Since the enemy has advantages only in one respect but shortcomings in all others and we have shortcomings in only one respect but advantages in all others, why has this

produced not a balance, but, on the contrary, a superior position for him and an inferior position for us at the present time? Quite clearly, we cannot consider the question in such a formal way. The fact is that the disparity between the enemy's strength and our own is now so great that the enemy's shortcomings have not developed, and for the time being cannot develop, to a degree sufficient to offset his strength, while our advantages have not developed, and for the time being cannot develop, to a degree sufficient to compensate for our weakness. Therefore there can as yet be no balance, only imbalance.

32. Although our efforts in persevering in the War of Resistance and the united front have somewhat changed the enemy's strength and superiority as against our weakness and inferiority, there has as yet been no basic change. Hence during a certain stage of the war, to a certain degree the enemy will be victorious and we shall suffer defeat. But why is it that in this stage the enemy's victories and our defeats are definitely restricted in degree and cannot be transcended by complete victory or complete defeat? The reason is that, first, from the very beginning the enemy's strength and our weakness have been relative and not absolute, and that, second, our efforts in persevering in the War of Resistance and in the united front have further accentuated this relativeness. In comparison with the original situation, the enemy is still strong, but unfavourable factors have reduced his strength, although not yet to a degree sufficient to destroy his superiority, and similarly we are still weak, but favourable factors have compensated for our weakness, although not yet to a degree sufficient to transform our inferiority. Thus it turns out that the enemy is relatively strong and we are relatively weak, that the enemy is in a relatively superior and we are in a relatively inferior position. On both sides, strength and weakness, superiority and inferiority, have never been absolute, and besides, our efforts in persevering in resistance to Japan and in

the united front during the war have brought about further changes in the original balance of forces between us and the enemy. Therefore, in this stage the enemy's victory and our defeat are definitely restricted in degree, and hence the war becomes protracted.

33. But circumstances are continually changing. In the course of the war, provided we employ correct military and political tactics, make no mistakes of principle and exert our best efforts, the enemy's disadvantages and China's advantages will both grow as the war is drawn out, with the inevitable result that there will be a continual change in the difference in comparative strength and hence in the relative position of the two sides. When a new stage is reached, a great change will take place in the balance of forces, resulting in the enemy's defeat and our victory.

34. At present the enemy can still manage to exploit his strength, and our War of Resistance has not yet fundamentally weakened him. The insufficiency in his manpower and material resources is not yet such as to prevent his offensive; on the contrary, they can still sustain his offensive to a certain extent. The reactionary and barbarous nature of his war, a factor which intensifies both class antagonisms within Japan and the resistance of the Chinese nation, has not yet brought about a situation which radically impedes his advance. The enemy's international isolation is increasing but is not yet complete. In many countries which have indicated they will help us, the capitalists dealing in munitions and war materials and bent solely on profit are still furnishing Japan with large quantities of war supplies, [12] and their governments [13] are still reluctant to join the Soviet Union in practical sanctions against Japan. From all this it follows that our War of Resistance cannot be won quickly and can only be a protracted war. As for China, although there has been some improvement with regard to her weakness in the military, economic, political and cultural

spheres in the ten months of resistance, it is still a long way from what is required to prevent the enemy's offensive and prepare our counteroffensive. Moreover, quantitatively speaking, we have had to sustain certain losses. Although all the factors favourable to us are having a positive effect, it will not be sufficient to halt the enemy's offensive and to prepare for our counter-offensive unless we make an immense effort. Neither the abolition of corruption and the acceleration of progress at home, nor the curbing of the pro-Japanese forces and the expansion of the anti-Japanese forces abroad, are yet accomplished facts. From all this it follows that our war cannot be won quickly but can only be a protracted war.

THE THREE STAGES OF THE PROTRACTED WAR

35. Since the Sino-Japanese war is a protracted one and final victory will belong to China, it can reasonably be assumed that this protracted war will pass through three stages. The first stage covers the period of the enemy's strategic offensive and our strategic defensive. The second stage will be the period of the enemy's strategic consolidation and our preparation for the counter-offensive. The third stage will be the period of our strategic counter-offensive and the enemy's strategic retreat. It is impossible to predict the concrete situation in the three stages, but certain main trends in the war may be pointed out in the light of present conditions. The objective course of events will be exceedingly rich and varied, with many twists and turns, and nobody can cast a horoscope for the Sino-Japanese war; nevertheless it is necessary for the strategic direction of the war to make a rough sketch of its trends. Although our sketch may not be in full accord with the subsequent facts and will be amended by them, it is still necessary to make it in order to give firm and purposeful strategic direction to the protracted war.

36. The first stage has not yet ended. The enemy's design is to occupy Canton, Wuhan and Lanchow and link up these three points. To accomplish this aim the enemy will have to use at least fifty divisions, or about one and a half million men, spend from one and a half to two years, and expend more than ten thousand million yen. In penetrating so deeply, he will encounter immense difficulties, with consequences disastrous beyond imagination. As for attempting to occupy the entire length of the Canton-Hankow Railway and the Sian-Lanchow Highway, he will have to fight perilous battles and even so may not fully accomplish his design. But in drawing up our operational plan we should base ourselves on the assumption that the enemy may occupy the three points and even certain additional areas, as well as link them up, and we should make

dispositions for a protracted war, so that even if he does so, we shall be able to cope with him. In this stage the form of fighting we should adopt is primarily mobile warfare, supplemented by guerrilla and positional warfare. Through the subjective errors of the Kuomintang military authorities, positional warfare was assigned the primary role in the first phase of this stage, but it is nevertheless supplementary from the point of view of the stage as a whole. In this stage, China has already built up a broad united front and achieved unprecedented unity. Although the enemy has used and will continue to use base and shameless means to induce China to capitulate in the attempt to realize his plan for a quick decision and to conquer the whole country without much effort, he has failed so far, nor is he likely to succeed in the future. In this stage, in spite of considerable losses, China will make considerable progress, which will become the main basis for her continued resistance in the second stage. In the present stage the Soviet Union has already given substantial aid to China. On the enemy side, there are already signs of flagging morale, and his army's momentum of attack is less in the middle phase of this stage than it was in the initial phase, and it will diminish still further in the concluding phase. Signs of exhaustion are beginning to appear in his finances and economy; war-weariness is beginning to set in among his people and troops; and within the clique at the helm of the war, "war frustrations" are beginning to manifest themselves and pessimism about the prospects of the war is growing.

37. The second stage may be termed one of strategic stalemate. At the tail end of the first stage, the enemy will be forced to fix certain terminal points to his strategic offensive owing to his shortage of troops and our firm resistance, and upon reaching them he will stop his strategic offensive and enter the stage of safeguarding his occupied areas. In the second stage, the enemy will attempt to safeguard the occupied areas and to make them his own by the fraudulent method of

setting up puppet governments, while plundering the Chinese people to the limit; but again he will be confronted with stubborn guerrilla warfare. Taking advantage of the fact that the enemy's rear is unguarded, our guerrilla warfare will develop extensively in the first stage, and many base areas will be established, seriously threatening the enemy's consolidation of the occupied areas, and so in the second stage there will still be widespread fighting. In this stage, our form; of fighting will be primarily guerrilla warfare, supplemented by mobile warfare. China will still retain a large regular army, but she will find it difficult to launch the strategic counter-offensive immediately because, on the one hand, the enemy will adopt a strategically defensive position in the big cities and along the main lines of communication under his occupation and, on the other hand, China will not yet be adequately equipped technically. Except for the troops engaged in frontal defence against the enemy, our forces will be switched in large numbers to the enemy's rear in comparatively dispersed dispositions, and, basing themselves on all the areas not actually occupied by the enemy and co-ordinating with the people's local armed forces, they will launch extensive, fierce guerrilla warfare against enemy-occupied areas, keeping the enemy on the move as far as possible in order to destroy him in mobile warfare, as is now being done in Shansi Province. The fighting in the second stage will be ruthless, and the country will suffer serious devastation. But the guerrilla warfare will be successful, and if it is well conducted the enemy may be able to retain only about one-third of his occupied territory, with the remaining two-thirds in our hands, and this will constitute a great defeat for the enemy and a great victory for China. By then the enemy-occupied territory as a whole will fall into three categories: first, the enemy base areas; second, our base areas for guerrilla warfare; and, third, the guerrilla areas contested by both sides. The duration of this stage will depend on the degree of change in the balance of forces between us and the enemy and on the changes in the international situation; generally speaking, we should be prepared to see this stage last a comparatively long time and to weather its hardships. It will be a very painful period for China; the two big problems will be economic difficulties and the disruptive activities of the traitors. The enemy will go all out to wreck China's united front, and the traitor organizations in all the occupied areas will merge into a so-called "unified government". Owing to the loss of big cities and the hardships of war, vacillating elements within our ranks will clamour for compromise, and pessimism will grow to a serious extent. Our tasks will then be to mobilize the whole people to unite as one man and carry on the war with unflinching perseverance, to broaden and consolidate the united front, sweep away all pessimism and ideas of compromise, promote the will to hard struggle and apply new wartime policies, and so to weather the hardships. In the second stage, we will have to call upon the whole country resolutely to maintain a united government, we will have to oppose splits and systematically improve fighting techniques, reform the armed forces, mobilize the entire people and prepare for the counter-offensive. The international situation will become still more unfavourable to Japan and the main international forces will incline towards giving more help to China, even though there may be talk of "realism" of the Chamberlain type which accommodates itself to fait accomplis. Japan's threat to Southeast Asia and Siberia will become greater, and there may even be another war. As regards Japan, scores of her divisions will be inextricably bogged down in China. Widespread guerrilla warfare and the people's anti-Japanese movement will wear down this big Japanese force, greatly reducing it and also disintegrating its morale by stimulating the growth of homesickness, war-weariness and even anti-war sentiment. Though it would be wrong to say that Japan will achieve no results at all in her plunder of China, yet, being short of capital and harassed by guerrilla warfare, she cannot possibly achieve rapid or substantial results. This second stage will be the transitional stage of the entire war; it will be the most trying period but also the pivotal one. Whether China becomes an independent country or is reduced to a colony will be determined not by the retention or loss of the big cities in the first stage but by the extent to which the whole nation exerts itself in the second. If we can persevere in the War of Resistance, in the united front and in the protracted war, China will in that stage gain the power to change from weakness to strength. It will be the second act in the three-act drama of China's War of Resistance. And through the efforts of the entire cast it will become possible to perform a most brilliant last act.

38.   The third stage will be the stage of the counter-offensive to recover our lost territories. Their recovery will depend mainly upon the strength which China has built up in the preceding stage and which will continue to grow in the third stage. But China's strength alone will not be sufficient, and we shall also have to rely on the support of international forces and on the changes that will take place inside Japan, or otherwise we shall not be able to win; this adds to China's tasks in international propaganda and diplomacy. In the third stage, our war will no longer be one of strategic defensive, but will turn into a strategic counter-offensive manifesting itself in strategic offensives; and it will no longer be fought on strategically interior lines, but will shift gradually to strategically exterior lines. Not until we fight our way to the Yalu River can this war be considered over. The third stage will be the last in the protracted war, and when we talk of persevering in the war to the end, we mean going all the way through this stage. Our primary form of fighting will still be mobile warfare, but positional warfare will rise to importance. While positional defence cannot be regarded as important in the first stage because of the prevailing circumstances, positional attack will become quite important in the third stage because of the changed conditions and the requirements of the task. In the third stage guerrilla warfare will again provide

strategic support by supplementing mobile and positional warfare, but it will not be the primary form as in the second stage.

39.   It is thus obvious that the war is protracted and consequently ruthless in nature. The enemy will not be able to gobble up the whole of China but will be able to occupy many places for a considerable time. China will not be able to oust the Japanese quickly, but the greater part of her territory will remain in her hands. Ultimately the enemy will lose and we will win, but we shall have a hard stretch of road to travel.

40.   The Chinese people will become tempered in the course of this long and ruthless war. The political parties taking part in the war will also be steeled and tested. The united front must be persevered in; only by persevering in the united front can we persevere in the war; and only by persevering in the united front and in the war can we win final victory. Only thus can all difficulties be overcome. After travelling the hard stretch of road we shall reach the highway to victory. This is the natural logic of the war.

41.   In the three stages the changes in relative strength will proceed along the following lines. In the first stage, the enemy is superior and we are inferior in strength. With regard to our inferiority we must reckon on changes of two different kinds from the eve of the War of Resistance to the end of this stage. The first kind is a change for the worse. China's original inferiority will be aggravated by war losses, namely, decreases in territory, population, economic strength, military strength and cultural institutions. Towards the end of the first stage, the decrease will probably be considerable, especially on the economic side. This point will be exploited by some people as a basis for their theories of national subjugation and of compromise. But the second kind of change, the change for the better, must also be noted. It includes the experience gained in

the war, the progress made by the armed forces, the political progress, the mobilization of the people, the development of culture in a new direction, the emergence of guerrilla warfare, the increase in international support, etc. What is on the downgrade in the first stage is the old quantity and the old quality, the manifestations being mainly quantitative. What is on the upgrade is the new quantity and the new quality, the manifestations being mainly qualitative. It is the second kind of change that provides a basis for our ability to fight a protracted war and win final victory.

42.   In the first stage, changes of two kinds are also occurring on the enemy's side. The first kind is a change for the worse and manifests itself in hundreds of thousands of casualties, the drain on arms and ammunition, deterioration of troop morale, popular discontent at home, shrinkage of trade, the expenditure of over ten thousand million yen, condemnation by world opinion, etc. This trend also provides a basis for our ability to fight a protracted war and win final victory. But we must likewise reckon with the second kind of change on the enemy's side, a change for the better, that is, his expansion in territory, population and resources. This too is a basis for the protracted nature of our War of Resistance and the impossibility of quick victory, but at the same time certain people will use it as a basis for their theories of national subjugation and of compromise. However, we must take into account the transitory and partial character of this change for the better on the enemy's side. Japan is an imperialist power heading for collapse, and her occupation of China's territory is temporary. The vigorous growth of guerrilla warfare in China will restrict her actual occupation to narrow zones. Moreover, her occupation of Chinese territory has created and intensified contradictions between Japan and other foreign countries. Besides, generally speaking, such occupation involves a considerable period in which Japan will make capital outlays without drawing any profits, as is shown by the experience in

the three northeastern provinces. All of which again gives us a basis for demolishing the theories of national subjugation and of compromise and for establishing the theories of protracted war and of final victory.

43. In the second stage, the above changes on both sides will continue to develop. While the situation cannot be predicted in detail, on the whole Japan will continue on the downgrade and China on the upgrade. [14] For example, Japan's military and financial resources will be seriously drained by China's guerrilla warfare, popular discontent will grow in Japan, the morale of her troops will deteriorate further, and she will become more isolated internationally. As for China, she will make further progress in the political, military and cultural spheres and in the mobilization of the people; guerrilla warfare will develop further; there will be some new economic growth on the basis of the small industries and the widespread agriculture in the interior; international support will gradually increase; and the whole picture will be quite different from what it is now. This second stage may last quite a long time, during which there will be a great reversal in the balance of forces, with China gradually rising and Japan gradually declining. China will emerge from her inferior position, and Japan will lose her superior position; first the two countries will become evenly matched, and then their relative positions will be reversed. Thereupon, China will in general have completed her preparations for the strategic counter-offensive and will enter the stage of the counter-offensive and the expulsion of the enemy. It should be reiterated that the change from inferiority to superiority and the completion of preparations for the counter-offensive will involve three things, namely, an increase in China's own strength, an increase in Japan's difficulties, and an increase in international support; it is the combination of all these forces that will bring about China's superiority and the completion of her preparations for the counter-offensive.

44.   Because of the unevenness in China's political and economic development, the strategic counter-offensive of the third stage will not present a uniform and even picture throughout the country in its initial phase but will be regional in character, rising here and subsiding there. During this stage, the enemy will not relax his divisive tricks to break China's united front, hence the task of maintaining internal unity in China will become still more important, and we shall have to ensure that the strategic counter-offensive does not collapse halfway through internal dissension. In this period the international situation will become very favourable to China. China's task will be to take advantage of it in order to attain complete liberation and establish an independent democratic state, which at the same time will mean helping the world anti-fascist movement.

45.   China moving from inferiority to parity and then to superiority, Japan moving from superiority to parity and then to inferiority; China moving from the defensive to stalemate and then to the counter-offensive, Japan moving from the offensive to the safeguarding of her gains and then to retreat -- such will be the course of the Sino-Japanese war and its inevitable trend.

46.   Hence the questions and the conclusions are as follows: Will China be subjugated? The answer is; No, she will not be subjugated, but will win final victory. Can China win quickly? The answer is, No, she cannot win quickly, and the war must be a protracted one. Are these conclusions correct? I think they are.

47.   At this point, the exponents of national subjugation and of compromise will again rush in and say, "To move from inferiority to parity China needs a military and economic power equal to Japan's, and to move from parity to superiority she will need a military and economic power greater than

Japan's. But this is impossible, hence the above conclusions are not correct."

48. This is the so-called theory that "weapons decide everything", [15] which constitutes a mechanical approach to the question of war and a subjective and one-sided view. Our view is opposed to this; we see not only weapons but also people. Weapons are an important factor in war, but not the decisive factor; it is people, not things, that are decisive. The contest of strength is not only a contest of military and economic power, but also a contest of human power and morale. Military and economic power is necessarily wielded by people. If the great majority of the Chinese, of the Japanese and of the people of other countries are on the side of our War of Resistance Against Japan, how can Japan's military and economic power, wielded as it is by a small minority through coercion, count as superiority? And if not, then does not China, though wielding relatively inferior military and economic power, become the superior? There is no doubt that China will gradually grow in military and economic power, provided she perseveres in the War of Resistance and in the united front. As for our enemy, weakened as he will be by the long war and by internal and external contradictions, his military and economic power is bound to change in the reverse direction. In these circumstances, is there any reason why China cannot become the superior? And that is not all. Although we cannot as yet count the military and economic power of other countries as being openly and to any great extent on our side, is there any reason why we will not be able to do so in the future? If Japan's enemy is not just China, if in future one or more other countries make open use of their considerable military and economic power defensively or offensively against Japan and openly help us, then will not our superiority be still greater? Japan is a small country, her war is reactionary and barbarous, and she will become more and more isolated internationally; China is a large country, her war is progressive and just, and

she will enjoy more and more support internationally. Is there any reason why the long-term development of these factors should not definitely change the relative position between the enemy and ourselves?

49.   The exponents of quick victory, however, do not realize that war is a contest of strength, and that before a certain change has taken place in the relative strength of the belligerents, there is no basis for trying to fight strategically decisive battles and shorten the road to liberation. Were their ideas to be put into practice, we should inevitably run our heads into a brick wall. Or perhaps they are just talking for their own pleasure without really intending to put their ideas into practice. In the end Mr. Reality will come and pour a bucket of cold water over these chatterers, showing them up as mere windbags who want to get things on the cheap, to have gains without pains. We have had this kind of idle chatter before and we have it now, though not very much so far; but there may be more as the war develops into the stage of stalemate and then of counter-offensive. But in the meantime, if China's losses in the first stage are fairly heavy and the second stage drags on very long, the theories of national subjugation and of compromise will gain great currency. Therefore, our fire should be directed mainly against them and only secondarily against the idle chatter about quick victory.

50. That the war will be protracted is certain, but nobody can predict exactly how many months or years it will last, as this depends entirely upon the degree of the change in the balance of forces. All those who wish to shorten the war have no alternative but to work hard to increase our own strength and reduce that of the enemy. Specifically, the only way is to strive to win more battles and wear down the enemy's forces, develop guerrilla warfare to reduce enemy-occupied territory to a minimum, consolidate and expand the united front to rally the forces of the whole nation, build up new armies and develop

new war industries, promote political, economic and cultural progress, mobilize the workers, peasants, businessmen, intellectuals and other sections of the people, disintegrate the enemy forces and win over their soldiers, carry on international propaganda to secure foreign support, and win the support of the Japanese people and other oppressed peoples. Only by doing all this can we reduce the duration of the war. There is no magic short-cut.

A WAR OF JIG-SAW PATTERN

51. We can say with certainty that the protracted War of Resistance Against Japan will write a splendid page unique in the war history of mankind. One of the special features of this war is the interlocking "jig-saw" pattern which arises from such contradictory factors as the barbarity of Japan and her shortage of troops on the one hand, and the progressiveness of China and the extensiveness of her territory on the other. There have been other wars of jig-saw pattern in history, the three years' civil war in Russia after the October Revolution being a case in point. But what distinguishes this war in China is its especially protracted and extensive character, which will set a record in history. Its jig-saw pattern manifests itself as follows.

52. Interior and exterior lines. The anti-Japanese war as a whole is being fought on interior lines; but as far as the relation between the main forces and the guerrilla units is concerned, the former are on the interior lines while the latter are on the exterior lines, presenting a remarkable spectacle of pincers around the enemy. The same can be said of the relationship between the various guerrilla areas. From its own viewpoint each guerrilla area is on interior lines and the other areas are on exterior lines; together they form many battle fronts, which hold the enemy in pincers. In the first stage of the war, the regular army operating strategically on interior lines is withdrawing, but the guerrilla units operating strategically on exterior lines will advance with great strides over wide areas to the rear of the enemy -- they will advance even more fiercely in the second stage -- thereby presenting a remarkable picture of both withdrawal and advance.

53. Possession and non-possession of a rear area. The main forces, which extend the front lines to the outer limits of the enemy's occupied areas, are operating from the rear area of the country as a whole. The guerrilla units, which extend the

battle lines into the enemy rear, are separated from the rear area of the country as a whole. But each guerrilla area has a small rear of its own, upon which it relies to establish its fluid battle lines. The case is different with the guerrilla detachments which are dispatched by a guerrilla area for short-term operations in the rear of the enemy in the same area; such detachments have no rear, nor do they have a battle line. "Operating without a rear area" is a special feature of revolutionary war in the new era, wherever a vast territory, a progressive people, and an advanced political party and army are to be found; there is nothing to fear but much to gain from it, and far from having doubts about it we should promote it.

54. Encirclement and counter-encirclement. Taking the war as a whole, there is no doubt that we are strategically encircled by the enemy because he is on the strategic offensive and operating on exterior lines while we are on the strategic defensive and operating on interior lines. This is the first form of enemy encirclement. We on our part can encircle one or more of the enemy columns advancing on us along separate routes, because we apply the policy of fighting campaigns and battles from tactically exterior lines by using numerically preponderant forces against these enemy columns advancing on us from strategically exterior lines. This is the first form of our counter-encirclement of the enemy. Next, if we consider the guerrilla base areas in the enemy's rear, each area taken singly is surrounded by the enemy on all sides, like the Wutai Mountains, or on three sides, like the northwestern Shansi area. This is the second form of enemy encirclement. However, if one considers all the guerrilla base areas together and in their relation to the positions of the regular forces, one can see that we in turn surround a great many enemy forces. In Shansi Province, for instance, we have surrounded the Tatung-Puchow Railway on three sides (the east and west flanks and the southern end) and the city of Taiynan on all sides; and there are many similar instances in Hopei and Shantung Provinces. This

is the second form of our counter-encirclement of the enemy. Thus there are two forms of encirclement by the enemy forces and two forms of encirclement by our own -- rather like a game of weichi. [16] Campaigns and battles fought by the two sides resemble the capturing of each other's pieces, and the establishment of enemy strongholds (such as Taiyuan) and our guerrilla base areas (such as the Wutai Mountains) resembles moves to dominate spaces on the board. If the game of weichi is extended to include the world, there is yet a third form of encirclement as between us and the enemy, namely, the interrelation between the front of aggression and the front of peace. The enemy encircles China, the Soviet Union, France and Czechoslovakia with his front of aggression, while we counter-encircle Germany, Japan and Italy with our front of peace. But our encirclement, like the hand of Buddha, will turn into the Mountain of Five Elements lying athwart the Universe, and the modern Sun Wu-kungs [17] -- the fascist aggressors -- will finally be buried underneath it, never to rise again. Therefore, if on the international plane we can create an anti-Japanese front in the Pacific region, with China as one strategic unit, with the Soviet Union and other countries which may join it as other strategic units, and with the Japanese people's movement as still another strategic unit, and thus form a gigantic net from which the fascist Sun Wu-kungs can kind no escape, then that will be our enemy's day of doom. Indeed, the day when this gigantic net is formed will undoubtedly be the day of the complete overthrow of Japanese imperialism. We are not jesting; this is the inevitable trend of the war.

55. Big areas and little areas. There is a possibility that the enemy will occupy the greater part of Chinese territory south of the Great Wall, and only the smaller part will be kept intact. That is one aspect of the situation. But within this greater part, which does not include the three northeastern provinces, the enemy can actually hold only the big cities, the main lines of communication and some of the plains -- which

may rank first in importance, but will probably constitute only the smaller part of the occupied territory in size and population, while the greater part will be taken up by the guerrilla areas that will grow up everywhere. That is another aspect of the situation. If we go beyond the provinces south of the Great Wall and include Mongolia, Sinkiang, Chinghai and Tibet, then the unoccupied area will constitute the greater part of China's territory, and the enemy-occupied area will become the smaller part, even with the three northeastern provinces. That is yet another aspect of the situation. The area kept intact is undoubtedly important, and we should devote great efforts to developing it, not only politically, militarily and economically but, what is also important, culturally. The enemy has transformed our former cultural centres into culturally backward areas, and we on our part must transform the former culturally backward areas into cultural centres. At the same time, the work of developing extensive guerrilla areas behind the enemy lines is also extremely important, and we should attend to every aspect of this work, including the cultural. All in all, big pieces of China's territory, namely, the rural areas, will be transformed into regions of progress and light, while the small pieces, namely, the enemy-occupied areas and especially the big cities, will temporarily become regions of backwardness and darkness.

56. Thus it can be seen that the protracted and far-flung War of Resistance Against Japan is a war of a jig-saw pattern militarily, politically, economically and culturally. It is a marvellous spectacle in the annals of war, a heroic undertaking by the Chinese nation, a magnificent and earth-shaking feat. This war will not only affect China and Japan, strongly impelling both to advance, but will also affect the whole world, impelling all nations, especially the oppressed nations such as India, to march forward. Every Chinese should consciously throw himself into this war of a jig-saw pattern, for this is the form of war by which the Chinese nation is liberating itself, the

special form of war of liberation waged by a big semi-colonial country in the Nineteen Thirties and the Nineteen Forties.

FIGHTING FOR PERPETUAL PEACE

57. The protracted nature of China's anti-Japanese war is inseparably connected with the fight for perpetual peace in China and the whole world. Never has there been a historical period such as the present in which war is so close to perpetual peace. For several thousand years since the emergence of classes, the life of mankind has been full of wars; each nation has fought countless wars, either internally or with other nations. In the imperialist epoch of capitalist society, wars are waged on a particularly extensive scale and with a peculiar ruthlessness. The first great imperialist war of twenty years ago was the first of its kind in history, but not the last. Only the war which has now begun comes close to being the final war, that is, comes close to the perpetual peace of mankind. By now one-third of the world's population has entered the war. Look! Italy, then Japan; Abyssinia, then Spain, then China. The population of the countries at war now amounts to almost 600 million, or nearly a third of the total population of the world. The characteristics of the present war are its uninterruptedness and its proximity to perpetual peace. Why is it uninterrupted? After attacking Abyssinia, Italy attacked Spain, and Germany joined in; then Japan attacked China. What will come next? Undoubtedly Hitler will fight the great powers. "Fascism is war" [18] -- this is perfectly true. There will be no interruption in the development of the present war into a world war; mankind will not be able to avoid the calamity of war. Why then do we say the present war is near to perpetual peace? The present war is the result of the development of the general crisis of world capitalism which began with World War I; this general crisis is driving the capitalist countries into a new war and, above all, driving the fascist countries into new war adventures. This war, we can foresee, will not save capitalism, but will hasten its collapse. It will be greater in scale and more ruthless than the war of twenty years ago, all nations will inevitably be drawn in, it will drag on for a very long time, and

mankind will suffer greatly. But, owing to the existence of the Soviet Union and the growing political consciousness of the people of the world, great revolutionary wars will undoubtedly emerge from this war to oppose all counter-revolutionary wars, thus giving this war the character of a struggle for perpetual peace. Even if later there should be another period of war, perpetual world peace will not be far off. Once man has eliminated capitalism, he will attain the era of perpetual peace, and there will be no more need for war. Neither armies, nor warships, nor military aircraft, nor poison gas will then be needed. Thereafter and for all time, mankind will never again know war. The revolutionary wars which have already begun are part of the war for perpetual peace. The war between China and Japan, two countries which have a combined population of over 500 million, will take an important place in this war for perpetual peace, and out of it will come the liberation of the Chinese nation. The liberated new China of the future will be inseparable from the liberated new world of the future. Hence our War of Resistance Against Japan takes on the character of a struggle for perpetual peace.

58. History shows that wars are divided into two kinds, just and unjust. All wars that are progressive are just, and all wars that impede progress are unjust. We Communists oppose all unjust wars that impede progress, but we do not oppose progressive, just wars. Not only do we Communists not oppose just wars, we actively participate in them. As for unjust wars, World War I is an instance in which both sides fought for imperialist interests; therefore the Communists of the whole world firmly opposed that war. The way to oppose a war of this kind is to do everything possible to prevent it before it breaks out and, once it breaks out, to oppose war with war, to oppose unjust war with just war, whenever possible. Japan's war is an unjust war that impedes progress, and the peoples of the world, including the Japanese people, should oppose it and are opposing it. In our country the people and the government, the

Communist Party and the Kuomintang, have all raised the banner of righteousness in the national revolutionary war against aggression. Our war is sacred and just, it is progressive and its aim is peace. The aim is peace not just in one country but throughout the world, not just temporary but perpetual peace. To achieve this aim we must wage a life-and-death struggle, be prepared for any sacrifice, persevere to the end and never stop short of the goal. However great the sacrifice and however long the time needed to attain it, a new world of perpetual peace and brightness already lies clearly before us. Our faith in waging this war is based upon the new China and the new world of perpetual peace and brightness for which we are striving. Fascism and imperialism wish to perpetuate war, but we wish to put an end to it in the not too distant future. The great majority of mankind should exert their utmost efforts for this purpose. The 450 million people of China constitute one quarter of the world's population, and if by their concerted efforts they overthrow Japanese imperialism and create a new China of freedom and equality, they will most certainly be making a tremendous contribution to the struggle for perpetual world peace. This is no vain hope, for the whole world is approaching this point in the course of its social and economic development, and provided that the majority of mankind work together, our goal will surely be attained in several decades.

MAN'S DYNAMIC ROLE IN WAR

59. We have so far explained why the war is a protracted war and why the final victory will be China's, and in the main dealt with what protracted war is and what it is not. Now we shall turn to the question of what to do and what not to do. How to conduct protracted war and how to win the final victory? These are the questions answered below. We shall therefore successively discuss the following problems: man's dynamic role in war, war and politics, political mobilization for the War of Resistance, the object of war, offence within defence, quick decisions within a protracted war, exterior lines within interior lines, initiative, flexibility, planning, mobile warfare, guerrilla warfare' positional warfare, war of annihilation, war of attrition, the possibilities of exploiting the enemy's mistakes, the question of decisive engagements in the anti-Japanese war, and the army and the people as the foundation of victory. Let us start with the problem of man's dynamic role.

60. When we say we are opposed to a subjective approach to problems, we mean that we must oppose ideas which are not based upon or do not correspond to objective facts, because such ideas are fanciful and fallacious and will lead to failure if acted on. But whatever is done has to be done by human beings; protracted war and final victory will not come about without human action. For such action to be effective there must be people who derive ideas, principles or views from the objective facts, and put forward plans, directives, policies, strategies and tactics. Ideas, etc. are subjective, while deeds or actions are the subjective translated into the objective, but both represent the dynamic role peculiar to human beings. We term this kind of dynamic role "man's conscious dynamic role", and it is a characteristic that distinguishes man from all other beings. All ideas based upon and corresponding to objective facts are correct ideas, and all

deeds or actions based upon correct ideas are correct actions. We must give full scope to these ideas and actions, to this dynamic role. The anti-Japanese war is being waged to drive out imperialism and transform the old China into a new China; this can be achieved only when the whole Chinese people are mobilized and full scope is given to their conscious dynamic role in resisting Japan. If we just sit by and take no action, only subjugation awaits us and there will be neither protracted war nor final victory.

61. It is a human characteristic to exercise a conscious dynamic role. Man strongly displays this characteristic in war. True, victory or defeat in war is decided by the military, political, economic and geographical conditions on both sides, the nature of the war each side is waging and the international support each enjoys, but it is not decided by these alone; in themselves, all these provide only the possibility of victory or defeat but do not decide the issue. To decide the issue, subjective effort must be added, namely, the directing and waging of war, man's conscious dynamic role in war.

62. In seeking victory, those who direct a war cannot overstep the limitations imposed by the objective conditions; within these limitations, however, they can and must play a dynamic role in striving for victory. The stage of action for commanders in a war must be built upon objective possibilities, but on that stage they can direct the performance of many a drama, full of sound and colour, power and grandeur. Given the objective material foundations, the commanders in the anti-Japanese war should display their prowess and marshal all their forces to crush the national enemy, transform the present situation in which our country and society are suffering from aggression and oppression, and create a new China of freedom and equality; here is where our subjective faculties for directing war can and must be exercised. We do not want any of our commanders in the war to detach himself from the

objective conditions and become a blundering hothead, but we decidedly want every commander to become a general who is both bold and sagacious. Our commanders should have not only the boldness to overwhelm the enemy but also the ability to remain masters of the situation throughout the changes and vicissitudes of the entire war. Swimming in the ocean of war, they must not flounder but make sure of reaching the opposite shore with measured strokes. Strategy and tactics, as the laws for directing war, constitute the art of swimming in the ocean of war.

WAR AND POLITICS

63. "War is the continuation of politics." In this sense war is politics and war itself is a political action; since ancient times there has never been a war that did not have a political character. The anti-Japanese war is a revolutionary war waged by the whole nation, and victory is inseparable from the political aim of the war -- to drive out Japanese imperialism and build a new China of freedom and equality -- inseparable from the general policy of persevering in the War of Resistance and in the united front, from the mobilization of the entire people, and from the political principles of the unity between officers and men, the unity between army and people and the disintegration of the enemy forces, and inseparable from the effective application of united front policy, from mobilization on the cultural front, and from the efforts to win international support and the support of the people inside Japan. In a word, war cannot for a single moment be separated from politics. Any tendency among the anti-Japanese armed forces to belittle politics by isolating war from it and advocating the idea of war as an absolute is wrong and should be corrected.

64. But war has its own particular characteristics and in this sense it cannot be equated with politics in general. "War is the continuation of politics by other . . . means." [19] When politics develops to a certain stage beyond which it cannot proceed by the usual means, war breaks out to sweep the obstacles from the way. For instance, the semi-independent status of China is an obstacle to the political growth of Japanese imperialism, hence Japan has unleashed a war of aggression to sweep away that obstacle. What about China? Imperialist oppression has long been an obstacle to China's bourgeois-democratic revolution, hence many wars of liberation have been waged in the effort to sweep it away. Japan is now using war for the purpose of oppressing China and completely blocking the advance of the Chinese

revolution, and therefore China is compelled to wage the War of Resistance in her determination to sweep away this obstacle. When the obstacle is removed, our political aim will be attained and the war concluded. But if the obstacle is not completely swept away, the war will have to continue till the aim is fully accomplished. Thus anyone who seeks a compromise before the task of the anti-Japanese war is fulfilled is bound to fail, because even if a compromise were to occur for one reason or another, the war would break out again, since the broad masses of the people would certainly not submit but would continue the war until its political objective was achieved. It can therefore be said that politics is war without bloodshed while war is politics with bloodshed.

65. From the particular characteristics of war there arise a particular set of organizations, a particular series of methods and a particular kind of process. The organizations are the armed forces and everything that goes with them. The methods are the strategy and tactics for directing war. The process is the particular form of social activity in which the opposing armed forces attack each other or defend themselves against one another, employing strategy and tactics favourable to themselves and unfavourable to the enemy. Hence war experience is a particular kind of experience. All who take part in war must rid themselves of their customary ways and accustom themselves to war before they can win victory.

POLITICAL MOBILIZATION FOR
THE WAR OF RESISTANCE

66. A national revolutionary war as great as ours cannot be won without extensive and thoroughgoing political mobilization. Before the anti-Japanese war there was no political mobilization for resistance to Japan, and this was a great drawback, as a result of which China has already lost a move to the enemy. After the war began, political mobilization was very far from extensive, let alone thoroughgoing. It was the enemy's gunfire and the bombs dropped by enemy aeroplanes that brought news of the war to the great majority of the people. That was also a kind of mobilization, but it was done for us by the enemy, we did not do it ourselves. Even now the people in the remoter regions beyond the noise of the guns are carrying on quietly as usual. This situation must change, or otherwise we cannot win in our life-and-death struggle. We must never lose another move to the enemy; on the contrary, we must make full use of this move, political mobilization, to get the better of him. This move is crucial; it is indeed of primary importance, while our inferiority in weapons and other things is only secondary. The mobilization of the common people throughout the country will create a vast sea in which to drown the enemy, create the conditions that will make up for our inferioritY in arms and other things, and create the prerequisites for overcoming every difficulty in the war. To win victory, we must persevere in the War of Resistance, in the united front and in the protracted war. But all these are inseparable from the mobilization of the common people. To wish for victory and yet neglect political mobilization is like wishing to "go south by driving the chariot north", and the result would inevitably be to forfeit victory.

67. What does political mobilization mean? First, it means telling the army and the people about the political aim of the war. It is necessary for every soldier and civilian to see why the war must be fought and how it concerns him. The political aim

of the war is "to drive out Japanese imperialism and build a new China of freedom and equality"; we must proclaim this aim to everybody, to all soldiers and civilians, before we can create an anti-Japanese upsurge and unite hundreds of millions as one man to contribute their all to the war. Secondly, it is not enough merely to explain the aim to them; the steps and policies for its attainment must also be given, that is, there must be a political programme. We already have the Ten-Point Programme for Resisting Japan and Saving the Nation and also the Programme of Armed Resistance and National Reconstruction; we should popularize both of them in the army and among the people and mobilize everyone to carry them out. Without a clear-cut, concrete political programme it is impossible to mobilize all the armed forces and the whole people to carry the war against Japan through to the end. Thirdly, how should we mobilize them? By word of mouth, by leaflets and bulletins, by newspapers, books and pamphlets, through plays and films, through schools, through the mass organizations and through our cadres. What has been done so far in the Kuomintang areas is only a drop in the ocean, and moreover it has been done in a manner ill-suited to the people's tastes and in a spirit uncongenial to them; this must be drastically changed. Fourthly, to mobilize once is not enough; political mobilization for the War of Resistance must be continuous. Our job is not to recite our political programme to the people, for nobody will listen to such recitations; we must link the political mobilization for the war with developments in the war and with the life of the soldiers and the people, and make it a continuous movement. This is a matter of immense importance on which our victory in the war primarily depends.

THE OBJECT OF WAR

68. Here we are not dealing with the political aim of war; the political aim of the War of Resistance Against Japan has been defined above as "to drive out Japanese imperialism and build a new China of freedom and equality". Here we are dealing with the elementary object of war, war as "politics with bloodshed", as mutual slaughter by opposing armies. The object of war is specifically "to preserve oneself and destroy the enemy" (to destroy the enemy means to disarm him or "deprive him of the power to resist", and does not mean to destroy every member of his forces physically). In ancient warfare, the spear and the shield were used, the spear to attack and destroy the enemy, and the shield to defend and preserve oneself To the present day, all weapons are still an extension of the spear and the shield. The bomber, the machine-gun, the long-range gun and poison gas are developments of the spear, while the air-raid shelter, the steel helmet, the concrete fortification and the gas mask are developments of the shield. The tank is a new weapon combining the functions of both spear and shield. Attack is the chief means of destroying the enemy, but defence cannot be dispensed with. In attack the immediate object is to destroy the enemy, but at the same time it is self-preservation, because if the enemy is not destroyed, you will be destroyed. In defence the immediate object is to preserve yourself, but at the same time defence is a means of supplementing attack or preparing to go over to the attack. Retreat is in the category of defence and is a continuation of defence, while pursuit is a continuation of attack. It should be pointed out that destruction of the enemy is the primary object of war and self-preservation the secondary, because only by destroying the enemy in large numbers can one effectively preserve oneself. Therefore attack, the chief means of destroying the enemy, is primary, while defence, a

supplementary means of destroying the enemy and a means of self-preservation, is secondary. In actual warfare the chief role is played by defence much of the time and by attack for the rest of the time, but if war is taken as a whole, attack remains primary.

69. How do we justify the encouragement of heroic sacrifice in war? Does it not contradict "self-preservation"? No, it does not; sacrifice and self-preservation are both opposite and complementary to each other. War is politics with bloodshed and exacts a price, sometimes an extremely high price. Partial and temporary sacrifice (non-preservation) is incurred for the sake of general and permanent preservation. This is precisely why we say that attack, which is basically a means of destroying the enemy, also has the function of self-preservation. It is also the reason why defence must be accompanied by attack and should not be defence pure and simple.

70. The object of war, namely, the preservation of oneself and the destruction of the enemy, is the essence of war and the basis of all war activities, an essence which pervades all war activities, from the technical to the strategic. The object of war is the underlying principle of war, and no technical, tactical, or strategic concepts or principles can in any way depart from it. What for instance is meant by the principle of "taking cover and making full use of fire-power" in shooting? The purpose of the former is self-preservation, of the latter the destruction of the enemy. The former gives rise to such techniques as making use of the terrain and its features, advancing in spurts, and spreading out in dispersed formation. The latter gives rise to other techniques, such as clearing the field of fire and organizing a fire-net. As for the assault force, the containing force and the reserve force in a tactical operation, the first is for annihilating the enemy, the second for preserving oneself, and the third is for either purpose according to circumstances --

either for annihilating the enemy (in which case it reinforces the assault force or serves as a pursuit force), or for self-preservation (in which case it reinforces the containing force or serves as a covering force). Thus, no technical, tactical, or strategical principles or operations can in any way depart from the object of war, and this object pervades the whole of a war and runs through it from beginning to end.

71. In directing the anti-Japanese war, leaders at the various levels must lose sight neither of the contrast between the fundamental factors on each side nor of the object of this war. In the course of military operations these contrasting fundamental factors unfold themselves in the struggle by each side to preserve itself and destroy the other. In our war we strive in every engagement to win a victory, big or small, and to disarm a part of the enemy and destroy a part of his men and matériel. We must accumulate the results of these partial destructions of the enemy into major strategic victories and so achieve the final political aim of expelling the enemy, protecting the motherland and building a new China.

OFFENSE WITHIN DEFENSE,
QUICK DECISIONS WITHIN A PROTRACTED WAR,
EXTERIOR LINES WITHIN INTERIOR LINES

72. Now let us examine the specific strategy of the War of Resistance Against Japan. We have already said that our strategy for resisting Japan is that of protracted war, and indeed this is perfectly right. But this strategy is general, not specific. Specifically, how should the protracted war be conducted? We shall now discuss this question. Our answer is as follows. In the first and second stages of the war, i.e., in the stages of the enemy's offensive and preservation of his gains, we should conduct tactical offensives within the strategic defensive, campaigns and battles of quick decision within the strategically protracted war, and campaigns and battles on exterior lines within strategically interior lines. In the third stage, we should launch the strategic counter-offensive.

73. Since Japan is a strong imperialist power and we are a weak semi-colonial and semi-feudal country, she has adopted the policy of the strategic offensive while we are on the strategic defensive. Japan is trying to execute the strategy of a war of quick decision; we should consciously execute the strategy of protracted war. Japan is using dozens of army divisions of fairly high combat effectiveness (now numbering thirty) and part of her navy to encircle and blockade China from both land and sea, and is using her air force to bomb China. Her army has already established a long front stretching from Paotow to Hangchow and her navy has reached Fukien and Kwangtung; thus exterior-line operations have taken shape on a vast scale. On the other hand, we are in the position of operating on interior lines. All this is due to the fact that the enemy is strong while we are weak. This is one aspect of the situation.

74. But there is another and exactly opposite aspect. Japan, though strong, does not have enough soldiers. China, though weak, has a vast territory, a large population and plenty of soldiers. Two important consequences follow. First, the enemy, employing his small forces against a vast country, can only occupy some big cities and main lines of communication and part of the plains. Thus there are extensive areas in the territory under his occupation which he has had to leave ungarrisoned, and which provide a vast arena for our guerrilla warfare. Taking China as a whole, even if the enemy manages to occupy the line connecting Canton, Wuhan and Lanchow and its adjacent areas, he can hardly seize the regions beyond, and this gives China a general rear and vital bases from which to carry on the protracted war to final victory. Secondly, in pitting his small forces against large forces, the enemy is encircled by our large forces. The enemy is attacking us along several routes, strategically he is on exterior lines while we are on interior lines, strategically he is on the offensive while we are on the defensive; all this looks very much to our disadvantage. However, we can make use of our two advantages, namely, our vast territory and large forces, and, instead of stubborn positional warfare, carry on flexible mobile warfare, employing several divisions against one enemy division, several tens of thousands of our men against ten thousand of his, several columns against one of his columns, and suddenly encircling and attacking a single column from the exterior lines of the battlefield. In this way, while the enemy is on exterior lines and on the offensive in strategic operations, he will be forced to fight on interior lines and on the defensive in campaigns and battles. And for us, interior lines and the defensive in strategic operations will be transformed into exterior lines and the offensive in campaigns and battles. This is the way to deal with one or indeed with any advancing enemy column. Both the consequences discussed above follow from the fact that the enemy is small while we are big. Moreover, the enemy forces,

though small, are strong (in arms and in training) while our forces, though large, are weak (in arms and in training but not in morale), and in campaigns and battles, therefore, we should not only employ large forces against small and operate from exterior against interior lines, but also follow the policy of seeking quick decisions. In general, to achieve quick decision, we should attack a moving and not a stationary enemy. We should concentrate a big force under cover beforehand alongside the route which the enemy is sure to take, and while he is on the move, advance suddenly to encircle and attack him before he knows what is happening, and thus quickly conclude the battle. If we fight well, we may destroy the entire enemy force or the greater part or some part of it, and even if we do not fight so well, we may still inflict heavy casualties. This applies to any and every one of our battles. If each month we could win one sizable victory like that at Pinghsingkuan or Taierhchuang, not to speak of more, it would greatly demoralize the enemy, stimulate the morale of our own forces and evoke international support. Thus our strate gically protracted war is translated in the held into battles of quick decision. The enemy's war of strategic quick decision is bound to change into protracted war after he is defeated in many campaigns and battles.

75. In a word, the above operational principle for fighting campaigns and battles is one of "quick-decision offensive warfare on exterior lines". It is the opposite of our strategic principle of "protracted defensive warfare on interior lines", and yet it is the indispensable principle for carrying out this strategy. If we should use "protracted defensive warfare on interior lines" as the principle for campaigns and battles too, as we did at the beginning of the War of Resistance, it would be totally unsuited to the circumstances in which the enemy is small while we are big and the enemy is strong while we are weak; in that case we could never achieve our strategic objective of a protracted war and we would be defeated by the

enemy. That is why we have always advocated the organization of the forces of the entire country into a number of large field armies, each counterposed to one of the enemy's field armies but having two, three or four times its strength, and so keeping the enemy engaged in extensive theatres of war in accordance with the principle outlined above. This principle of "quick-decision offensive warfare on exterior lines" can and must be applied in guerrilla as well as in regular warfare. It is applicable not only to any one stage of the war but to its entire course. In the stage of strategic counter-offensive, when we are better equipped technically and are no longer in the position of the weak fighting the strong, we shall be able to capture prisoners and booty on a large scale all the more effectively if we continue to employ superior numbers in quick-decision offensive battles from exterior lines. For instance, if we employ two, three or four mechanized divisions against one mechanized enemy division, we can be all the more certain of destroying it. It is common sense that several hefty fellows can easily beat one.

76. If we resolutely apply "quick-decision offensive warfare on exterior lines" on a battlefield, we shall not only change the balance of forces on that battlefield, but also gradually change the general situation. On the battlefield we shall be on the offensive and the enemy on the defensive, we shall be employing superior numbers on exterior lines and the enemy inferior numbers on interior lines, and we shall seek quick decisions, while the enemy, try as he may, will not be able to protract the fighting in the expectation of reinforcements; for all these reasons, the enemy's position will change from strong to weak, from superior to inferior, while that of our forces will change from weak to strong, from inferior to superior. After many such battles have been victoriously fought, the general situation between us and the enemy will change. That is to say, through the accumulation of victories on many battlefields by quick-decision offensive warfare on exterior lines, we shall

gradually strengthen ourselves and weaken the enemy, which will necessarily affect the general balance of forces and bring about changes in it. When that happens, these changes, together with other factors on our side and together with the changes inside the enemy camp and a favourable international situation, will turn the over-all situation between us and the enemy first into one of parity and then into one of superiority for us. That will be the time for us to launch the counter-offensive and drive the enemy out of the country.

77. War is a contest of strength, but the original pattern of strength changes in the course of war. Here the decisive factor is subjective effort -- winning more victories and committing fewer errors. The objective factors provide the possibility for such change, but in order to turn this possibility into actuality both correct policy and subjective effort are essential. It is then that the subjective plays the decisive role.

INITIATIVE, FLEXIBILITY AND PLANNING

78. In quick-decision offensive campaigns and battles on exterior lines, as discussed above, the crucial point is the "offensive"; "exterior lines" refers to the sphere of the offensive and "quick-decision" to its duration. Hence the name "quick-decision offensive warfare on exterior lines". It is the best principle for waging a protracted war and it is also the principle for what is known as mobile warfare. But it cannot be put into effect without initiative, flexibility and planning. Let us now study these three questions.

79. We have already discussed man's conscious dynamic role, so why tlo we talk about the initiative again? By conscious dynamic role we mean conscious action and effort, a characteristic distinguishing man from other beings, and this human characteristic manifests itself most strongly in war; all this has been discussed already. The initiative here means an army's freedom of action as distinguished from an enforced loss of freedom. Freedom of action is the very life of an army and, once it is lost, the army is close to defeat or destruction. The disarming of a soldier is the result of his losing freedom of action through being forced into a passive position. The same is true of the defeat of an army. For this reason both sides in war do all they can to gain the initiative and avoid passivity. It may be said that the quick-decision offensive warfare on exterior lines which we advocate and the flexibility and planning necessary for its execution are designed to gain the initiative and thus force the enemy into a passive position and achieve the object of preserving ourselves and destroying the enemy. But initiative or passivity is inseparable from superiority or inferiority in the capacity to wage war. Consequently it is also inseparable from the correctness or incorrectness of the subjective direction of war. In addition,

there is the question of exploiting the enemy's misconceptions and unpreparedness in order to gain the initiative and force the enemy into passivity. These points are analysed below.

80. Initiative is inseparable from superiority in capacity to wage war, while passivity is inseparable from inferiority in capacity to wage war. Such superiority or inferiority is the objective basis of initiative or passivity. It is natural that the strategic initiative can be better maintained and exercised through a strategic offensive, but to maintain the initiative always and everywhere, that is, to have the absolute initiative, is possible only when there is absolute superiority matched against absolute inferiority. When a strong, healthy man wrestles with an invalid, he has the absolute initiative. If Japan were not riddled with insoluble contradictions, if, for instance, she could throw in a huge force of several million or ten million men all at once, if her financial resources were several times what they are, if she had no opposition from her own people or from other countries, and if she did not pursue the barbarous policies which arouse the desperate resistance of the Chinese people, then she would be able to maintain absolute superiority and have the absolute initiative always and every where. In history, such absolute superiority rarely appears in the early stages of a war or a campaign but is to be found towards its end. For instance, on the eve of Germany's capitulation in World War I, the Entente countries became absolutely superior and Germany absolutely inferior, so that Germany was defeated and the Entente countries were victorious; this is an example of absolute superiority and inferiority towards the end of a war. Again, on the eve of the Chinese victory at Taierhchuang, the isolated Japanese forces there were reduced after bitter fighting to absolute inferiority while our forces achieved absolute superiority, so that the enemy was defeated and we were victorious; this is an example of absolute superiority and inferiority towards the end of a campaign. A war or campaign may also end in a situation of

relative superiority or of parity, in which case there is compromise in the war or stalemate in the campaign. But in most cases it is absolute superiority and inferiority that decide victory and defeat. All this holds for the end of a war or a campaign, and not for the beginning. The outcome of the Sino-Japanese war, it can be predicted, will be that Japan will become absolutely inferior and be defeated and that China will become absolutely superior and gain victory. But at present superiority or inferiority is not absolute on either side, but is relative. With the advantages of her military, economic and political-organizational power, Japan enjoys superiority over us with our military, economic and political-organizational weakness, which creates the basis for her initiative. But since quantitatively her military and other power is not great and she has many other disadvantages, her superiority is reduced by her own contradictions. Upon her invasion of China, her superiority has been reduced still further because she has come up against our vast territory, large population, great numbers of troops and resolute nation-wide resistance. Hence, Japan's general position has become one of only relative superiority, and her ability to exercise and maintain the initiative, which is thereby restricted, has likewise become relative. As for China, though placed in a somewhat passive position strategically because of her inferior strength, she is nevertheless quantitatively superior in territory, population and troops, and also superior in the morale of her people and army and their patriotic hatred of the enemy; this superiority, together with other advantages, reduces the extent of her inferiority in military, economic and other power, and changes it into a relative strategic inferiority. This also reduces the degree of China's passivity so that her strategic position is one of only relative passivity. Any passivity, however, is a disadvantage, and one must strive hard to shake it off. Militarily, the way to do so is resolutely to wage quick-decision offensive warfare on exterior lines, to launch guerrilla warfare in the rear of the enemy and so secure overwhelming local superiority and initiative in many campaigns of mobile and guerrilla warfare. Through such local superiority and local initiative in many campaigns, we can gradually create strategic superiority and strategic initiative and extricate ourselves from strategic inferiority and passivity. Such is the interrelation between initiative and passivity, between superiority and inferiority.

81. From this we can also understand the relationship between initiative or passivity and the subjective directing of war. As already explained, it is possible to escape from our position of relative strategic inferiority and passivity, and the method is to create local superiority and initiative in many campaigns, so depriving the enemy of local superiority and initiative and plunging him into inferiority and passivity. These local successes will add up to strategic superiority and initiative for us and strategic inferiority and passivity for the enemy. Such a change depends upon correct subjective direction. Why? Because while we seek superiority and the initiative, so does the enemy; viewed from this angle, war is a contest in subjective ability between the commanders of the opposing armies in their struggle for superiority and for the initiative on the basis of material conditions such as military forces and financial resources. Out of the contest there emerge a victor and a vanquished; leaving aside the contrast in objective material conditions, the victor will necessarily owe his success to correct subjective direction and the vanquished his defeat to wrong subjective direction. We admit that the phenomenon of war is more elusive and is characterized by greater uncertainty than any other social phenomenon, in other words, that it is more a matter of "probability". Yet war is in no way supernatural, but a mundane process governed by necessity. That is why Sun Wu Tzu's axiom, "Know the enemy and know yourself, and you can fight a hundred battles with no danger of defeat",[20] remains a scientific truth. Mistakes arise from ignorance about the enemy and about ourselves, and moreover the peculiar nature of war makes it impossible in

many cases to have full knowledge about both sides; hence the uncertainty about military conditions and operations, and hence mistakes and defeats. But whatever the situation and the moves in a war, one can know their general aspects and essential points. It is possible for a commander to reduce errors and give generally correct direction, first through all kinds of reconnaissance and then through intelligent inference and judgement. Armed with the weapon of "generally correct direction", we can win more battles and transform our inferiority into superiority and our passivity into initiative. This is how initiative or passivity is related to the correct or incorrect subjective direction of a war.

82. The thesis that incorrect subjective direction can change superiority and initiative into inferiority and passivity, and that correct subjective direction can effect a reverse change, becomes all the more convincing when we look at the record of defeats suffered by big and powerful armies and of victories won by small and weak armies. There are many such instances in Chinese and foreign history. Examples in China are the Battle of Chengpu between the states of Tsin and Chu,[21] the Battle of Chengkao between the states of Chu and Han,[22] the Battle in which Han Hsin defeated the Chao armies,[23] the Battle of Kunyang between the states of Hsin and Han,[24] the Battle of Kuantu between Yuan Shao and Tsao Tsao,[25] the Battle of Chihpi between the states of Wu and Wei,[26] the Battle of Yiling between the states of Wu and Shu,[27] the Battle of Feishui between the states of Chin and Tsin,[28] etc. Among examples to be found abroad are most of Napoleon's campaigns and the civil war in the Soviet Union after the October Revolution. In all these instances, victory was won by small forces over big and by inferior over superior forces. In every case, the weaker force, pitting local superiority and initiative against the enemy's local inferiority and passivity, first inflicted one sharp defeat on the enemy and then turned on the rest of his forces and smashed them one by one, thus

transforming the over-all situation into one of superiority and initiative. The reverse was the case with the enemy who originally had superiority and held the initiative; owing to subjective errors and internal contradictions, it sometimes happened that he completely lost an excellent or fairly good position in which he enjoyed superiority and ipitiative, and became a general without an army or a king without a kingdom. Thus it can be seen that although superiority or inferiority in the capacity to wage war is the objective basis determining initiative or passivity, it is not in itself actual initiative or passivity; it is only through a struggle, a contest of ability, that actual initiative or passivity can emerge. In the struggle, correct subjective direction can transform inferiority into superiority and passivity into initiative, and incorrect subjective direction can do the opposite. The fact that every ruling dynasty was defeated by revolutionary armies shows that mere superiority in certain respects does not guarantee the initiative, much less the final victory. The inferior side can wrest the initiative and victory from the superior side by securing certain conditions through active subjective endeavour in accordance with the actual circumstances.

83. To have misconceptions and to be caught unawares may mean to lose superiority and initiative. Hence, deliberately creating misconceptions for the enemy and then springing surprise attacks upon him are two ways -- indeed two important means -- of achieving superiority and seizing the initiative. What are misconceptions? "To see every bush and tree on Mount Pakung as an enemy soldier"[29] is an example of misconception. And "making a feint to the east but attacking in the west" is a way of creating misconceptions among the enemy. When the mass support is sufficiently good to block the leakage of news, it is often possible by various ruses to succeed in leading the enemy into a morass of wrong judgements and actions so that he loses his superiority and the initiative. The

saying, "There can never be too much deception in war", means precisely this. What does "being caught unawares" mean? It means being unprepared. Without preparedness superiority is not real superiority and there can be no initiative either. Having grasped this point, a force which is inferior but prepared can often defeat a superior enemy by surprise attack We say an enemy on the move is easy to attack precisely because he is then off guard, that is, unprepared. These two points -- creating mis conceptions among the enemy and springing surprise attacks on him -- mean transferring the uncertainties of war to the enemy while securing the greatest possible certainty for ourselves and thereby gaining superiority, the initiative and victory. Excellent organization of the masses is the prerequisite for attaining all this. Therefore it is extremely important to arouse all the people who are opposed to the enemy, to arm themselves to the last man, make widespread raids on the enemy and also prevent the leakage of news and provide a screen for our own forces; in this way the enemy will be kept in the dark about where and when our forces will attack, and an objective basis will be created for misconceptions and unpreparedness on his part. It was largely owing to the organized, armed masses of the people that the weak and small force of the Chinese Red Army was able to win many battles in the period of the Agrarian Revolutionary War. Logically, a national war should win broader mass support than an agrarian revolutionary war; however, as a result of past mistakes [30] the people are in an unorganized state, cannot be promptly drawn in to serve the cause and are sometimes even made use of by the enemy. The resolute rallying of the people on a broad scale is the only way to secure inexhaustible resources to meet all the requirements of the war. Moreover, it will definitely play a big part in carrying out our tactics of defeating the enemy by misleading him and catching him unawares. We are not Duke Hsiang of Sung and have no use for his asinine ethics.[31] In order to achieve victory we must as far as possible make the enemy blind and deaf by sealing his eyes and ears and drive his commanders to distraction by creating confusion in their minds. The above concerns the way in which the initiative or passivity is related to the subjective direction of the war. Such subjective direction is indispensable for defeating Japan.

84. By and large, Japan has held the initiative in the stage of her offensive by reason of her military power and her exploitation of our subjective errors, past and present. But her initiative is beginning to wane to some extent because of her many inherent disadvantages and of the subjective errors she too has committed in the course of the war (of which more later) and also because of our many advantages. The enemy's defeat at Taierhchuang and his predicament in Shansi prove this clearly. The widespread development of guerrilla warfare in the enemy's rear has placed his garrisons in the occupied areas in a completely passive position. Although he is still on the offensive strategically and still holds the initiative, his initiative will end when his strategic offensive ends. The first reason why the enemy will not be able to maintain the initiative is that his shortage of troops renders it impossible for him to carry on the offensive indefinitely. Our offensive warfare in campaigns and our guerrilla warfare behind the enemy lines, together with other factors, constitute the second reason why he will have to cease his offensive at a certain limit and will not be able to keep his initiative. The existence of the Soviet Union and changes in the international situation constitute the third reason. Thus it can be seen that the enemy's initiative is limited and can be shattered. If, in military operations, China can keep up offensive warfare by her main forces in campaigns and battles, vigorously develop guerrilla warfare in the enemy's rear and mobilize the people on a broad scale politically, we can gradually build up a position of strategic initiative.

85. Let us now discuss flexibility. What is flexibility? It is the concrete realization of the initiative in military operations;

it is the flexible employment of armed forces. The flexible employment of armed forces is the central task in directing a war, a task most difficult to perform well. In addition to organizing and educating the army and the people, the business of war consists in the employment of troops in combat, and all these things are done to win the fight. Of course it is difficult to organize an army, etc., but it is even more difficult to employ it, particularly when the weak are fighting the strong. To do so requires subjective ability of a very high order and requires the overcoming of the confusion, obscurity and uncertainty peculiar to war and the discovery of order, clarity and certainty in it; only thus can flexibility in command be realized.

86. The basic principle of field operations for the War of Resistance Against Japan is quick-decision offensive warfare on exterior lines. There are various tactics or methods for giving effect to this principle, such as dispersion and concentration of forces, diverging advance and converging attack, the offensive and the defensive, assault and containment, encirclement and outflanking, advance and retreat. It is easy to understand these tactics, but not at all easy to employ and vary them flexibly. Here the three crucial links are the time, the place and the troops. No victory can be won unless the time, the place and the troops are well chosen. For example, in attacking an enemy force on the move, if we strike too early, we expose ourselves and give the enemy a chance to prepare, and if we strike too late, the enemy may have encamped and concentrated his forces, presenting us with a hard nut to crack. This is the question of the time. If we select a point of assault on the left flank which actually turns out to be the enemy's weak point, victory will be easy; but if we select the right flank and hit a snag, nothing will be achieved. This is the question of the place. If a particular unit of our forces is employed for a particular task, victory may be easy; but if another unit is employed for the same task, it may be hard to achieve results. This is the question of the troops. We should

know not only how to employ tactics but how to vary them. For flexibility of command the important task is to make changes such as from the offensive to the defensive or from the defensive to the offensive, from advance to retreat or from retreat to advance, from containment to assault or from assault to containment, from encirclement to outflanking or from outflanking to encirclement, and to make such changes properly and in good time according to the circumstances of the troops and terrain on both sides. This is true of command in campaigns and strategic command as well as of command in battles.

87. The ancients said: "Ingenuity in varying tactics depends on mother wit"; this "ingenuity", which is what we mean by flexibility, is the contribution of the intelligent commander. Flexibility does not mean recklessness; recklessness must be rejected. Flexibility consists in the intelligent commander's ability to take timely and appropriate measures on the basis of objective conditions after "judging the hour and sizing up the situation" (the "situation" includes the enemy's situation, our situation and the terrain), and this flexibility is "ingenuity in varying tactics". On the basis of this ingenuity, we can win more victories in quick-decision offensive warfare on exterior lines, change the balance of forces in our favour, gain the initiative over the enemy, and overwhelm and crush him so that the final victory will be ours.

88. Let us now discuss the question of planning. Because of the uncertainty peculiar to war, it is much more difficult to prosecute war according to plan than is the case with other activities. Yet, since "preparedness ensures success and unpreparedness spells failure", there can be no victory in war without advance planning and preparations. There is no absolute certainty in war, and yet it is not without some degree of relative certainty. We are comparatively certain about our own situation. We are very uncertain about the enemy's, but

here too there are signs for us to read, clues to follow and sequences of phenomena to ponder. These form what we call a degree of relative certainty, which provides an objective basis for planning in war. Modern technical developments (telegraphy, radio, aeroplanes, motor vehicles, railways, steamships, etc.) have added to the possibilities of planning in war. However, complete or stable planning is difficult because there is only very limited and transient certainty in war; such planning must change with the movement (flow or change) of the war and vary in degree according to the scale of the war. Tactical plans, such as plans for attack or defence by small formations or units, often have to be changed several times a day. A plan of campaign, that is, of action by large formations, can generally stand till the conclusion of the campaign, in the course of which, however, it is often changed partially or sometimes even wholly. A strategic plan based on the over-all situation of both belligerents is still more stable, but it too is applicable only in a given strategic stage and has to be changed when the war moves towards a new stage. The making and changing of tactical, campaign and strategic plans in accordance with scope and circumstance is a key factor in directing a war; it is the concrete expression of flexibility in war, in other words, it is also ingenuity in varying one's tactics. Commanders at all levels in the anti-Japanese war should take note.

89. Because of the fluidity of war, some people categorically deny that war plans or policies can be relatively stable, describing such plans or policies as "mechanical". This view is wrong. In the preceding section we fully recognized that, because the circumstances of war are only relatively certain and the flow (movement or change) of war is rapid, war plans or policies can be only relatively stable and have to be changed or revised in good time in accordance with changing circumstances and the flow of the war; otherwise we would become mechanists. But one must not deny the need for war

plans or policies that are relatively stable over given periods; to negate this is to negate everything, including the war itself as well as the negator himself. As both military conditions and operations are relatively stable, we must grant the relative stability of the war plans and policies resulting from them. For example, since both the circumstances of the war in northern China and the dispersed nature of the Eighth Route Army's operations are relatively stable for a particular stage, it is absolutely necessary during this stage to acknowledge the relative stability of the Eighth Route Army's strategic principle of operation, namely, "Guerrilla warfare is basic, but lose no chance for mobile warfare under favourable conditions." The period of validity of a plan for a campaign is shorter than that of a strategic plan, and for a tactical plan it is shorter still, but each is stable over a given period. Anyone denying this point would have no way of handling warfare and would become a relativist in war with no settled views, for whom one course is just as wrong or just as right as another. No one denies that even a plan valid for a given period is fluid; otherwise, one plan would never be abandoned in favour of another. But it is fluid within limits, fluid within the bounds of the various war operations undertaken for carrying it out, but not fluid as to its essence; in other words, it is quantitatively but not qualitatively fluid. Within such a given period of time, this essence is definitely not fluid, which is what we mean by relative stability within a given period. In the great river of absolute fluidity throughout the war there is relative stability at each particular stretch -- such is our fundamental view regarding war plans or policies.

90. Having dealt with protracted defensive warfare on interior lines in strategy and with quick-decision offensive warfare on exterior lines in campaigns and battles, and also with the initiative, flexibility and planning, we can now sum up briefly. The anti-Japanese war must have a plan. War plans, which are the concrete application of strategy and tactics, must

be flexible so that they can be adapted ta the circumstances of the war. We should always seek to transform our inferiority into superiority and our passivity into the initiative so as to change the situation as between the enemy and ourselves. All these find expression in quick-decision offensive warfare on exterior lines in campaigns and battles and protracted defensive warfare on interior lines in strategy.

MOBILE WARFARE, GUERRILLA WARFARE AND POSITIONAL WARFARE

91. A war will take the form of mobile warfare when its content is quick-decision offensive warfare on exterior lines in campaigns and battles within the framework of the strategy of interior lines, protracted war and defence. Mobile warfare is the form in which regular armies wage quick-decision offensive campaigns and battles on exterior lines along extensive fronts and over big areas of operation. At the same time, it includes "mobile defence", which is conducted when necessary to facilitate such offensive battles; it also includes positional attack and positional defence in a supplementary role. Its characteristics are regular armies, superiority of forces in campaigns and battles, the offensive, and fluidity.

92. China has a vast territory and an immense number of soldiers, but her troops are inadequately equipped and trained; the enemy's forces, on the other hand, are inadequate in number, but better equipped and trained. In this situation, there is no doubt that we must adopt offensive mobile warfare as our primary form of warfare, supplementing it by others and integrating them all into mobile warfare. We must oppose "only retreat, never advance", which is flightism, and at the same time oppose "only advance, never retreat", which is desperate recklessness.

93. One of the characteristics of mobile warfare is fluidity, which not only permits but requires a field army to advance and to withdraw in great strides. However, it has nothing in common with flightism of the Han Fu-chu brand.[32] The primary requirement of war is to destroy the enemy, and the other requirement is self-preservation. The object of self-preservation is to destroy the enemy, and to destroy the enemy is in turn the most effective means of self-preservation. Hence mobile warfare is in no way an excuse for people like Han Fu-

chu and can never mean moving only backward, and never forward; that kind of "moving" which negates the basic offensive character of mobile warfare would, in practice, "move" China out of existence despite her vastness.

94. However, the other view, which we call the desperate recklessness of "only advance, never retreat", is also wrong. The mobile warfare we advocate, the content of which is quick-decision offensive warfare on exterior lines in campaigns and battles, includes positional warfare in a supplementary role, "mobile defence" and retreat, with out all of which mobile warfare cannot be fully carried out. Desperate recklessness is military short-sightedness, originating often from fear of losing territory. A man who acts with desperate recklessness does not know that one characteristic of mobile warfare is fluidity, which not only permits but requires a field army to advance and to withdraw in great strides. On the positive side, in order to draw the enemy into a fight unfavourable to him but favourable to us, it is usually necessary that he should be on the move and that we should have a number of advantages, such as favourable terrain, a vulnerable enemy, a local population that can prevent the leakage of information, and the enemy's fatigue and unpreparedness. This requires that the enemy should advance, and we should not grudge a temporary loss of part of our territory. For the temporary loss of part of our territory is the price we pay for the permanent preservation of all our territory, including the recovery of lost territory. On the negative side, whenever we are forced into a disadvantageous position which fundamentally endangers the preservation of our forces, we should have the courage to retreat, so as to preserve our forces and hit the enemy when new opportunities arise. In their ignorance of this principle, the advocates of desperate action will contest a city or a piece of ground even when the position is obviously and definitely unfavourable; as a result, they not only lose the city or ground but fail to preserve their forces. We have always advocated the policy of

"luring the enemy in deep", precisely because it is the most effective military policy for a weak army strategically on the defensive to employ against a strong army.

95. Among the forms of warfare in the anti-Japanese war mobile warfare comes first and guerrilla warfare second. When we say that in the entire war mobile warfare is primary and guerrilla warfare supplementary, we mean that the outcome of the war depends mainly on regular warfare, especially in its mobile form, and that guerrilla warfare cannot shoulder the main responsibility in deciding the out come. It does not follow, however, that the role of guerrilla warfare is unimportant in the strategy of the war. Its role in the strategy of the war as a whole is second only to that of mobile warfare, for without its support we cannot defeat the enemy. In saying this we also have in mind the strategic task of developing guerrilla warfare into mobile warfare. Guerrilla warfare will not remain the same throughout this long and cruel war, but will rise to a higher level and develop into mobile warfare. Thus the strategic role of guerrilla warfare is twofold, to support regular warfare and to transform itself into regular warfare. Considering the unprecedented extent and duration of guerrilla warfare in China's War of Resistance, it is all the more important not to underestimate its strategic role. Guerrilla warfare in China, therefore, has not only its tactical but also its peculiar strategic problems. I have already discussed this in "Problems of Strategy in Guerrilla War Against Japan". As indicated above, the forms of warfare in the three strategic stages of the War of Resistance are as follows. In the first stage mobile warfare is primary, while guerrilla and positional warfare are supplementary. In the second stage guerrilla warfare will advance to the first place and will be supplemented by mobile and positional warfare. In the third stage mobile warfare will again become the primary form and will be supplemented by positional and guerrilla warfare. But the mobile warfare of the third stage will no longer be

undertaken solely by the original regular forces; part, possibly quite an important part, will be undertaken by forces which were originally guerrillas but which will have progressed from guerrilla to mobile warfare. From the view point of all three stages in China's War of Resistance Against Japan, guerrilla warfare is definitely indispensable. Our guerrilla war will present a great drama unparalleled in the annals of war. For this reason, out of the millions of China's regular troops, it is absolutely necessary to assign at least several hundred thousand to disperse through all enemy-occupied areas, arouse the masses to arm themselves, and wage guerrilla warfare in co-ordination with the masses. The regular forces so assigned should shoulder this sacred task conscientiously, and they should not think their status lowered because they fight fewer big battles and for the time being do not appear as national heroes. Any such thinking is wrong. Guerrilla warfare does not bring as quick results or as great renown as regular warfare, but "a long road tests a horse's strength and a long task proves a man's heart", and in the course of this long and cruel war guerrilla warfare will demonstrate its immense power; it is indeed no ordinary under taking. Moreover, such regular forces can conduct guerrilla warfare when dispersed and mobile warfare when concentrated, as the Eighth Route Army has been doing. The principle of the Eighth Route Army is, "Guerrilla warfare is basic, but lose no chance for mobile warfare under favourable conditions." This principle is perfectly correct; the views of its opponents are wrong.

96. At China's present technical level, positional warfare, defensive or offensive, is generally impracticable, and this is where our weakness manifests itself. Moreover, the enemy is also exploiting the vastness of our territory to bypass our fortified positions. Hence positional warfare cannot be an important, still less the principal, means for us. But in the first and second stages of the war, it is possible and essential, within the scope of mobile warfare, to employ localized positional

warfare in a supplementary role in campaigns. Semi-positional "mobile defence" is a still more essential part of mobile warfare undertaken for the purpose of resisting the enemy at every step, thereby depleting his forces and gaining extra time. China must strive to increase her supplies of modern weapons so that she can fully carry out the tasks of positional attack in the stage of the strategic counter-offensive. In this third stage positional warfare will undoubtedly play a greater role, for then the enemy will be holding fast to his positions, and we shall not be able to recover our lost territory unless we launch powerful positional attacks in support of mobile warfare. Nevertheless, in the third stage too, we must exert our every effort to make mobile warfare the primary form of warfare. For the art of directing war and the active role of man are largely nullified in positional warfare such as that fought in Western Europe in the second half of World War I. It is only natural that the war should be taken "out of the trenches", since the war is being fought in the vast expanses of China and since our side will remain poorly equipped technically for quite a long time. Even during the third stage, when China's technical position will be better, she will hardly surpass her enemy in that respect, and so will have to concentrate on highly mobile warfare, without which she cannot achieve final victory. Hence, throughout the War of Resistance China will not adopt positional warfare as primary; the primary or important forms are mobile warfare and guerrilla warfare. These two forms of warfare will afford full play to the art of directing war and to the active role of man -- what a piece of good fortune out of our misfortune!

WAR OF ATTRITION AND WAR OF ANNIHILATION

97. As we have said before, the essence, or the object, of war is to preserve oneself and destroy the enemy. Since there are three forms of warfare, mobile, positional and guerrilla, for achieving this object, and since they differ in degrees of effectiveness, there arises the broad distinction between war of attrition and war of annihilation.

98. To begin with, we may say that the anti-Japanese war is at once a war of attrition and a war of annihilation. Why? Because the enemy is still exploiting his strength and retains strategic superiority and strategic initiative, and therefore, unless we fight campaigns and battles of annihilation, we cannot effectively and speedily reduce his strength and break his superiority and initiative. We still have our weakness and have not yet rid ourselves of strategic inferiority and passivity; therefore, unless we fight campaigns and battles of annihilation, we cannot win time to improve our internal and international situation and alter our unfavourable position. Hence campaigns of annihilation are the means of attaining the objective of strategic attrition. In this sense war of annihilation is war of attrition. It is chiefly by using the method of attrition through annihilation that China can wage protracted war.

99. But the objective of strategic attrition may also be achieved by campaigns of attrition. Generally speaking, mobile warfare performs the task of annihilation, positional warfare performs the task of attrition, and guerrilla warfare performs both simultaneously; the three forms of warfare are thus distinguished from one another. In this sense war of annihilation is different from war of attrition. Campaigns of attrition are supplementary but necessary in protracted war.

100. Speaking theoretically and in terms of China's needs, in order to achieve the strategic objective of greatly depleting the enemy's forces, China in her defensive stage should not only exploit the function of annihilation, which is fulfilled primarily by mobile warfare and partially by guerrilla warfare, but also exploit the function of attrition, which is fulfilled primarily by positional warfare (which itself is supplementary) and partially by guerrilla warfare. In the stage of stalemate we should continue to exploit the functions of annihilation and attrition fulfilled by guerrilla and mobiie warfare for further large-scale depletion of the enemy's forces. All this is aimed at protracting the war, gradually changing the general balance of forces and preparing the conditions for our counter-offensive. During the strategic counter-offensive, we should continue to employ the method of attrition through annihilation so as finally to expel the enemy.

101. But as a matter of fact, it was our experience in the last ten months that many or even most of the mobile warfare campaigns became campaigns of attrition, and guerrilla warfare did not adequately fulfil its proper function of annihilation in certain areas. The positive aspect is that at least we depleted the enemy's forces, which is important both for the protracted warfare and for our final victory, and did not shed our blood in vain. But the drawbacks are first, that we did not sufficiently deplete the enemy, and second, that we were unable to avoid rather heavy losses and captured little war booty. Although we should recognize the objective cause of this situation, namely, the disparity between us and the enemy in technical equipment and in the training of troops, in any case it is necessary, both theoretically and practically, to urge that our main forces should fight vigorous battles of annihilation whenever circumstances are favourable. And although our guerrilla units have to wage battles of pure attrition in performing specific tasks such as sabotage and harassment, it is necessary to advocate and vigorously carry out campaigns and battles of

annihilation whenever circumstances are favourable, so as greatly to deplete the enemy's forces and greatly replenish our own.

102. The "exterior lines", the "quick-decision" and the "offensive" in quick-decision offensive warfare on exterior lines and the "mobility" in mobile warfare find their main operational expression in the use of encircling and outflanking tactics; hence the necessity for concentrating superior forces. Therefore concentration of forces and the use of encircling and outflanking tactics are the prerequisites for mobile warfare, that is, for quick-decision offensive warfare on exterior lines. All this is aimed at annihilating the enemy forces.

103. The strength of the Japanese army lies not only in its weapons but also in the training of its officers and men -- its degree of organization, its self-confidence arising from never having been defeated, its superstitious belief in the Mikado and in supernatural beings, its arrogance, its contempt for the Chinese people and other such characteristics, all of which stem from long years of indoctrination by the Japanese warlords and from the Japanese national tradition. This is the chief reason why we have taken very few prisoners, although we have killed and wounded a great many enemy troops. It is a point that has been underestimated by many people in the past. To destroy these enemy characteristics will be a long process. The first thing to do is to give the matter serious attention, and then patiently and systematically to work at it in the political field and in the fields of international propaganda and the Japanese people's movement; in the military sphere war of annihilation is of course one of the means. In these enemy characteristics pessimists may and a basis for the theory of national subjugation, and passively minded military men a basis for opposition to war of annihilation. We, on the contrary, maintain that these strong points of the Japanese army can be destroyed and that their destruction has already begun. The

chief method of destroying them is to win over the Japanese soldiers politically. We should understand, rather than hurt, their pride and channel it in the proper direction and, by treating prisoners of war leniently, lead the Japanese soldiers to see the anti-popular character of the aggression committed by the Japanese rulers. On the other hand, we should demonstrate to the Japanese soldiers the indomitable spirit and the heroic, stubborn fighting capacity of the Chinese army and the Chinese people, that is, we should deal them blows in battles of annihilation. Our experience in the last ten months of military operations shows that it is possible to annihilate enemy forces -- witness the Pinghsingkuan and Taierhchuang campaigns. The Japanese army's morale is beginning to sag, its soldiers do not understand the aim of the war, they are engulfed by the Chinese armies and by the Chinese people, in assault they show far less courage than the Chinese soldiers, and so on; all these are objective factors favourable to waging battles of annihilation, and they will, moreover, steadily develop as the war becomes protracted. From the viewpoint of destroying the enemy's overweening arrogance through battles of annihilation, such battles are one of the prerequisites for shortening the war and accelerating the emancipation of the Japanese soldiers and the Japanese people. Cats make friends with cats, and nowhere in the world do cats make friends with mice.

104. On the other hand, it must be admitted that for the present we are inferior to the enemy in technical equipment and in troop training. Therefore, it is often difficult to achieve the maximum in annihilation, such as capturing the whole or the greater part of an enemy force, especially when hghting on the plains. In this connection the excessive demands of the theorists of quick victory are wrong. What should be demanded of our forces in the anti-Japanese war is that they should fight battles of annihilation as far as possible. In favourable circumstances, we should concentrate superior forces in every battle and employ encircling and outflanking tactics -- encircle

part if not all of the enemy forces, capture part if not all of the encircled forces, and inflict heavy casualties on part of the encircled forces if we cannot capture them. In circumstances which are unfavourable for battles of annihilation, we should fight battles of attrition. In favourable circumstances, we should employ the principle of concentration of forces, and in unfavourable circumstances that of their dispersion. As for the relationship of command in campaigns, we should apply the principle of centralized command in the former and that of decentralized command in the latter. These are the basic principles of field operations for the War of Resistance Against Japan.

THE POSSIBILITIES OF EXPLOITING
THE ENEMY'S MISTAKES

105. The enemy command itself provides a basis for the possibility of defeating Japan. History has never known an infallible general, and the enemy makes mistakes just as we ourselves can hardly avoid making them; hence, the possibility exists of exploiting the enemy's errors. In the ten months of his war of aggression the enemy has already made many mistakes in strategy and tactics. There are five major ones.

First, piecemeal reinforcement. This is due to the enemy's underestimation of China and also to his shortage of troops. The enemy has always looked down on us. After grabbing the four northeastern provinces at small cost, he occupied eastern Hopei and northern Chahar, all by way of strategic reconnaissance. The conclusion the enemy came to was that the Chinese nation is a heap of loose sand. Thus, thinking that China would crumble at a single blow, he mapped out a plan of "quick decision", attempting with very small forces to send us scampering in panic. He did not expect to find such great unity and such immense powers of resistance as China has shown during the past ten months, forgetting as he did that China is already in an era of progress and already has an advanced political party, an advanced army and an advanced people. Meeting with setbacks, the enemy then increased his forces piecemeal from about a dozen to thirty divisions. If he wants to advance, he will have to augment his forces still further. But because of Japan's antagonism with the Soviet Union and her inherent shortage of manpower and finances, there are inevitable limits to the maximum number of men she can throw in and to the furthest extent of her advance.

Second, absence of a main direction of attack. Before the Taierhchuang campaign, the enemy had divided his forces more or less evenly between northern and central China and had again divided them inside each of these areas. In northern China, for instance, he divided his forces among the Tientsin-Pukow, the Peiping-Hankow and the Tatung-Puchow Railways, and along each of these lines he suffered some casualties and left some garrisons in the places occupied, after which he lacked the forces for further advances. After the Taierhchuang defeat, from which he learned a lesson, the enemy concentrated his main forces in the direction of Hsuchow, and so temporarily corrected this mistake.

Third, lack of strategic co-ordination. On the whole co-ordination exists within the groups of enemy forces in northern China and in central China, but there is glaring lack of co ordination between the two. When his forces on the southern section of the Tientsin-Pukow Railway attacked Hsiaopengpu, those on the northern section made no move, and when his forces on the northern section attacked Taierhchuang, those on the southern section made no move. After the enemy came to grief at both places, the Japanese minister of war arrived on an inspection tour and the chief of general staff turned up to take charge, and for the moment, it seemed, there was co-ordination. The landlord class, the bourgeoisie and the warlords of Japan have very serious internal contradictions, which are growing, and the lack of military co-ordination is one of the concrete manifestations of this fact.

Fourth, failure to grasp strategic opportunities. This failure was conspicuously shown in the enemy's halt after the occupation of Nanking and Taiyuan, chiefly because of his shortage of troops and his lack of a strategic pursuit force.

Fifth, encirclement of large, but annihilation of small, numbers. Before the Taierhchuang campaign, in the campaigns of Shanghai, Nanking, Tsangchow, Paoting, Nankow, Hsinkou and Linfen, many Chinese troops were routed but few were taken prisoner, which shows the stupidity of the enemy command.

These five errors -- piecemeal reinforcement, absence of a main direction of attack, lack of strategic co-ordination, failure to grasp opportunities, and encirclement of large, but annihilation of small, numbers -- were all points of incompetence in the Japanese command before the Taierhchuang campaign. Although the enemy has since made some improvements, he cannot possibly avoid repeating his errors because of his shortage of troops, his internal contradictions and other factors. In addition, what he gains at one point he loses at another. For instance, when he concentrated his forces in northern China on Hsuchow, he left a great vacuum in the occupied areas in northern China, which gave us full scope for developing guerrilla warfare. These mistakes were of the enemy's own making and not induced by us. On our part, we can deliberately make the enemy commit errors, that is, we can mislead him and manoeuvre him into the desired position by ingenious and effective moves with the help of a well-organized local population, for example, by "making a feint to the east but attacking in the west". This possibility has already been discussed. All the above shows that in the enemy's command, too, we can find some basis for victory. Of course, we should not take it as an important basis for our strategic planning; on the contrary, the only reliable course is to base our planning on the assumption that the enemy will make few mistakes. Besides, the enemy can exploit our mistakes just as we can exploit his. It is the duty of our command to allow him the minimum of opportunities for doing so. Actually, the enemy command has committed errors, will again commit errors in the future, and can be made to do so through our endeavours. All these errors we can exploit, and it is the business of our generals in the War of Resistance to do their utmost to seize upon them. However, although much of the enemy's strategic and campaign command is incompetent, there are quite a few excellent points in his battle command, that is, in his unit and small formation tactics, and here we should learn from him.

THE QUESTION OF DECISIVE ENGAGEMENTS
IN THE ANTI-JAPANESE WAR

106. The question of decisive engagements in the anti-Japanese war should be approached from three aspects: we should resolutely fight a decisive engagement in every campaign or battle in which we are sure of victory; we should avoid a decisive engagement in every campaign or battle in which we are not sure of victory; and we should absolutely avoid a strategically decisive engagement on which the fate of the whole nation is staked. The characteristics differentiating our War of Resistance Against Japan from many other wars are also revealed in this question of decisive engagements. In the first and second stages of the war, which are marked by the enemy's strength and our weakness, the enemy's objective is to have us concentrate our main forces for a decisive engagement. Our objective is exactly the opposite. We want to choose conditions favourable to us, concentrate superior forces and fight decisive campaigns or battles only when we are sure of victory, as in the battles at Pinghsingkuan, Taierhchuang and other places; we want to avoid decisive engagements under unfavourable conditions when we are not sure of victory, this being the policy we adopted in the Changteh and other campaigns. As for fighting a strategically decisive engagement on which the fate of the whole nation is staked, we simply must not do so, as witness the recent withdrawal from Hsuchow. The enemy's plan for a "quick decision" was thus foiled, and now he cannot help fighting a protracted war with us. These principles are impracticable in a country with a small territory, and hardly practicable in a country that is very backward politically. They are practicable in China because she is a big country and is in an era of progress. If strategically decisive engagements are avoided, then "as long as the green mountains are there, one need not worry about firewood", for even though

some of our territory may be lost, we shall still have plenty of room for manoeuvre and thus be able to promote and await domestic progress, international support and the internal disintegration of the enemy; that is the best policy for us in the anti-Japanese war. Unable to endure the arduous trials of a protracted war and eager for an early triumph, the impetuous theorists of quick victory clamour for a strategically decisive engagement the moment the situation takes a slightly favour able turn. To do what they want would be to inflict incalculable damage on the entire war, spell finis to the protracted war, and land us in the enemy's deadly trap; actually, it would be the worst policy. Undoubtedly, if we are to avoid decisive engagements, we shall have to abandon territory, and we must have the courage to do so when (and only when) it becomes completely unavoidable. At such times we should not feel the slightest regret, for this policy of trading space for time is correct. History tells us how Russia made a courageous retreat to avoid a decisive engagement and then defeated Napoleon, the terror of his age. Today China should do likewise.

107. Are we not afraid of being denounced as "non-resisters"? No, we are not. Not to fight at all but to compromise with the enemy -- that is non-resistance, which should not only be denounced but must never be tolerated. We must resolutely fight the War of Resistance, but in order to avoid the enemy's deadly trap, it is absolutely necessary that we should not allow our main forces to be finished off at one blow, which would make it difficult to continue the War of Resistance -- in brief, it is absolutely necessary to avoid national subjugation. To have doubts on this point is to be short sighted on the question of the war and is sure to lead one into the ranks of the subjugationists. We have criticized the desperate recklessness of "only advance, never retreat" precisely because, if it became the fashion, this doctrine would make it impossible to continue the War of Resistance and would lead to the danger of ultimate national subjugation.

108. We are for decisive engagements whenever circumstances are favourable, whether in battles or in major or minor campaigns, and in this respect we should never tolerate passivity. Only through such decisive engagements can we achieve the objective of annihilating or depleting the enemy forces, and every soldier in the anti-Japanese war should resolutely play his part. For this purpose considerable partial sacrifices are necessary; to avoid any sacrifice whatsoever is the attitude of cowards and of those afflicted by the fear of Japan and must be firmly opposed. The execution of Li Fu-ying, Han Fu-chu and other flightists was justified. Within the scope of correct war planning, encouraging the spirit and practice of heroic self-sacrifice and dauntless advance in battle is absolutely necessary and inseparable from the waging of protracted war and the achievement of final victory. We have strongly condemned the flightism of "only retreat, never advance" and have supported the strict enforcement of discipline, because it is only through heroic decisive engagements, fought under a correct plan, that we can vanquish the powerful enemy; flightism, on the contrary, gives direct support to the theory of national subjugation.

109. Is it not self-contradictory to fight heroically first and then abandon territory? Will not our heroic fighters have shed their blood in vain? That is not at all the way questions should be posed. To eat and then to empty your bowels -- is this not to eat in vain? To sleep and then to get up -- is this not to sleep in vain? Can questions be posed in such a way? I would suppose not. To keep on eating, to keep on sleeping, to keep on fighting heroically all the way to the Yalu River without a stop -- these are subjectivist and formalist illusions, not realities of life. As everybody knows, although in fighting and shedding our blood in order to gain time and prepare the counter-offensive we have had to abandon some territory, in fact we have gained time, we have achieved the objective of annihilating and depleting

enemy forces, we have acquired experience in fighting, we have aroused hitherto inactive people and improved our international standing. Has our blood been shed in vain? Certainly not. Territory has been given up in order to preserve our military forces and indeed to preserve territory, because if we do not abandon part of our territory when conditions are unfavourable but blindly fight decisive engagements without the least assurance of winning, we shall lose our military forces and then be unable to avoid the loss of all our territory, to say nothing of recovering territory already lost. A capitalist must have capital to run his business, and if he loses it all he is no longer a capitalist. Even a gambler must have money to stake, and if he risks it all on a single throw and his luck fails, he cannot gamble any more. Events have their twists and turns and do not follow a straight line, and war is no exception; only formalists are unable to comprehend this truth.

110. I think the same will also hold true for the decisive engagements in the stage of strategic counter-offensive. Although by then the enemy will be in the inferior and we in the superior position, the principle of "fighting profitable decisive engagements and avoiding unprofitable ones" will still apply and will continue to apply until we have fought our way to the Yalu River. This is how we will be able to maintain our initiative from beginning to end, and as for the enemy's "challenges" and other people's "taunts", we should imperturbably brush them aside and ignore them. In the War of Resistance only those generals who show this kind of firmness can be deemed courageous and wise. This is beyond the ken of those who "jump whenever touched". Even though we are in a more or less passive position strategically in this first stage of the war, we should have the initiative in every campaign; and of course we should have the initiative throughout the later stages. We are for protracted war and final victory, we are not gamblers who risk everything on a single throw.

Mao Tse-tung

THE ARMY AND THE PEOPLE ARE
THE FOUNDATION OF VICTORY

111. Japanese imperialism will never relax in its aggression against and repression of revolutionary China; this is determined by its imperialist nature. If China did not resist, Japan would easily seize all China without firing a single shot, as she did the four northeastern provinces. Since China is resisting, it is an inexorable law that Japan will try to repress this resistance until the force of her repression is exceeded by the force of China's resistance. The Japanese landlord class and bourgeoisie are very ambitious, and in order to drive south to Southeast Asia and north to Siberia, they have adopted the policy of breaking through in the centre by first attacking China. Those who think that Japan will know where to stop and be content with the occupation of northern China and of Kiangsu and Chekiang Provinces completely fail to perceive that imperialist Japan, which has developed to a new stage and is approaching extinction, differs from the Japan of the past. When we say that there is a definite limit both to the number of men Japan can throw in and to the extent of her advance, we mean that with her available strength, Japan can only commit part of her forces against China and only penetrate China as far as their capacity allows, for she also wants to attack in other directions and has to defend herself against other enemies; at the same time China has given proof of progress and capacity for stubborn resistance, and it is inconceivable that there should be fierce attacks by Japan without in evitable resistance by China. Japan cannot occupy the whole of China, but she will spare no effort to suppress China's resistance in all the areas she can reach, and will not stop until internal and external developments push Japanese imperialism to the brink of the grave. There are only two possible outcomes to the political situation in Japan. Either the downfall of her entire ruling class occurs rapidly, political power passes to the people and war thus comes to an end, which is impossible at the moment; or

her landlord class and bourgeoisie become more and more fascist and maintain the war until the day of their downfall, which is the very road Japan is now travelling. There can be no other outcome. Those who hope that the moderates among the Japanese bourgeoisie will come forward and stop the war are only harbouring illusions. The reality of Japanese politics for many years has been that the bourgeois moderates of Japan have fallen captive to the landlords and the financial magnates. Now that Japan has launched war against China, so long as she does not suffer a fatal blow from Chinese resistance and still retains sufficient strength, she is bound to attack Southeast Asia or Siberia, or even both. She will do so once war breaks out in Europe; in their wishful calculations, the rulers of Japan have it worked out on a grandiose scale. Of course. it is possible that Japan will have to drop her original plan of invading Siberia and adopt a mainly defensive attitude towards the Soviet Union on account of Soviet strength and of the serious extent to which Japan herself has been weakened by her war against China. But in that case, so far from relaxing her aggression against China she will intensify it, because then the only way left to her will be to gobble up the weak. China's task of persevering in the War of Resistance, the united front and the protracted war will then become all the more weighty, and it will be all the more necessary not to slacken our efforts in the slightest.

112. Under the circumstances the main prerequisites for China's victory over Japan are nation-wide unity and all-round progress on a scale ten or even a hundred times greater than in the past. China is already in an era of progress and has achieved a splendid unity, but her progress and unity are still far from adequate. That Japan has occupied such an extensive area is due not only to her strength but also to China's weakness; this weakness is entirely the cumulative effect of the various historical errors of the last hundred years, and especially of the last ten years, which have confined progress

to its present bounds. It is impossible to vanquish so strong an enemy without making an extensive and long-term effort. There are many things we have to exert ourselves to do; here I will deal only with two fundamental aspects, the progress of the army and the progress of the people.

113. The reform of our military system requires its modernization and improved technical equipment, without which we cannot drive the enemy back across the Yalu River. In our employment of troops we need progressive, flexible strategy and tactics, without which we likewise cannot win victory. Nevertheless, soldiers are the foundation of an arrny; unless they are imbued with a progressive political spirit, and unless such a spirit is fostered through progressive political work, it will be impossible to achieve genuine unity between officers and men, impossible to arouse their enthusiasm for the War of Resistance to the full, and impossible to provide a sound basis for the most effective use of all our technical equipment and tactics. When we say that Japan will finally be defeated despite her technical superiority, we mean that the blows we deliver through annihilation and attrition, apart from inflicting losses, will eventually shake the morale of the enemy army whose weapons are not in the hands of politically conscious soldiers. With us, on the contrary, officers and men are at one on the political aim of the War of Resistance. This gives us the foundation for political work among all the anti-Japanese forces. A proper measure of democracy should be put into effect in the army, chiefly by abolishing the feudal practice of bullying and beating and by having officers and men share weal and woe. Once this is done, unity will be achieved between officers and men, the combat effectiveness of the army will be greatly increased, and there will be no doubt of our ability to sustain the long, cruel war.

114. The richest source of power to wage war lies in the masses of the people. It is mainly because of the unorganized

state of the Chinese masses that Japan dares to bully us. When this defect is remedied, then the Japanese aggressor, like a mad bull crashing into a ring of flames, will be surrounded by hundreds of millions of our people standing upright, the mere sound of their voices will strike terror into him, and he will be burned to death. China's armies must have an uninterrupted flow of reinforcements, and the abuses of press-ganging and of buying substitutes,[33] which now exist at the lower levels, must immediately be banned and replaced by widespread and enthusiastic political mobilization, which will make it easy to enlist millions of men. We now have great difficulties in raising money for the war, but once the people are mobilized, finances too will cease to be a problem. Why should a country as large and populous as China suffer from lack of funds? The army must become one with the people so that they see it as their own army. Such an army will be invincible, and an imperialist power like Japan will be no match for it.

115. Many people think that it is wrong methods that make for strained relations between officers and men and between the army and the people, but I always tell them that it is a question of basic attitude (or basic principle), of having respect for the soldiers and the people. It is from this attitude that the various policies, methods and forms ensue. If we depart from this attitude, then the policies, methods and forms will certainly be wrong, and the relations between officers and men and between the army and the people are bound to be unsatisfactory. Our three major principles for the army's political work are, first, unity between officers and men; second, unity between the army and the people; and third, the disintegration of the enemy forces. To apply these principles effectively, we must start with this basic attitude of respect for the soldiers and the people, and of respect for the human dignity of prisoners of war once they have laid down their arms. Those who take all this as a technical matter and not one

of basic attitude are indeed wrong, and they should correct their view.

116. At this moment when the defence of Wuhan and other places has become urgent, it is a task of the utmost importance to arouse the initiative and enthusiasm of the whole army and the whole people to the full in support of the war. There is no doubt that the task of defending Wuhan and other places must be seriously posed and seriously performed. But whether we can be certain of holding them depends not on our subjective desires but on concrete conditions. Among the most important of these conditions is the political mobilization of the whole army and people for the struggle. If a strenuous effort is not made to secure all the necessary conditions, indeed even if one of these conditions is missing, disasters like the loss of Nanking and other places are bound to be repeated. China will have her Madrids in places where the conditions are present. So far China has not had a Madrid, and from now on we should work hard to create several, but it all depends on the conditions. The most fundamental of these is extensive political mobilization of the whole army and people.

117. In all our work we must persevere in the Anti-Japanese National United Front as the general policy. For only with this policy can we persevere in the War of Resistance and in protracted warfare, bring about a widespread and profound improvement in the relations between officers and men and between the army and the people, arouse to the full the initiative and enthusiasm of the entire army and the entire people in the fight for the defence of all the territory still in our hands and for the recovery of what we have lost, and so win final victory.

118. This question of the political mobilization of the army and the people is indeed of the greatest importance. We have dwelt on it at the risk of repetition precisely because victory is

impossible with out it. There are, of course, many other conditions indispensable to victory, but political mobilization is the most fundamental. The Anti-Japanese National United Front is a united front of the whole army and the whole people, it is certainly not a united front merely of the headquarters and members of a few political parties; our basic objective in initiating the Anti-Japanese National United Front is to mobilize the whole army and the whole people to participate in it.

CONCLUSIONS

119. What are our conclusions? They are:

"Under what conditions do you think China can defeat and destroy the forces of Japan?" "Three conditions are required: first, the establishment of an anti-Japanese united front in China; second, the formation of an international anti-Japanese united front; third, the rise of the revolutionary movement of the people in Japan and the Japanese colonies. From the standpoint of the Chinese people, the unity of the people of China is the most important of the three conditions."

"How long do you think such a war would last?" "That depends on the strength of China's anti-Japanese united front and many other conditioning factors involving China and Japan."

"If these conditions are not realized quickly, the war will be prolonged. But in the end, just the same, Japan will certainly be defeated and China will certainly be victorious. Only the sacrifices will be great and there will be a very painful period."

"Our strategy should be to employ our main forces to operate over an extended and fluid front. To achieve success, the Chinese troops must conduct their warfare with a high degree of mobility on extensive battlefields."

"Besides employing trained armies to carry on mobile warfare, we must organize great numbers of guerrilla units among the peasants."

"In the course of the war, China will be able to . . . reinforce the equipment of her troops gradually. Therefore China will be able to conduct positional warfare in the latter period of the war and make positional attacks on the Japanese-occupied areas. Thus Japan's economy will crack under the strain of China's long resistance and the morale of the Japanese forces will break under the trial of innumerable battles. On the

Chinese side, however, the growing latent power of resistance will be constantly brought into play and large numbers of revolutionary people will be pouring into the front lines to fight for their freedom. The combination of all these and other factors will enable us to make the final and decisive attacks on the fortifications and bases in the Japanese occupied areas and drive the Japanese forces of aggression out of China." (From an interview with Edgar Snow in July 1936.)

"Thus a new stage has opened in China's political situation. . . . In the present stage the central task is to mobilize all the nation's forces for victory in the War of Resistance."

"The key to victory in the war now lies in developing the resistance that has already begun into a war of total resistance by the whole nation. Only through such a war of total resistance can final victory be won."

"The existence of serious weaknesses in the War of Resistance may lead to setbacks, retreats, internal splits, betrayals, temporary and partial compromises and other such reverses. Therefore it should be realized that the war will be arduous and protracted. But we are confident that, through the efforts of our Party and the whole people, the resistance already started will sweep aside all obstacles and continue to advance and develop." ("Resolution on the Present Situation and the Tasks of the Party", adopted by the Central Committee of the Communist Party of China, August 1937.)

These are our conclusions. In the eyes of the subjugationists the enemy are supermen and we Chinese are worthless, while in the eyes of the theorists of quick victory we Chinese are supermen and the enemy are worthless. Both are wrong. We take a different view; the War of Resistance Against Japan is a protracted war, and the final victory will be China's. These are our conclusions.

120. My lectures end here. The great War of Resistance Against Japan is unfolding, and many people are hoping for a summary of experience to facilitate the winning of complete victory. What I have discussed is simply the general experience of the past ten months, and it may perhaps serve as a kind of summary. The problem of protracted war deserves wide attention and discussion; what I have given is only an outline, which I hope you will examine and discuss, amend and amplify.

NOTES

[1] This theory of national subjugation was the view held by the Kuomintang. The Kuomintang was unwilling to resist Japan and fought Japan only under compulsion. After the Lukouchiao Incident (July 7. 1937), the Chiang Kai-shek clique reluctantly took part in the War of Resistance, while the Wang Ching-wei clique became the representatives of the theory of national subjugation, was ready to capitulate to Japan and in fact subsequently did so. However, the idea of national subjugation not only existed in the Kuomintang, but also affected certain sections of the middle strata of society and even certain backward elements among the labouring people. As the cortupt and impotent Kuomintang government lost one battle after another and the Japanese troops advanced unchecked to the vicinity of Wuhan in the first year of the War of Resistance, some backward people became profoundly pessimistic.

[2] These views were to be found within the Communist Party. During the first six months of the War of Resistance, there was a tendency to take the enemy lightly among some members of the Party, who held the view that Japan could be defeated at a single blow. It was not that they felt our own forces to be so strong, since they well knew that the troops and the organized people's forces led by the Communist Party were still small, but that the Kuomintang had begun to resist Japan. In their opinion, the Kuomintang was quite powerful, and, in co-ordination with the Communist Party, could deal Japan telling blows. They made this erroneous appraisal because they saw only one aspect of the Kuomintang, that it was resisting Japan, but overlooked the other aspect, that it was reactionary and corrupt.

[3] Such was the view of Chiang Kai-shek and company. Though they were compelled to resist Japan, Chiang Kai-shek

and the Kuomintang pinned their hopes solely on prompt foreign aid and had no confidence in their own strength, much less in the strength of the people.

[4] Taierhchuang is a town in southern Shantung where the Chinese army fought a battle in March 1938 against the Japanese invaders. By pitting 400,000 men against Japan's 70,000 to 80,000, the Chinese army defeated the Japanese.

[5] This view was put forward in an editorial in the Ta Kung Pao, then the organ of the Political Science Group in the Kuomintang. Indulging in wishful thinking, this clique hoped that a few more victories of the Taierhchuang type would stop Japan's advance and that there would be no need to mobilize the people for a protracted war, which would threaten the security of its own class. This wishful thinking then pervaded the Kuomintang as a whole.

[6] For many decades, beginning with the end of the 18th century, Britain exported an increasing quantity of opium to China. This traffic not only subjected the Chinese people to drugging but also plundered China of her silver. It aroused fierce opposition in China. In 1840, under the pretext of safeguarding its trade with China, Britain launched armed aggression against her. The Chinese troops led by Lin Tse-hsu put up resistance, and the people in Canton spontaneously organized the "Quell-the British Corps", which dealt serious blows to the British forces of aggression. In 1842, however, the corrupt Ching regime signed the Treaty of Ninking with Britain. This treaty provided for the payment of indemnities and the cession of Hongkong to Britain, and stipulated that Shanghai, Foochow, Amoy, Ningpo and Canton were to be opened to British trade and that tariff rates for British goods imported into China were to be jointly fixed by China and Britain.

[7] The Taiping Revolution, or the Movement of the Taiping Heavenly Kingdom, was the mid-19th century revolutionary peasant movemem against the feudal rule and national oppression of the Ching Dynasty. In Janualy 1851 Hung Hsiu-chuan, Yang Hsiu-ching and other leaders launched an uprising in Chintien Village in Kueiping County, Kwangsi Province, and proclaimed the founding of the Taiping Heavenly Kingdom. Proceeding northward from Kwangsi, their peasant army at tacked and occupied Hunan and Hupeh in 1852. In 1853 it marched through Kiangsi and Anhwei and captured Nanking. A section of the force then continued the drive north and pushed on to the vicinity of Tientsin. However the Taiping army failed to build stable base areas in the places it occupied; moreover, after establishing its capital in Nanking, its leading group committed many political and military errors. Therefore it was unable to withstand the combined onslaughts of the counter revolutionary forces of the Ching government and the British, U.S. and French aggressors, and was finally defeated in 1864.

[8] The Reform Movement of 1898, whose leading spirits were Kang Yu-wei, Liang Chi-chao and Tan Szu-tung represented the interests of the liberal bourgeoisie and the enlightened landlords. The movement was favoured and supported by Emperor Kuang Hsu, but had no mass basis. Yuan Shih-kai, who had an army behind him, betrayed the reformers to Empress Dowager Tzu Hsi, the leader of the die-hards, who seized power again and had Emperor Kuang Hsu imprisoned and Tan Szu-tung and five others beheaded. Thus the movement ended in tragic defeat.

[9] The Revolution of 1911 was the bourgeois revolution which overthrew the autocratic regime of the Ching Dynasty. On October 10 of that year, a section of the Ching Dynasty's New Army who were under revolutionary influence staged an uprising in Wuchang, Hupeh Province. The existing bourgeois

and petty-bourgeois revolutionary societies and the broad masses of the workers, peasants and soldiers responded enthusiastically, and very soon the rule of the Ching Dynasty crumbled. In January 1912, the Provisional Government of the Republic of China was set up in Nanking, with Sun Yat-sen as the Provisional President. Thus China's feudal monarchic system which had lasted for more than two thousand years was brought to an end. The idea of a democratic republic had entered deep in the hearts of the people. But the bourgeoisie which led the revolution was strongly conciliationist in nature. It did not mobilize the peasant masses on an extensive scale to crush the feudal rule of the landlord class in the countryside, but instead handed state power over to the Northern warlord Yuan Shih-kai under imperialist and feudal pressure. As a result, the revolution ended in defeat.

[10] The Northern Expedition was the punitive war against the Northern war lords launched by the revolutionary army which marched north from Kwangtung Province in May-July 1926. The Northern Expeditionary Army, with the Communist Party of China taking part in its leadership and under the Party's influence (the political work in the army was at that time mostly under the charge of Communist Party members), gained the warm support of the broad masses of workers and peasants. In the second half of 1926 and the first half of 1927 it occupied most of the provinces along the Yangtse and Yellow Rivers and defeated the Northern warlords. In April 1927 this revolutionary war failed as a result of betrayal by the reactionary clique under Chiang Kai-shek within the revolutionary army.

[11] On January 16, 1938, the Japanae cabinet declared in a policy statement that Japan would subjugate China by force. At the same time it tried by threats and blandishments to make the Kuomintang government capitulate, declaring that if the Kuomintang government "continued to plan resistance", the

Japanese government would foster a new puppet regime in China and no longer accept the Kuomintang as "the other party" in negotiations.

[12] The capitalists referred to here are chiefly those of the United States.

[13] By "their governments" Comrade Mao Tse-tung is here referring to the governments of the imperialist countries -- Britain, the United States and France.

[14] Comrade Mao Tse-tung's prediction that there would be an upswing in China during the stage of stalemate in the War of Resistance Against Japan was completely confirmed in the case of the Liberated Areas under the leadership of the Chinese Communist Party. But there was actually a decline instead of an upswing in the Kuomintang areas, because the ruling clique headed by Chiang Kai-shek was passive in tesisting Japan and active in opposing the Communist Parq and the people. This roused opposition among the broad masses of the people and raised their political consciousness.

[15] According to the theory that "weapons decide everything", China which was inferior to Japan in regard to arms was bound to be defeated in the war. This view was current among all the leaders of the Kuomintang reaction, Chiang Kai-shek included.

[16] See "Problems of Srategy in Guerrilla War Against Japan", Note 9, p. 112 of this volume.

[17] Sun Wu-kung is the monkey king in the Chinese novel Hsi Yu Chi (Pilgrimage to thc West), written in the 16th century. He could cover 108,000 li by turning a somersault. Yet once in the palm of the Buddha, he could not escape from it, however many somersaults he turned. With a flick of his

palm Buddha transformed his fingers into the five-peak Mountain of Five Elements, and buried Sun Wu-kung.

[18] "Fascism is unbridled chauvinism and predatory war," said Comrade Georgi Dimitrov in his report to the Seventh World Congress of the Communist International in August 1935, entitled "The Fascist Offensive and the Tasks of the Communist International" (see Selected Articles and Speeches, Eng. ed., Lawrence & Wishart, London, 1951, p. 44). In July 1937, Comrade Dimitrov published an article entitled Fascism Is War.

[19] V. I. Lenin, Socialism and War, Eng. ed., FLPH, Moscow, 1950, p. 19.

[20] Sun Tzu, Chapter 3, "The Strategy of Attack".

[21] Chengpu, situated in. the southwest of the present Chuancheng County in Shantung Province, was the scene of a great battle between the states of Tsin and Chu in 632 B.C. At the beginning of the battle the Chu troops got the upper hand. The Tsin troops, after making a retreat of 90 li, chose the right and left flanks of the Chu troops, their weak spots, and inflicted heavy defeats on them.

[22] The ancient town of Chengkao, in the northwest of the present Chengkao County, Honan Province, was of great military importance. It was the scene of battles fought in 203 B.C. between Liu Pang, King of Han, and Hsiang Yu, King of Chu. At first Hsiang Yu captured Hsingyang and Chengkao and Liu Pang's troops were almost routed. Liu Pang waited until the opportune moment when Hsiang Yu's troops were in midstream crossing the Szeshui River, and then crushed them and recaptured Chengkao.

[23] In 204 B.C., Han Hsin, a general of the state of Han, led his men in a big battle with Chao Hsieh at Chinghsing. Chao Hsieh's army, said to be 200,000 strong, was several times that of Han. Deploying his troops with their backs to a river, Han Hsin led them in valiant combat, and at the same time dispatched some units to attack and occupy the enemy's weakly garrisoned rear. Caught in a pincer, Chao Hsieh's troops were utterly defeated.

[24] The ancient town of Kunyang, in the north of the present Yehhsien County, Honan Province, was the place where Liu Hsiu, founder of thc Eastern Han Dynasty, defeated the troops of Wang Mang, Emperor of the Hsin Dynasty, in A.D. 23. There was a huge numerical disparity between the two sides, Liu Hsiu's forces totalling 8,000 to 9,000 men as against Wang Mang's 400,000. But taking advantage of the negligence of Wang Mang's generals, Wang Hsun and Wang Yi, who underestimated the enemy, Liu Hsiu with only three thousand picked troops put Wang Mang's main forces to rout. He followed up this victory by crushing the rest of the enemy troops.

[25] Kuantu was in the northeast of the present Chungmou County, Honan Province, and the scene of the battle between the armies of Tsao Tsao and Yuan Shao in A.D.

200. Yuan Shao had an army of 100,000, while Tsao Tsao had only a meagre force and was short of supplies. Taking advantage of the lack of vigilance on the part of Yuan Shao's troops, who belittled the enemy, Tsao Tsao dispatched his light-footed soldiers to spring a surprise attack on them and set their supplies on fire. Yuan Shao's army was thrown into confusion and its main force wiped out.

[26] The sute of Wu was ruled by Sun Chuan, and the sute of Wei by Tsao Tsao. Chihpi is situated on the south bank of the

Yangtse River, to the northeast of Chiayu, Hupeh Province. In A.D. 208 Tsao Tsao led an army of over 500,000 men, which he proclaimed to be 800,000 strong, to launch an attack on Sun Chuan. The latter, in alliance with Tsao Tsao's antagonist Liu Pei, mustered a force of 30,000. Knowing that Tsao Tsao's army was plagued by epidemics and was unaccustomed to action afloat, the allied forces of Sun Chuan and Liu Pei set fire to Tsao Tsao's fleet and crushed his army.

[27] Yiling, to the east of the present Ichang, Hupeh Province, was the place where Lu Sun, a general of the sute of Wu, defeated the army of Liu Pei, ruler of Shu, in A.D. 222. Liu Pei's troops scored successive victories at the beginning of the war and penetrated five or six hundred li into the territory of Wu as far as Yiling. Lu Sun, who was defending Yiling, avoided battle for over seven months until Liu Pei "was at his wits' end and his troops were exhausted and demoralized". Then he crushed Liu Pei's troops by taking advantage of a favourable wind to set fire to their tents.

[28] Hsieh Hsuan, a general of Eastern Tsin Dynasty, defeated Fu Chien, ruler of the state of Chin, in A.D. 383 at the Feishui River in Anhwei Province. Fu Chien had an infantry force of more than 600,000, a cavalry force of 270,000 and a guards corps of more than 30,000, while the land and river forces of Eastern Tsin numbered only 80,000. When the armies lined up on opposite banks of the Feishui River, Hsieh Hsuan, taking advantage of the overconfidence and conceit of the enemy troops, requested Fu Chien to move his troops back so as to leave room for the Eastern Tsin troops to cross the river and fight it out. Fu Chien complied, but when he ordered withdrawal, his troops got into a panic and could not be stopped. Seizing the opportunity, the Eastern Tsin troops crossed the river, launched an offensive and crushed the enemy.

[29] In A.D. 383, Fu Chien, the ruler of the state of Chin, belittled the forces of Tsin and attacked them. The Tsin troops defeated the enemy's advance units at Lochien, Shouyang County, Anhwei Province, and pushed forward by land and water. Ascending the city wall of Shouyang, Fu Chien observed the excellent alignment of the Tsin troops and, mistaking the woods and bushes on Mount Pakung for enemy soldiers, was frightened by the enemy's apparent strength.

[30] Comrade Mao Tse-tung is here referring to the fact that Chiang Kai-shek and Wang Ching-wei, having betrayed the first national democratic united front of the Kuomintang and the Communist Party in 1927, launched a ten-year war against the people, and thus made it impossible for the Chinese people to be organized on a large scale. For this the Kuomintang reactionaries headed by Chiang Kai-shek must be held responsible.

[31] Duke Hsiang of Sung ruled in the Spring and Autumn Era. In 638 B.C., the state of Sung fought with the powerful state of Chu. The Sung forces were already deployed in battle positions when the Chu troops were crossing the river. One of the Sung officers suggested that, as the Chu troops were numerically stronger, this was the moment for attack. But the Duke said, "No, a gentleman should never attack one who is unprepared." When the Chu troops had crossed the river but had not yet completed their battle alignment, the officer again proposed an immediate attack, and once again the Duke said, "No, a gentleman should never attack an army which has not yet completed its battle alignment." The Duke gave the order for attack only after the Chu troops wete fully prepared. As a result, the Sung troops met with a disastrous defeat and the Duke himself was wounded.

[32] Han Fu-chu, a Kuomintang warlord, was for several years governor of Shantung. When the Japanese invaders thrust

southward to Shantung along the Tientsin-pukow Railway after occupying Peiping and Tientsin in 1937, Han Fu-chu fled all the way from Shantung to Honan without fighting a single battle.

[33] The Kuomintang expanded its army by press-ganging. Its military and police seized people everywhere, roping them up and treating them like convicts. Those who had money would bribe the Kuomintang officials or pay for substitutes.

Mao Tse-tung

THE ART OF WAR

PART 4

PROBLEMS OF WAR

AND STRATEGY

by

Mao Tse-tung

November 6, 1938

Mao Tse-tung

Preface

This article is part of Comrade Mao Tse-tung's concluding speech at the Sixth Plenary Session of the Sixth Central Committee of the Party. In his "Problems of Strategy in Guerrilla War Against Japan" and "On Protracted War", Comrade Mao Tse-tung had already settled the question of the Party's leading role in the War of Resistance Against Japan. But some comrades, committing Right opportunist errors, denied that the Party must maintain its independence and initiative in the united front, and so doubted and even opposed the Party's line on the war and on strategy.

In order to overcome this Right opportunism, bring the whole Party to a clearer understanding of the prime importance of the problems of war and strategy in the Chinese revolution and mobilize it for serious work in this connection, Comrade Mao Tse-tung again stressed the importance of the subject at this plenary session, approaching it from the viewpoint of the history of China's political struggles, and analyzed the development of the Party's military work and the specific changes in its strategy. The result was unanimity of thought in the Party leadership and unanimity of action throughout the Party.

Mao Tse-tung

I CHINA'S CHARACTERISTICS
AND REVOLUTIONARY WAR

The seizure of power by armed force, the settlement of the issue by war, is the central task and the highest form of revolution. This Marxist-Leninist principle of revolution holds good universally, for China and for all other countries.

But while the principle remains the same, its application by the party of the proletariat finds expression in varying ways according to the varying conditions. Internally, capitalist countries practise bourgeois democracy (not feudalism) when they are not fascist or not at war; in their external relations, they are not oppressed by, but themselves oppress, other nations. Because of these characteristics, it is the task of the party of the proletariat in the capitalist countries to educate the workers and build up strength through a long period of legal struggle, and thus prepare for the final overthrow of capitalism. In these countries, the question is one of a long legal struggle, of utilizing parliament as a platform, of economic and political strikes, of organizing trade unions and educating the workers. There the form of organization is legal and the form of struggle bloodless (non-military). On the issue of war, the Communist Parties in the capitalist countries oppose the imperialist wars waged by their own countries; if such wars occur, the policy of these Parties is to bring about the defeat of the reactionary governments of their own countries. The one war they want to fight is the civil war for which they are preparing.[1] But this insurrection and war should not be launched until the bourgeoisie becomes really helpless, until the majority of the proletariat are determined to rise in arms and fight, and until the rural masses are giving willing help to the proletariat. And when the time comes to launch such an insurrection and war, the first step will be to seize the cities, and then advance into the countryside, and not the other way about. All this has been done by Communist Parties in capitalist countries, and it has been proved correct by the October Revolution in Russia.

China is different however. The characteristics of China are that she is not independent and democratic but semi-colonial and semi-feudal, that internally she has no democracy but is under feudal oppression and that in her external relations she has no national independence but is oppressed by imperialism. It follows that we have no parliament to make use of and no legal right to organize the workers to strike. Basically, the task of the Communist Party here is not to go through a long period of legal struggle before launching insurrection and war, and not to seize the big cities first and then occupy the countryside, but the reverse.

When imperialism is not making armed attacks on our country, the Chinese Communist Party either wages civil war jointly with the bourgeoisie against the warlords (lackeys of imperialism), as in 1924-27 in the wars in Kwangtung Province[2] and the Northern Expedition, or unites with the peasants and the urban petty bourgeoisie to wage civil war against the landlord class and the comprador bourgeoisie (also lackeys of imperialism), as in the War of Agrarian Revolution of 1927-36. When imperialism launches armed attacks on China, the Party unites all classes and strata in the country opposing the foreign aggressors to wage a national war against the foreign enemy, as it is doing in the present War of Resistance Against Japan.

All this shows the difference between China and the capitalist countries. In China war is the main form of struggle and the army is the main form of organization. Other forms such as mass organization and mass struggle are also extremely important and indeed indispensable and in no circumstances to be overlooked, but their purpose is to serve the war. Before the outbreak of a war all organization and struggle are in preparation for the war, as in the period from the May 4th Movement of 1919 to the May 30th Movement of 1925. After war breaks out, all organization and struggle are coordinated with the war either directly or indirectly, as, for instance in the period of the Northern Expedition when all organization and struggle in the rear areas of the revolutionary army were coordinated with the war directly, and those in the Northern warlord areas were coordinated with the war indirectly. Again in the period of the War of Agrarian Revolution all organization and struggle inside the Red areas were coordinated with the war directly, and outside the Red areas indirectly. Yet again in the present period, the War of Resistance, all organization and struggle in the rear areas of the anti-Japanese forces and in the areas occupied by the enemy are directly or indirectly coordinated with the war.

"In China the armed revolution is fighting the armed counter-revolution. That is one of the specific features and one of the advantages of the Chinese revolution."[3] This thesis of Comrade Stalin's is perfectly correct and is equally valid for the Northern Expedition, the War of Agrarian Revolution, and the present War of Resistance Against Japan. They are all revolutionary wars, all directed against counter-revolutionaries and all waged mainly by the revolutionary people, differing only in the sense that a civil war differs from a national war, and that a war conducted by the Communist Party differs from a war it conducts jointly with the Kuomintang. Of course, these differences are important. They indicate the breadth of the main forces in the war (an alliance of the workers and peasants, or of the workers, peasants and bourgeoisie) and whether our antagonist in the war is internal or external (whether the war is against domestic or foreign foes, and, if domestic, whether against the Northern warlords or against the Kuomintang); they also indicate that the content of China's revolutionary war differs at different stages of its history. But all these wars are instances of armed revolution fighting armed counter-revolution, they are all revolutionary wars, and all exhibit the specific features and advantages of the Chinese revolution. The thesis that revolutionary war "is one of the specific features and one of the advantages of the Chinese revolution" fits China's conditions perfectly. The main task of the party of the Chinese proletariat, a task confronting it almost from its very inception, has been to unite with as many allies as possible and, according to the circumstances, to organize armed struggles for national and social liberation against armed counter-revolution, whether internal or external. Without armed struggle the proletariat and the Communist Party would have no standing at all in China, and it would be impossible to accomplish any revolutionary task.

Our Party did not grasp this point fully during the first five or six years after it was founded, that is, from 1921 to its participation in the Northern Expedition in 1926. It did not then understand the supreme importance of armed struggle in China, or seriously prepare for war and organize armed forces, or apply itself to the study of military strategy and tactics. During the Northern Expedition it neglected to win over the army but laid one-sided stress on the mass movement, with the result that the whole mass movement collapsed the moment the Kuomintang turned reactionary. For a long time after 1927 many comrades continued to make it the Party's central task to prepare for insurrections in the cities and to work in the White areas. It was only after our victory in repelling the enemy's third "encirclement and suppression" campaign in 1931 that some comrades fundamentally changed their attitude on this question. But this was not true of the whole Party, and there were other comrades who did not think along the lines presented here.

Experience tells us that China's problems cannot be settled without armed force. An understanding of this point will help us in successfully waging the War of Resistance Against Japan from now on. The fact that the whole nation is rising in armed resistance in the war against Japan should inculcate a better understanding of the importance of this question in the whole Party, and every Party member should be prepared to take up arms and go to the front at any moment. More over, our present session has clearly defined the direction for our efforts by deciding that the Party's main fields of work are in the battle zones and in the enemy's rear. This is also an excellent antidote against the tendency of some Party members to be willing only to work in Party organizations and in the mass movement but to be unwilling to study or participate in warfare, and against the failure of some schools to encourage students to go to the front, and other such phenomena. In most of China, Party organizational work and mass work are directly linked with armed struggle; there is not and cannot be, any Party work or mass work that is isolated and stands by itself. Even in rear areas remote from the battle zones (like Yunnan, Kweichow and Szechuan) and in enemy-occupied areas (like Peiping, Tientsin, Nanking and Shanghai), Party organizational work and mass work are co-ordinated with the war, and should and must exclusively serve the needs of the front. In a word, the whole Party must pay great attention to war, study military matters and prepare itself for fighting.

II. THE WAR HISTORY OF THE KUOMINTANG

It will be useful for us to look at the history of the Kuomintang and see what attention it pays to war.

From the start, when he organized a small revolutionary group, Sun Yat-sen staged armed insurrections against the Ching Dynasty.[4] The period of Tung Meng Hui (the Chinese Revolutionary League) was replete with armed insurrections, [5] right up to the armed overthrow of the Ching Dynasty by the Revolution of 1911. Then, during the period of the Chinese Revolutionary Party, he carried out a military campaign against Yuan Shih-kai.[6] Subsequent events such as the southern movement of the naval units,[7] the northern expedition from Kweilin [8] and the founding of the Whampoa Military Academy [9] were also among Sun Yat-sen's military undertakings.

After Sun Yat-sen came Chiang Kai-shek, who brought the Kuomintang's military power to its zenith. He values the army as his very life and has had the experience of three wars, namely, the Northern Expedition, the Civil War and the War of Resistance Against Japan. For the last ten years Chiang Kai-shek has been a counter-revolutionary. He has created a huge "Central Army" for counter-revolutionary purposes. He has held firmly to the vital point that whoever has an army has power and that war decides everything. In this respect we ought to learn from him. In this respect both Sun Yat-sen and Chiang Kai-shek are our teachers. Since the Revolution of 1911, all the warlords have clung to their armies for dear life, setting great store by the principle, "Whoever has an army has power."

Tan Yen-kai,[10] a clever bureaucrat who had a chequered career in Hunan, was never a civil governor pure and simple but always insisted on being both the military governor and the civil governor. Even when he became President of the National Government first in Canton and then in Wuhan, he was concurrently the commander of the Second Army.

There are many such warlords who understand this peculiarity of China's. There have also been parties in China, notably the Progressive Party,[11] which did not want to have an army; yet even this party recognized that it could not get government positions without some warlord backing. Among its successive patrons have been Yuan Shih-kai,[12] Tuan Chijui [13] and Chiang Kai-shek (to whom the Political Science Group,[14] formed out of a section of the Progressive Party, has attached itself).

A few small political parties with a short history, e.g., the Youth Party,[15] have no army, and so have not been able to get anywhere.

In other countries there is no need for each of the bourgeois parties to have an armed force under its direct command. But things are different in China, where, because of the feudal division of the country, those landlord or bourgeois groupings or parties which have guns have power, and those which have more guns have more power. Placed in such an environment, the party of the proletariat should see clearly to the heart of the matter.

Communists do not fight for personal military power (they must in no circumstances do that, and let no one ever again follow the example of Chang Kuo-tao), but they must fight for military power for the Party, for military power for the people. As a national war of resistance is going on, we must also fight for military power for the nation. Where there is naivety on the question of military power, nothing whatsoever can be achieved. It is very difficult for the labouring people, who have been deceived and intimidated by the reactionary ruling classes for thousands of years, to awaken to the importance of having guns in their own hands. Now that Japanese imperialist oppression and the nation-wide resistance to it have pushed our labouring people into the arena of war, Communists should prove themselves the most politically conscious leaders in this war.

Every Communist must grasp the truth, "Political power grows out of the barrel of a gun." Our principle is that the Party commands the gun, and the gun must never be allowed to command the Party. Yet, having guns, we can create Party organizations, as witness the powerful Party organizations which the Eighth Route Army has created in northern China. We can also create cadres, create schools, create culture, create mass movements. Everything in Yenan has been created by having guns. All things grow out of the barrel of a gun. According to the Marxist theory of the state, the army is the chief component of state power. Whoever wants to seize and retain state power must have a strong army. Some people ridicule us as advocates of the "omnipotence of war". Yes, we are advocates of the omnipotence of revolutionary war; that is good, not bad, it is Marxist. The guns of the Russian Communist Party created socialism. We shall create a democratic republic. Experience in the class struggle in the era of imperialism teaches us that it is only by the power of the gun that the working class and the labouring masses can defeat the armed bourgeoisie and landlords; in this sense we may say that only with guns can the whole world be transformed.

We are advocates of the abolition of war, we do not want war; but war can only be abolished through war, and in order to get rid of the gun it is necessary to take up the gun.

III THE WAR HISTORY OF THE CHINESE COMMUNIST PARTY

Our Party failed to grasp the importance of engaging itself directly in preparations for war and in the organization of armed forces for a period of three or four years, that is, from 1921 (when the Chinese Communist Party was founded) to 1924 (when the First National Congress of the Kuomintang was held), and it still lacked adequate understanding of this issue in the 1924-27 period and even later; nevertheless, after 1924, when it began to participate in the Whampoa Military Academy, it entered a new stage and began to see the importance of military affairs.

Through helping the Kuomintang in the wars in Kwangtung Province and participating in the Northern Expedition, the Party gained leadership over some armed forces.[16] Then, having learned a bitter lesson from the failure of the revolution, the Party organized the Nanchang Uprising,[17] the Autumn Harvest Uprising [18] and the Canton Uprising, and entered on a new period, the founding of the Red Army. That was the crucial period in which our Party arrived at a thorough understanding of the importance of the army. Had there been no Red Army and no war fought by the Red Army in this period, that is, had the Communist Party adopted Chen Tu-hsiu's liquidationism, the present War of Resistance would have been inconceivable or could not have been sustained for long.

At its emergency meeting held on August 7, 1927, the Centra Committee of the Party combated Right opportunism in the political sphere, thus enabling the Party to take a big stride forward. At its fourth plenary session in January 1931, the Sixth Central Committee nominally combated "Left" opportunism in the political sphere, but in fact itself committed the error of "Left" opportunism anew. The two meetings differed in their content and historical role, but neither of them dealt seriously with the problems of war and strategy, a fact which showed that war had not yet been made the centre of gravity in the Party's work. After the central leadership of the Party moved into the Red areas in 1933, this situation underwent a radical change, but mistakes in principle were again committed on the problem of war (and all other major problems), bringing serious losses to the revolutionary war. The Tsunyi Meeting of 1935, on the other hand, was mainly a fight against opportunism in the military sphere and gave top priority to the question of war, and this was a reflection of the war conditions of the time. Today we can say with confidence that in the struggles of the past seventeen years the Chinese Communist Party has forged not only a firm Marxist political line but also a firm Marxist military line. We have been able to apply Marxism in solving not only political but also military problems; we have trained not only a large core of cadres capable of running the Party and the state, but also a large core of cadres capable of running the army.

These achievements are the flower of the revolution, watered by the blood of countless martyrs, a glory that belongs not only to the Chinese Communist Party and the Chinese people, but also to the Communist Parties and the peoples of the whole world. There are only three armies in the whole world which belong to the proletariat and the labouring people, the armies led by the Communist Parties of the Soviet Union, of China and of Spain, and as yet Communist Parties in other countries have had no military experience; hence our army and our military experience are all the more precious.

In order to carry the present War of Resistance Against Japan to victory, it is extremely important to expand and consolidate the Eighth Route Army, the New Fourth Army and all the guerrilla forces led by our Party. Acting on this principle, the Party should dispatch a sufficient number of its best members and cadres to the front. Everything must serve victory at the front, and the organizational task must be subordinated to the political task.

IV. CHANGES IN THE PARTY'S MILITARY STRATEGY IN THE CIVIL WAR AND THE NATIONAL WAR

The changes in our Party's military strategy are worth studying. Let us deal separately with the two processes, the civil war and the national war.

The civil war can be roughly divided into two strategic periods. Guerrilla warfare was primary in the first period and regular warfare in the second. But this regular warfare was of the Chinese type, regular only in its concentration of forces for mobile warfare and in a certain degree of centralization and planning in command and organization; in other respects it retained a guerrilla character and, as regular warfare, was on a low level and not comparable with the regular warfare of foreign armies or, in some ways, even with that of the Kuomintang army. Thus, in a sense, this type of regular warfare was only guerrilla warfare raised to a higher level.

The War of Resistance Against Japan can also be roughly divided into two strategic periods, so far as our Party's military tasks are concerned. In the first period (comprising the stages of the strategic defensive and strategic stalemate) it is guerrilla warfare which is primary, while in the second (the stage of the strategic counter-offensive) it is regular warfare which will be primary. However, the guerrilla warfare of the first period of the War of Resistance differs considerably in content from that of the first period of the civil war, because the dispersed guerrilla tasks are being carried out by the regular (i.e., regular to a certain degree) Eighth Route Army. Likewise, the regular warfare of the second period of the War of Resistance will be different from that of the second period of the civil war because we can assume that, given up-to-date equipment, a great change will take place both in the army and in its operations. Our army will then attain a high degree of centralization and organization, and its operations will lose much of their guerrilla character and attain a high degree of regularity; what is now on a low level will then be raised to a higher level, and the Chinese type of regular warfare will change into the general type. That will be our task in the stage of the strategic counter-offensive.

Thus we see that the two processes, the civil war and the War of Resistance Against Japan, and their four strategic periods, contain three changes in strategy. The first was the change from guerrilla warfare to regular warfare in the civil war. The second was the change from regular warfare in the civil war to guerrilla warfare in the War of Resistance. And the third will be the change from guerrilla warfare to regular warfare in the War of Resistance.

The first of the three changes encountered great difficulties. It involved a twofold task. On the one hand, we had to combat the Right tendency of localism and guerrilla-ism, which consisted in clinging to guerrilla habits and refusing to make the turn to regularization, a tendency which arose because our cadres underestimated the changes in the enemy's situation and our own tasks. In the Central Red Area it was only after much painstaking education that this tendency was gradually corrected. On the other hand, we also had to combat the "Left" tendency of over-centralization and adventurism which put undue stress on regularization, a tendency which arose because some of the leading cadres overestimated the enemy, set the tasks too high and mechanically applied foreign experience regardless of the actual conditions. For three long years (before the Tsunyi Meeting) this tendency imposed enormous sacrifices on the Central Red Area, and it was corrected only after we had learned lessons for which we paid in blood. Its correction was the achievement of the Tsunyi Meeting.

The second change in strategy took place in the autumn of 1937 (after the Lukouchiao Incident), at the juncture of the two different wars. We faced a new enemy, Japanese imperialism, and had as our ally our former enemy, the Kuomintang (which was still hostile to us), and the theatre of war was the vast expanse of northern China (which was temporarily our army's front but would soon be the enemy's rear and would remain so for a long time). In this special situation, our change in strategy was an extremely serious one. In this special situation we had to transform the regular army of the past into a guerrilla army (in respect to its dispersed operations, and not to its sense of organization or to its discipline), and transform the mobile warfare of the past into guerrilla warfare, so that we could adapt ourselves to the kind of enemy facing us and to the tasks before us. But this change was, to all appearances, a step backward and therefore necessarily very difficult. Both underestimation and morbid fear of Japan, tendencies likely to occur at such a time, did actually occur among the Kuomintang. When the Kuomintang changed over from civil war to national war, it suffered many needless losses mainly because of its underestimation of the enemy, but also because of its morbid fear of Japan (as exemplified by Han Fu-chu and Liu Chih[19]). On the other hand, we have effected the change fairly smoothly and, instead of suffering losses, have won big victories. The reason is that the great majority of our cadres accepted the correct guidance of the Central Committee in good time and skilfully sized up the actual situation, even though there were serious arguments between the Central Committee and some of the army cadres. The extreme importance of this change for persevering in, developing and winning the War of Resistance as a whole, as well as for the future of the Communist Party of China, can be seen immediately if we think of the historic signihcance of anti-Japanese guerrilla warfare in determining the fate of the national liberation struggle in China. In its extraordinary breadth and protractedness, China's anti-Japanese guerrilla war is without precedent, not only in the East but perhaps in the whole history of mankind.

The third change, from guerrilla to regular warfare against Japan, belongs to the future development of the war, which will presumably give rise to new circumstances and new difficulties. We need not discuss it now.

V THE STRATEGIC ROLE OF GUERRILLA WARFARE AGAINST JAPAN

In the anti-Japanese war as a whole, regular warfare is primary and guerrilla warfare supplementary, for only regular warfare can decide the final outcome of the war. Of the three strategic stages (the defensive, the stalemate and the counter-offensive) in the entire process of the war in the country as a whole, the first and last are stages in which regular warfare is primary and guerrilla warfare supplementary. In the intermediate stage guerrilla warfare will become primary and regular warfare supplementary, because the enemy will be holding on to the areas he has occupied and we will be preparing for the counter-offensive but will not yet be ready to launch it. Though this stage will possibly be the longest, it is still only one of the three stages in the entire war. If we take the war as a whole, therefore, regular

It is also beyond doubt that in the long course of struggle the guerrilla units and guerrilla warfare will not remain as they are but will develop to a higher stage and evolve gradually into regular units and regular warfare. Through guerrilla warfare, we shall build up our strength and turn ourselves into a decisive element in the crushing of Japanese imperialism.

VI PAY GREAT ATTENTION TO THE STUDY OF MILITARY MATTERS

All the issues between two hostile armies depend on war for their solution, and China's survival or extinction depends on her victory or defeat in the present war. Hence our study of military theory, of strategy and tactics and of army political work brooks not a moment's delay. Though our study of tactics is still inadequate, our comrades who are engaged in military work have achieved a great deal in the last ten years and, on the basis of Chinese conditions, have brought forth much that is new; the shortcoming here is that there has been no general summing-up. But so far only a few people have taken up the study of the problems of strategy and the theory of war. First-rate results have been achieved in the study of our political work, which, in wealth of experience and in the number and quality of its innovations, ranks second only to that of the Soviet Union; here too the shortcoming is insufficient synthesis and systematization. The popularization of military knowledge is an urgent task for the Party and the whole country. We must now pay great attention to all these things, but most of all to the theory of war and strategy. I deem it imperative that we arouse interest in the study of military theory and direct the attention of the whole membership to the study of military matters.

NOTES

[1] See V. I. Lenin, "The War and Russian Social-Democracy" (Collected Works, Eng. ed., Progress Publishers, Moscow, 1964, Vol. XXI, pp. 27-34), "The Conference of the R.S.D.L.P. Groups Abroad" (ibid., pp. 158-64), "The Defeat of One's Own Government in the Imperialist War" (ibid. pp. 275-80), "The Defeat of Russia and the Revolutionary Crisis" (ibid. pp. 378-82). These articles, written in 1914-15, deal specifically with the imperialist war of that time. See also History of the Communist Party of tbe Soviet Union (Bolsheviks) Short Course Eng. ed., FLPH, Moscow, , pp. 258-67.]

[2] In 1924, Dr. Sun Yat-sen, in alliance with the Communist Party and the revolutionary workers and peasants, defeated the "Merchants' Corps", an armed force of the compradors and landlords which engaged in counter-revolutionaq activities in Canton in collaboration with the British imperialists. The revolutionary army, which had been founded on the basis of co-operation between the Kuomintang and the Communist Party, set out from Canton early in 1925, fought the Eastern Campaign and, with the support of the peasants, defeated the troops of the warlord Chen Chiung-ming. It then returned to Canton and overthrew the Yunnan and Kwangsi warlords who had entrenched themselves there. That autumn it conducted the Second Eastern Campaign and finally wiped out Chen Chiung-ming's forces. These campaigns, in which members of the Communist Party and the Communist Youth League fought heroically in the van, brought about the political unification of Kwangtung Province and paved the way for the Northern Expedition.

[3] J. V. Stalin, "The Prospects of the Revolution in China", Works, Eng. ed., FLPH, Moscow, 1954, Vol. VIII, p. 379.

[4] In 1894, Dr. Sun Yat-sen formed a small revolutionary organization in Honolulu called the Hsing Chung Hui (Society for China's Regeneration). With the support of the secret societies among the people, he staged two armed insurrections in Kwangtung Province against the Ching government after its defeat in the Sino-Japanese war in 1895, one at Canton in 1895 and the other at Huichow in 1900

[5] Tung Meng Hui, or the Chinese Revolutionary League (a united front organization of the bourgeoisie, the petty bourgeoisie and a section of the landed gentry opposed to the Ching government), was formed in 1905 through the merging of the Hsing Chung Hui (see note above) and two other groups, the Hua Hsing Hui (Society for China's Regeneration) and the Kuang Fu Hui (Society for Breaking the Foreign Yoke). It put forward a programme of bourgeois revolution advocating "the expulsion of the Tartars (Manchus), the recovery of China, the establishment of a republic and the equalization of landownership". In the period of the Chinese Revolutionary League, Dr. Sun Yat-sen, allying himself with the secret societies and a part of the New Army of the Ching government, launched a number of armed insurrections against the Ching regime, notably those at Pinghsiang (Kiangsi Province), Liuyang and Liling (Hunan Province) in 1906, at Huangkang, Chaochow and Chinchow (Kwangtung Province), and at Chennankuan (Kwangsi Province) in 1907, at Hokou (Yunnan Province) in 1908 and at Canton in 1911. The last was followed in the same year by the Wuchang Uprising which resulted in the overthrow of the Ching Dynasty.

[6] In 1912, the Chinese Revolutionary League was reorganized into the Kuomintang and made a compromise with the Northern warlord regime headed by Yuan Shih-kai. In 1913 Yuan's troops marched southward to suppress the forces which had emerged in the provinces of Kiangsi, Anhwei and

Kwangtung in the course of the 1911 revolution. Armed resistance was organized by Dr. Sun Yat-sen but it was soon crushed. In 1914, realizing the error of the Kuomintang's policy of compromise, Dr. Sun formed the Chung Hua Ke Ming Tang (Chinese Revolutionary Party) in Tokyo, Japan, in order to distinguish his organization from the Kuomintang of the time. The new party was actually an alliance of the political representatives of a section of the petty bourgeoisie and a section of the bourgeoisie against Yuan Shih-kai. Through this alliance, Dr. Sun Yat-sen staged a minor insurrection in Shanghai in 1914. In 1915 when Yuan Shih-kai proclaimed himself emperor, Tsai Ngo and others set out fronn Yunnan to take action against him, and Dr. Sun was also very active in advocating and promoting armed opposition to Yuan Shih-kai.

[7] In 1917 Dr. Sun Yat-sen went from Shanghai to Canton at the head of a naval force which was under his influence. Using Kwangtung as a base and co-operating with the Southwestern warlords who were opposed to the Northern warlord Tuan Chi-jui, he set up a military government opposed to Tuan Chi-jui.

8] In 1921 Dr. Sun Yat-sen planned a northern expedition from Kweilin, Kwangsi Province. But his plan was frustrated by the mutiny of his subordinate, Chen Chiung-ming, who was in league with the Northern warlords.

[9] The Whampoa Military Academy, located at Whampoa near Canton, was established by Dr. Sun Yat-sen in 1924 after the reorganization of the Kuomintang with the help of the Chinese Communist Party and the Soviet Union. Before Chiang Kai-shek's betrayal of the revolution in 1927, the academy was run jointly by the Kuomintang and the Communist Party. Comrades Chou En-lai, Yeh Chien-ying, Yun Tai-ying, Hsiao Chu-nu and others held responsible posts in the academy at one time or another. Many of the cadets were members of the Communist Party or the Communist Youth

League, and they formed the revolutionary core of the academy.

[10] Tan Yen-kai was a native of Hunan who had been a Hanlin, a member of the highest official scholastic body under the Ching Dynasty. He was a careerist who first advocated a constitutional monarchy and then took part in the Revolution of 1911. His later adherence to the Kuomintang reflected the contradiction between the Hunan landlords and the Northern warlords.

[11] The Progressive Party was organized by Liang Chi-chao and others under the aegis of Yuan Shih-kai during the first years of the Republic.

[12] Yuan Shih-kai was the head of the Northern warlords in the last years of the Ching Dynasty. After the Ching Dynasty was overthrown by the Revolution of 1911, he usurped the presidency of the Republic and organized the first government of the Northern warlords, which represented the big landlord and big comprador classes. He did this by relying on counter-revolutionary armed force and on the support of the imperialists and by taking advantage of the conciliationist character of the bourgeoisie, which was then leading the revolution. In 1915 he wanted to make himself emperor and, to gain the support of the Japanese imperialists, accepted the Twenty-one Demands with which Japan aimed at obtaining exclusive control of all China. In December of the same year an uprising against his assumption of the throne took place in Yunnan Province and promptly won nation-wide response and support. Yuan Shih-kai died in Peking in June 1916.

[13] Tuan Chi-jui was an old subordinate of Yuan Shih-kai and head of the Anhwei clique of Northern warlords. After Yuan's death he more than once controlled the Peking government.

[14] The extremely right-wing Political Science Group was formed in 1916 by a section of the Progressive Party and a section of the Kuomintang. It gambled now on the Southern, now on the Northern, warlords in order to grab government posts. During the Northern Expedition of 1926-27, its pro-Japanese members, such as Huang Fu, Chang Chun and Yang Yung-tai, began to collaborate with Chiang Kai-shek and, using their reactionary political experience, helped him build up a counter-revolutionary regime.

[15] The Youth Party, also called the Chinese Youth Party or the Etatiste Party, was formed by a handful of unscrupulous fascist politicians. They made counter revolutionary careers for themselves by opposing the Communist Party and the Soviet Union and received subsidies from the various groups of reactionaries in power and from the imperialists.

[16] Comrade Mao Tse-tung is here referring mainly to the independent regiment commanded by General Yeh Ting, a Communist, during the Northern Expedition. See "The Struggle in the Chingkang Mountains", Note 14, Selected Works of Mao Tse-tung, Eng. ed., FLP, Peking, 1961, Vol. I.

[17] Nanchang, capital of Kiangsi Province, was the scene of the famous uprising on August 1, 1927 led by the Communist Party of China in order to combat the counter-revolution of Chiang Kai-shek and Wang Ching-wei and to continue the revolution of 1924-27. More than thirty thousand troops took part in the uprising which was led by Comrades Chou En-lai, Chu Teh, Ho Lung and Yeh Ting. The insurrectionary army withdrew from Nanchang on August 5 as planned, but suffered a defeat when approaching Chaochow and Swatow in Kwangtung Province. Led by Comrades Chu Teh, Chen Yi and Lin Piao, part of the troops later fought their way to the Chingkang Mountains and joined forces with the First Division

of the First Workers' and Peasants' Revolutionary Army under Comrade Mao Tse-tung.

[18] The famous Autumn Harvest Uprising under the leadership of Comrade Mao Tse-tung was launched in September 1927 by the people's armed forces of Hsiushui, Pinghsiang, Pingkiang and Liuyang Counties on the Hunan-Kiangsi border, who formed the First Division of the First Workers' and Peasants' Revolutionary Army. Comrade Mao Tse-tung led this force to the Chingkang Mountains where a revolutionary base was established.

[19] Han Fu-chu was a Kuomintang warlord in Shantung Province. Liu Chih, another warlord, who commanded Chiang Kai-shek's personal troops in Honan Province, was responsible for the defence of the Paoting area in Hopei after the outbreak of the War of Resistance Against Japan. Both of them fled before the Japanese without firing a shot.

Made in the USA
Lexington, KY
31 March 2010